Homosexuality

OPPOSING VIEWPOINTS®

Other Books of Related Interest in the Opposing
Viewpoints Series:

AIDS
American Values
America's Children
Civil Liberties
Constructing a Life Philosophy
The Family in America
Male/Female Roles
Sexual Values
Social Justice
Suicide
Teenage Sexuality

Homosexuality

OPPOSING VIEWPOINTS®

David Bender & Bruno Leone, *Series Editors*

William Dudley, *Book Editor*

OPPOSING
VIEWPOINTS
SERIES®

Greenhaven Press, Inc.   PO Box 289009 San Diego, CA   92198-9009

Library of Congress Cataloging-in-Publication Data

Homosexuality : opposing viewpoints / William Dudley, book editor.
    p.   cm. — (Opposing viewpoints series)
    Includes bibliographical references and index.
    Summary: Presents opposing viewpoints on such aspects of homosexuality as what causes it, how society should treat homosexuals, and whether sexual orientation can be changed.
    ISBN 0-89908-481-8 (alk. paper) — ISBN 0-89908-456-7 (pbk. : alk. paper)
    1. Homosexuality—United States. 2. Gays—United States. [1. Homosexuality.] I. Dudley, William, 1964–   . II. Series: Opposing viewpoints series (Unnumbered)
HQ76.3.U5H675 1993
305.9′0664—dc20   92-40705
                                                                        CIP
                                                                        AC

"Congress shall make no law . . .
abridging the freedom of speech,
or of the press."

First Amendment to the U.S. Constitution

The basic foundation of our democracy is the first amendment
guarantee of freedom of expression. The Opposing Viewpoints
Series is dedicated to the concept of this basic freedom and the
idea that it is more important to practice it than to enshrine it.

Contents

Page

Why Consider Opposing Viewpoints?   9

Introduction   12

Chapter 1: What Causes Homosexuality?

Chapter Preface   16

1. Differences in Brain Structure May Cause
   Homosexuality   17
   Marcia Barinaga

2. The Link Between Brain Structure and
   Homosexuality Remains Unproven   23
   Barbara Grizzuti Harrison

3. Poor Parent-Child Relationships Cause Homosexuality   28
   Roy Masters

4. Parent-Child Relationships Do Not Affect
   Homosexuality   36
   *Carolyn Welch Griffin, Marian J. Wirth
   & Arthur G. Wirth*

5. The Causes of Homosexuality Are Uncertain   45
   Deborah A. Miller & Alex Waigandt

6. The Causes of Homosexuality Are Unimportant   52
   Patricia Hersch

A Critical Thinking Activity:
   Recognizing Statements That Are Provable   58

Periodical Bibliography   60

Chapter 2: Should Society Encourage Increased Acceptance of Homosexuality?

Chapter Preface   62

1. Society Should Accept Homosexuality   63
   Jeff Peters

2. Society Does Not Need to Accept Homosexuality   69
   Carl F. Horowitz

3. Homosexuals Need Civil Rights Protection   78
   Matthew A. Coles

4. Homosexuals Do Not Need Civil Rights Protection   87
   Roger J. Magnuson

5. The Military Should Accept Homosexuals   96
   Eric Konigsberg

6. The Military Should Not Accept Homosexuals 102
   David Hackworth

7. School Programs Should Stress Acceptance of
   Homosexuality 106
   Bruce Mirken

8. School Programs Should Not Stress Acceptance of
   Homosexuality 113
   Patricia Smith

A Critical Thinking Activity:
   Distinguishing Between Fact and Opinion 120

Periodical Bibliography 122

Chapter 3: Can Homosexuals Change Their Sexual Orientation?

Chapter Preface 125

1. Psychotherapy Can Change Sexual Orientation 126
   Joseph Nicolosi

2. Psychotherapy Should Help Gay Men Accept Their
   Homosexuality 133
   Richard A. Isay

3. Christianity Can Help Gays Change Their Sexual
   Orientation 140
   Colin Cook

4. Gay Christians Should Accept Their Homosexuality 148
   Chris Glaser

A Critical Thinking Activity:
   Evaluating Sources of Information 156

Periodical Bibliography 158

Chapter 4: Should Society Legally Sanction Gay Relationships?

Chapter Preface 160

1. Society Should Sanction Gay Partnerships 161
   Thomas B. Stoddard & Patricia Horn

2. Society Should Not Sanction Gay Partnerships 167
   Bruce Fein & Dinesh D'Souza

3. Legalizing Gay Marriage Would Help Homosexuals 172
   Craig R. Dean

4. Marriage Is Not a Path to Liberation 177
   Paula L. Ettelbrick

5. Homosexuals Should Have Greater Parental Rights   184
   Scott Harris

6. Homosexuals Should Not Have Greater Parental
   Rights   192
   Human Events

A Critical Thinking Activity:
   Recognizing Deceptive Arguments   198

Periodical Bibliography   200

Organizations to Contact   201
Bibliography of Books   207
Index   211

Why Consider Opposing Viewpoints?

"The only way in which a human being can make some approach to knowing the whole of a subject is by hearing what can be said about it by persons of every variety of opinion and studying all modes in which it can be looked at by every character of mind. No wise man ever acquired his wisdom in any mode but this."

John Stuart Mill

In our media-intensive culture it is not difficult to find differing opinions. Thousands of newspapers and magazines and dozens of radio and television talk shows resound with differing points of view. The difficulty lies in deciding which opinion to agree with and which "experts" seem the most credible. The more inundated we become with differing opinions and claims, the more essential it is to hone critical reading and thinking skills to evaluate these ideas. Opposing Viewpoints books address this problem directly by presenting stimulating debates that can be used to enhance and teach these skills. The varied opinions contained in each book examine many different aspects of a single issue. While examining these conveniently edited opposing views, readers can develop critical thinking skills such as the ability to compare and contrast authors' credibility, facts, argumentation styles, use of persuasive techniques, and other stylistic tools. In short, the Opposing Viewpoints Series is an ideal way to attain the higher-level thinking and reading skills so essential in a culture of diverse and contradictory opinions.

In addition to providing a tool for critical thinking, Opposing Viewpoints books challenge readers to question their own strongly held opinions and assumptions. Most people form their opinions on the basis of upbringing, peer pressure, and personal, cultural, or professional bias. By reading carefully balanced opposing views, readers must directly confront new ideas as well as the opinions of those with whom they disagree. This is not to simplistically argue that everyone who reads opposing views will—or should—change his or her opinion. Instead, the series enhances readers' depth of understanding of their own views by encouraging confrontation with opposing ideas. Careful examination of others' views can lead to the readers' understanding of the logical inconsistencies in their own opinions, perspective on why they hold an opinion, and the consideration of the possibility that their opinion requires further evaluation.

Evaluating Other Opinions

To ensure that this type of examination occurs, Opposing Viewpoints books present all types of opinions. Prominent spokespeople on different sides of each issue as well as well-known professionals from many disciplines challenge the reader. An additional goal of the series is to provide a forum for other, less known, or even unpopular viewpoints. The opinion of an ordinary person who has had to make the decision to cut off life support from a terminally ill relative, for example, may be just as valuable and provide just as much insight as a medical ethicist's professional opinion. The editors have two additional purposes in including these less known views. One, the editors encourage readers to respect others' opinions—even when not enhanced by professional credibility. It is only by reading or listening to and objectively evaluating others' ideas that one can determine whether they are worthy of consideration. Two, the inclusion of such viewpoints encourages the important critical thinking skill of objectively evaluating an author's credentials and bias. This evaluation will illuminate an author's reasons for taking a particular stance on an issue and will aid in readers' evaluation of the author's ideas.

As series editors of the Opposing Viewpoints Series, it is our hope that these books will give readers a deeper understanding of the issues debated and an appreciation of the complexity of even seemingly simple issues when good and honest people disagree. This awareness is particularly important in a democratic society such as ours in which people enter into public debate to determine the common good. Those with whom one disagrees should not be regarded as enemies but rather as people whose views deserve careful examination and may shed light on one's own.

Thomas Jefferson once said that "difference of opinion leads to inquiry, and inquiry to truth." Jefferson, a broadly educated man, argued that "if a nation expects to be ignorant and free . . . it expects what never was and never will be." As individuals and as a nation, it is imperative that we consider the opinions of others and examine them with skill and discernment. The Opposing Viewpoints Series is intended to help readers achieve this goal.

David L. Bender & Bruno Leone,
Series Editors

Introduction

"In the 1990s homosexuality will be what the abortion issue has been in the 1980s."

Morris Chapman, *Newsweek*, September 14, 1992

On June 27, 1969, police raided a gay bar in New York City called the Stonewall Inn to enforce vice laws against homosexual acts. Such raids, in which police often harassed homosexuals, were a common occurrence in the 1950s and 1960s in many U.S. cities. In this case, however, as the people arrested were being led out of the bar, streetside onlookers, most of them also gay, began to taunt and throw objects at the police. Eventually the raid erupted into a full-scale riot between the police and the gay community, with clashes continuing sporadically for two days. The incident, which became known as the Stonewall Rebellion, brought a sense of empowerment to homosexuals and marked a turning point in gay life in the United States. Gay author Roger E. Biery wrote that the event brought visibility and togetherness to many gays and lesbians who had previously felt isolated: "For the first time in history, it was okay to be gay."

Inspired both by Stonewall and by the civil rights and antiwar movements of the 1960s, gays and lesbians greatly increased their efforts to improve their social acceptance and to make their presence publicly known. The number of gay and lesbian organizations in the United States grew from around fifty in 1969 to almost eight hundred in 1973 and several thousand by 1990. At first the primary aim of many of these groups was to encourage all lesbians and gays to "come out of the closet"—to publicly acknowledge their sexual orientation. An increasing number of people did just that. In 1970 about five thousand gays and lesbians marched in New York City to commemorate the Stonewall incident. Over the next two decades "gay pride" parades became increasingly larger and more common. In October 1987 more than 600,000 gays and lesbians marched in Washington, D.C., to demand equality and civil rights.

This increased visibility has been coupled with other efforts. In part due to gay lobbying, homosexuality was removed from the official list of mental disorders by the American Psychiatric Association in 1973, and in 1975 the Civil Service Commission

Good intro

12

lifted its 1953 ban against hiring homosexuals for most federal jobs. By 1992, gay and lesbian activists had also succeeded in having statutes enacted in 21 states and 130 municipalities that provide legal protection against discrimination based on sexual orientation. A growing number of religious groups have recognized and affirmed homosexuality and gay relationships, and some denominations have welcomed gay and lesbian clergy.

The gay movement has not progressed unimpeded, however. It has faced setbacks both from within and without. AIDS has devastated the male gay community and it absorbed much of the energy of the movement in the 1980s and 1990s. The gay movement has also faced divisions within itself between lesbians and gay men, who often have differing experiences and agendas, and between homosexuals who wish to assimilate within society and those who seek to create their own subculture. Such relatively new groups as Queer Nation, which seeks to combat prejudice against homosexuality with civil disobedience and public confrontational tactics rather than legal and political lobbying, are controversial both outside and within the gay community.

In addition to divisions within itself, the gay and lesbian community faces opposition from the general public. Many Americans view homosexuality as an immoral lifestyle or a mental disorder that should be treated rather than encouraged. Some, such as writer Samuel McCracken, view homosexuality as simply unnatural. He writes in *Commentary*:

> I use the term "natural" here to mean "appropriate to the nature of man," for I am at a loss to know what other term to use in dealing with the obvious fact that human bodies seem more obviously designed for heterosexual intercourse than for homosexual, both as to technique and to purpose. . . .

> And it seems to me that one cannot honestly ignore the relation of sex to reproduction. . . . The fact is that homosexuality generally entails a renunciation of responsibility for the continuance of the human race.

Many of the opinions people have about homosexuality are influenced by religious beliefs, which have traditionally condemned homosexuality. The leadership of the movement against gay rights has come largely from conservative religious leaders such as Jerry Falwell and Pat Robertson. They and others have strongly opposed any government actions that grant special rights to homosexuals or in any way condone or signal approval of homosexuality. Conservative commentator and Republican presidential candidate Patrick Buchanan, speaking at the 1992 Republican convention, asserted that gay rights have no place "in a nation we still call God's country."

Many Americans without religious reasons for opposing homosexuality still feel uncomfortable about it. An August 1992 *New York Times*/CBS News poll found about 80 percent believed homosexuals have equal rights to job opportunity, but only 57 percent supported having homosexuals in the military, and only 38 percent thought it was an acceptable alternative lifestyle. In Colorado in 1992 voters approved a measure preventing local governments from enacting laws that would protect gays from discrimination. Critics of the measure stated that besides depriving homosexuals needed legal protection, it tacitly sanctioned prejudice and violence against gays and lesbians. "Colorado is a test case," argued Robert Bray of the National Gay and Lesbian Task Force, a civil rights organization. "The ultraconservative right . . . intends to export Colorado-style initiatives around the country." Supporters of the measures say they are not against homosexuals, only against giving any group special status. "Our position has never been to discriminate," stated Will Perkins, head of the organization Colorado for Family Values, which supported the measure. "Our position is that sexual orientation is not an acceptable criterion for special rights."

Clearly, many Americans remain ambivalent about the increased visibility of the homosexual rights movement. *Homosexuality: Opposing Viewpoints* examines these conflicts in the following chapters: What Causes Homosexuality? Should Society Encourage Increased Acceptance of Homosexuality? Can Homosexuals Change Their Sexual Orientation? Should Society Legally Sanction Gay Relationships? The viewpoints presented here demonstrate that homosexuality, the formerly invisible "love that dared not speak its name," will remain a prominent and controversial issue in the American social and political scene.

What Causes Homosexuality?

Homosexuality

Chapter Preface

The question of what causes some people to be sexually attracted to members of their own gender generates many different answers.

Most scientific theories on the causes of homosexuality reflect the classic debate on whether a person's makeup is the product of biology or environment. Many researchers speculate that homosexuality is a by-product of upbringing, especially a child's relationship with his or her parents. Other researchers have focused instead on physical causes, such as brain structure or hormone exposure while in the womb. Recent research locating differences within the brains of heterosexual and homosexual men has added new ammunition to the biological side of the nature vs. nurture controversy.

The question of causation has important political implications for gays and lesbians. Some hope that if homosexuality is proven to be inherent in a person's physical makeup, prejudice and discrimination will decrease. "It would reduce being gay to something like being left-handed," writes noted gay journalist and author Randy Shilts, "which is in fact all that it is." Others are not so sure whether evidence demonstrating physical causes of homosexuality would have such a favorable impact on society's attitudes toward homosexuals. Science writer Denise Grady writes in *Discover* that some homosexuals "fear that the brain difference will be viewed as a defect, fueling homophobia—a pretext to screen fetuses and abort homosexual ones, or inject them with 'corrective' hormones, or even to press for brain-cell transplants to 'cure' homosexuality."

Clearly, the cause of homosexuality is of more than scientific interest—it is an issue that may have social repercussions as well. The viewpoints in this chapter examine several theories on the causes of homosexuality.

"Several independent studies have shown that various brain structures are different between people of different sexual orientation. "

Differences in Brain Structure May Cause Homosexuality

Marcia Barinaga

In 1991 Simon LeVay, a biologist at the Salk Institute for Biological Studies in San Diego, California, published research indicating that variations in sexual orientation may be the result of differences in brain structure. His findings received much attention and renewed the debate over whether homosexuality is caused by innate biological differences. In the following viewpoint, Marcia Barinaga, a writer for *Science* magazine, describes the significance of LeVay's research and other studies that suggest a biological cause of homosexuality.

As you read, consider the following questions:

1. What were LeVay's specific findings concerning the human brain and homosexuality, according to Barinaga?
2. How has LeVay's research been criticized, according to the author?
3. What other studies concerning homosexuality does Barinaga describe?

"I've always known I'm fundamentally different," is a frequent claim of homosexuals who feel that their sexual orientation is innate and not formed by choice or by social environment. Whether they're right has been the subject of heated debate on many fronts: scientific, social, political—even religious. An article in *Science* steps right into the middle of that controversy, presenting new evidence suggesting that homosexuality is at least in part a biological phenomenon.

Simon LeVay, a neuroscientist at the Salk Institute in San Diego, has found that in homosexual men part of the anterior hypothalamus—a brain region that governs sexual behavior—has the anatomical form usually found in women rather than the form typical of heterosexual men. LeVay's is the second report of a difference between the brains of homosexuals and heterosexuals (the first was published in 1990 in *Brain Research*)—though it is the first to find such a difference in the hypothalamus, which is known to be a source of sexual urges. That connection raises the possibility that this difference may not only correlate with homosexuality but also play a role in causing it.

Biological Differences

Either interpretation—correlation or cause—suggests that some biological difference is at the root of homosexuality. And that is a potentially explosive notion. Homophobes could exploit the result by pointing to the brain "defect" in homosexuals; they might even envisage screening for homosexuality in utero. Others may interpret the data as evidence that homosexuality is as natural a variation from the average brain as left-handedness. And many gays will see LeVay's finding as welcome confirmation of what they have always believed. "If it's true, the implications are amazing," says Dennis Landis, a neurologist who studies brain structure at Case Western Reserve University. "It would begin to suggest why male homosexuality is present in most human populations, despite cultural constraints. It suggests it's a biological phenomenon."

Indeed, the finding has important implications for science as well as society. Not only does it link sexual orientation to a structure within the brain, it also adds to a small but growing body of observations suggesting that many structural differences in the brain—including those that distinguish typical male and female brains—may be determined by prenatal hormone levels. Some of those differences may play a role in sexual behavior as well as in cognitive differences between men and women.

Lest eager believers jump to too many conclusions, LeVay points out that his finding contains no direct evidence that the difference he has observed actually causes homosexuality. He and others in the field acknowledge that the paper needs replication, since such studies are difficult and somewhat subjective. "Simon is very good; he's extremely well-equipped to make those observations," said one neuroscientist who is familiar with LeVay's work. "But we ought to put off big speculation until it is confirmed."

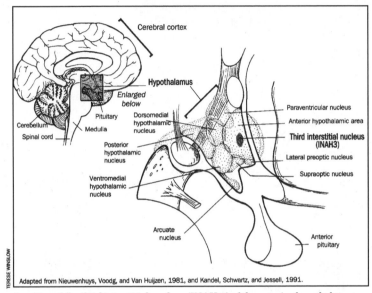

Location of the third interstitial nucleus (INAH 3) of the anterior hypothalamus, reported to be smaller in homosexual men than in heterosexual men. Nuclei are about the size of the head of a pin.

Source: *Journal of NIH Research.*

Ironically, given the potential impact of his work, LeVay, whose main research focuses on the visual areas of the brain, says he began this study as a "hobby project." He knew that the research team of Roger Gorski at the University of California, Los Angeles, had examined postmortem human brains and found two regions, or "nuclei," in the anterior hypothalamus that are more than twice as large in men as they are in women. LeVay extended the study to homosexual men, using brains of men who had died of AIDS. In most of the 19 homosexuals he looked at, he found that one of these nuclei, called INAH-3, was smaller than it is in heterosexual men—in fact it was the same size as it is in women.

The finding "fits in well with the animal research that shows [hypothalamic differences] that correlate with sexual behavior," says Gloria Hoffman, a neuroendocrine anatomist at the University of Pittsburgh. Indeed, while there is no animal model for studying homosexuality, some researchers have observed that experimental lesions in the anterior hypothalamus of male monkeys reduce behavior such as the mounting of females, while leaving unperturbed other sexual activities such as masturbation—the closest any animal evidence comes to showing a physical effect on sexual orientation.

AIDS provides the first chance to study the brains of homosexual men, LeVay says, since male homosexuality is a risk factor for the disease, and AIDS patients are often categorized by risk group. The brains of lesbians are more difficult to obtain for research, since lesbians are not generally at risk for AIDS, and sexual orientation is rarely recorded in deaths from other causes.

Could the differences LeVay saw be due to AIDS rather than to homosexuality? "AIDS pathologies . . . could influence the size of the nuclei," says Laura Allen, a postdoc with Gorski at UCLA who studies the INAH nuclei. But she notes that LeVay found that heterosexual men had large INAH-3 nuclei, whether they had died from AIDS or from other causes. That leads Allen to conclude that "LeVay is probably correct," though she reserves final approval until another lab has reproduced the finding.

Problems in Brain Research

One reason the work begs for confirmation is that the study of sexual dimorphism in the human brain has had a history of controversy and contradiction. Not only are the structures hard to see clearly in tissue slices, but researchers argue about what is the most reliable measure of size—the volume measurements used by LeVay, or actual cell counts. There is also the nagging possibility that some unknown factors may influence the size of the structures, according to one of the major players in the field, Dick Swaab, a neuroscientist at the Netherlands Institute for Brain Research in Amsterdam.

Despite his words of caution, Swaab says he is glad to hear of LeVay's finding, because it builds on his own group's discovery, reported in 1990 in Brain Research, of the first known structural difference between the brains of homosexual and heterosexual men. Swaab's team found that the suprachiasmatic nucleus (SCN), a part of the brain that governs daily rhythms, is twice as large in homosexual men as it is in the typical heterosexual brain.

But the suprachiasmatic nucleus is not known to play a role in sexual behavior, LeVay points out. So while it might be influenced by the same factors that cause homosexuality, it is less likely than the anterior hypothalamus to be part of the cause. Gorski postdoc Allen agrees that the anterior hypothalamus is "exactly where we would expect some nucleus that may control [sexual orientation] to be located."

But what factors might influence the development of this part of the brain? A possible answer comes from studies in rats, which also have a sexually dimorphic area in their anterior hypothalamus, larger in males than in females, that governs sexual behavior. In rats, the development of the area is dependent on testosterone levels before and immediately after birth. Male rat pups that are castrated at birth, reducing their testosterone levels, have a smaller sexually dimorphic nucleus than normal males, and when they grow up they show less male-type sexual behavior, such as mounting. Testosterone injections enlarge the nucleus in female pups. The resulting adults show more "male" sexual behavior.

Extending that kind of data to humans involves a huge step, but that's just the step some researchers are trying to take. Sandra J. Witelson and her colleagues at McMaster University have found lesbians to be twice as likely as heterosexual women to show lefthand preference on a variety of tasks; gay men also show such a tendency. Since studies of people with abnormal sex-hormone levels suggest that handedness is a brain feature that can be influenced by sex hormones during brain development, Witelson says her team's results suggest there "might be atypical brain organization" in homosexuals, also caused by atypical sex-hormone levels.

Hormones and the Brain

In a paper in *Psychoneuroendocrinology* (v.16, p.131), Witelson proposes that the brain is a mosaic of areas that may respond to sex hormones at various times during early development. Typical female or male hormone levels would produce a typical female or male brain, she says. But unusual levels of sex hormones at any given time may switch the development of susceptible brain areas. "This could cause different areas in the same brain to undergo different sexual differentiation," says Witelson. Depending on levels and timing, sex-hormones could influence handedness, sexual orientation, or other characteristics.

Witelson emphasizes that her model is speculative, based on a rather eclectic assortment of data. But that model—and LeVay's finding—raises questions that offer a program for future research. Does INAH-3 have sex-hormone receptors, for example, indicating that it could be influenced by those hormones? And when during brain development does the difference between the sexes emerge?

No matter how such questions are answered, it may be difficult ever to establish that INAH-3 or any other brain structure actually causes homosexuality, or to rule out the possibility that childhood or adolescent experience may have altered the size of

INAH-3 in homosexuals. But Witelson, for one, is not discouraged. "The important [point] is that several independent studies have shown that various brain structures are different between people of different sexual orientation," she says. And Swaab agrees with Witelson that this is what one would expect. The difference between homosexuals and heterosexuals, he quips, "should be in the brain, not in the heart."

"Scientists, in their haste to determine the 'causes' of homosexuality, have been wrong before."

The Link Between Brain Structure and Homosexuality Remains Unproven

Barbara Grizzuti Harrison

Barbara Grizzuti Harrison is a writer and columnist for *Mademoiselle* magazine. Her books include *Unlearning the Lie: Sexism in School* and *This Astonishing World*, a collection of interviews and essays. In the following viewpoint, she expresses doubts about studies that conclude differences in brain structure might account for differences in sexual orientation. Harrison criticizes such theories as being too simplistic to explain human sexuality. She argues that society should spend more effort on reducing social prejudice against gays and lesbians rather than searching for biological causes.

As you read, consider the following questions:

1. What flaws does Harrison find in LeVay's research and conclusions?
2. Why does the author doubt the ability of science to adequately explain human sexuality?
3. What should be the important questions society asks concerning homosexuality, according to Harrison?

How many angels can dance on the head of a pin?

Nowadays, such ostensibly medieval inquiries have taken the form of scientific research; and what substance and solace the debatable answers afford us is beyond me—unless it is to give rise to yet more questions. This is what I mean:

In September 1991, respected neurobiologist Simon LeVay, Ph.D., of San Diego's Salk Institute, reported in the prestigious journal *Science* that one tiny portion of the hypothalamus region of the brains of homosexual men is less than half the size of that of heterosexual men. *Tiny:* We are talking about a volume of cells—not even a cluster—that is smaller in heterosexual men than a grain of sand, and that is arguably nonexistent, and certainly almost undetectable, in the brains of women and homosexual men.

Well, we all know—we've been told often enough—that size, as it relates to sex, doesn't count. . . .

I suppose I ought not to engage in such expressions of levity. God knows, this study is being taken extremely seriously: More ink has been given over to a discussion of the possible psychosexual and social consequences of Dr. LeVay's conclusions than to any recent scientific research I can think of. This is inevitable whenever scientific evidence suggests that sexual adaptation or orientation is biologically determined. Anything that appears to prove we are biologically *destined* to be one thing or another is bound to arouse controversy.

Preliminary Findings

We would do well to bear in mind that these are very preliminary findings. (Too preliminary, one would think, upon which to expend so much intellectual passion.) On the other hand, all of us—homosexuals, heterosexuals and bisexuals—have something to gain and something to lose depending on how the results of this study are interpreted; so here goes.

Dr. LeVay examined thin slices of autopsied brain tissue from 19 homosexual men, 16 men presumed to be heterosexual and 6 women presumed to be heterosexual (he was unable to find any lesbians for his purposes)—a very small sampling, indeed.

On the face of it, there are evidentiary problems: First, inasmuch as all the homosexual men autopsied died of AIDS—which infiltrates the central nervous system—might there not be some relationship between the disease and the size of the hypothalamus?

Dr. LeVay says no, pointing to the fact that six of the men presumed to have been heterosexual also died of AIDS (contracted as a result of IV [intravenous] drug use); yet the structure of their brains was several times larger than that of the homosexual men who died as a result of AIDS.

Okay, let's yield that point to him. But here's another issue: He diagnosed tissue samples from 16 men *presumed* to be heterosexual and 6 women *presumed* to be heterosexual. Suppose—since not everyone has come out of the closet of secrecy—there were "hidden" homosexuals among this group. And what if there were bisexuals among those tested? If that were the case, the study wouldn't be worth fussing about.

Lesbianism a Conscious Choice

I personally don't think I was "born this way." (In fact, when I'm feeling hostile, I've been known to tell right-wingers that I'm a successfully "cured" hetero.) Until I was in my early thirties, I fell in love with men, took pleasure in sleeping with them, and even married one. But like most women, I experienced most of my closest emotional relationships with female friends. The only thing that made me different was that at some point I got curious about lesbian feminist claims that it was possible to combine that intense female intimacy with good sex. The good sex part turned out to be vastly easier than I anticipated. Even so, there was no immediate *biological* reason to stop having sex with men or to start living as a lesbian. Coming out was, for me, a conscious decision—every step of the way.

Lindsy Van Gelder, *Ms.*, May/June 1991.

Scientists, in their haste to determine the "causes" of homosexuality, have been wrong before. In a letter to the *New York Times*, William M. Byne, M.D., of Columbia University, cites several such errors. One occurred when Harvard neurologist Norman Geshwind, M.D., Ph.D., "conjectured that homosexuals contracted AIDS because of prenatal hormonal conditions that disrupted their immune systems and determined their sexual orientation." On another occasion, writes Dr. Byne, a study in *Science* claiming to demonstrate "a sex difference in the splenium, a portion of the brain connecting its two halves," was "interpreted as the biological explanation for gender differences in social roles, aptitudes and achievements." And in still another study published in *Science*, researchers claimed that a hormonal test could "distinguish between homosexual and heterosexual men," which is demonstrably untrue.

Nothing Proven

Let's give Dr. LeVay the benefit of the doubt; let's assume that his study will be duplicated with the same results. What will have been proven? Other anatomical differences will not have

25

been ruled out, nor will hormonal influences, nor will environmental factors, nor will the role of free will and choice. It is entirely possible that a number of different factors, anatomical, social and personal are at work in determining sexual preference.

Do we care?

Yes. Some gay men have been pleased by Dr. LeVay's studies. They contend that if the difference between homosexuals and heterosexuals is found to be innate, factored in at birth, homosexuals may be better tolerated by society at large—inasmuch as choice was in no way involved.

But this is too simple: For one thing, the structural difference Dr. LeVay found may be a *consequence* of homosexual activity, not a cause; according to my understanding of the way we learn language, the brain is capable of being "rewired." As John Money, M.D., professor emeritus at Johns Hopkins School of Medicine in Baltimore, says, "The really interesting questions are, When did it happen and how did it get there?"

Negative Consequences

For another thing, society may, if Dr. LeVay's studies are reckoned to be of crucial importance, not respond tolerantly at all. We live in strange biotechnical times. Suppose some clown comes along and suggests surgery, or hormone treatments, a vaccine, testosterone injections, or whatever, to "cure" the brains of homosexuals? Suppose Dr. LeVay's studies are used to prove that homosexuals are "diseased," handicapped, incompletely human? That deplorable result is just as likely, it seems to me. I truly believe that people who scorn and despise homosexuals are capable of predicating their antipathies on any evidence at all . . . or on no evidence at all.

(And, not so incidentally, what would be the consequences to women—whose hypothalamus is said to resemble more closely that of male homosexuals than that of male heterosexuals—if this brain structure were seen as "aberrant"? Would that make women "aberrant," too?)

And what about bisexuals?

And, if we adhere to a "single cause" theory, will we then conclude that a "tomboy" is the product of a diseased brain—no wonder she plays with blocks instead of dolls; it's that darned hypothalamus!

To cleave to this theory, in other words, is just as likely to be straitjacketing as liberating.

I know scientists have to do what they do; but what next? Are we going to look for the area of the brain that determines why some gay men like leather? Why some straight men are into S & M? Why some homosexuals and some heterosexuals are promiscuous and why some are monogamous?

What about transsexuals? Is there ever going to be anything that satisfactorily explains that phenomenon? It's sometimes made to sound like a biological glitch: "I felt like a woman trapped in a man's body." But what do those words mean, exactly? That he wants to have sex with men as a woman? Some transsexuals say it means simply that they want to do "feminine" things—like wearing silk underwear or doing needlework. Well, for Pete's sake, can't they do that as men?

Sexuality and Science

Sexuality is all so complicated. I doubt very much that anything that happens in a laboratory is going to provide us with the answers. God and sex are two subjects you're not going to reduce to scientific formulas.

"The behavioral sciences have not identified any sexual expression that can be empirically demonstrated to be, of itself, in a culture-free way detrimental to full human existence." That sentence, it may surprise you to know, comes from a study published by the Catholic Theological Society of America (not all Catholics are gay-bashers). The study also says that the question to be asked of any specific form of behavior is: Is it "harmful to the full flowering of personhood"? Social acceptability or lack of it is not a proper guideline: What a person does in bed has to be judged—if we're into the judging business, which I, happily, am not—in the context of his or her whole life. Is it good, is it kind, is it intelligent, is it beautiful? Does it hurt you? Those are far more important questions than how many cells dance in someone's hypothalamus.

"There are many types of dysfunctional family disorders. One of them, of course, is overt homosexuality."

Poor Parent-Child Relationships Cause Homosexuality

Roy Masters

Many theories of homosexual causation focus on childhood experiences, especially those within the family. In the following viewpoint, Roy Masters states that male homosexuality is an emotional/mental disorder caused by poor father-son relationships. Masters is a stress management consultant who hosts a syndicated radio show and has written several books, including *How to Control Your Negative Emotions*.

As you read, consider the following questions:

1. How does Masters distinguish between racism and criticism of homosexuality?
2. What basic family pattern leads to homosexuality, according to Masters?
3. Why is the father so important to the family, according to the author?

From Roy Masters, "Gays and Society: The Growing Clash," *New Dimensions*, July 1990. Reprinted with permission.

The question of whether homosexuality is caused by life's experience or is an inborn quality is, indeed, an extremely sensitive subject. The topic invokes strong emotion and prejudice, no matter which side one takes. Like abortion, it seems to be one of America's almost unsolvable problems. To understand the causes of homosexuality, a great deal of objectivity and compassion are required.

As is the case with so many other forms of aberrant behavior, we are dealing with victims who are in denial that they are victims. The very concept of gay pride was, of course, in imitation of racial minorities' call for ethnic pride in the '60s. However, the difference between the two is obvious to most Americans. One is simply a racial matter, but the other is behavioral. Of course, homosexual organizations deny that being gay is a behavioral problem because their claim to political power is based on convincing the country that being critical of homosexuality is equivalent to being racist. In order to make that stick, they must first convince the public that gays were born that way and that their inclinations have nothing to do with upbringing or moral choice.

Sickness and Denial

Thus homosexuals have been drawn into their sickness, siding with their torment rather than face the painful truth about their troubled childhood. Denial is a powerful thing for any individual to overcome. But added to this problem is the fact that the whole gay movement is there to be supportive of a deviant lifestyle. Such unhealthy support groups are common in our society and are, sadly, very effective in keeping people from finding themselves. Of course, these organizations believe that they are helping and being compassionate. But in reality, they provide the troubled individual with all the excuses and rationalizations he could ever need to justify his aberrant lifestyle. Often, these organizations are simply after power. . . .

The average person is unaware of the depth and breadth of the childhood traumas that have formed his adult modus operandi. It is very important not to underestimate the effect parents can have on their children. If we take a moment to think about it, all of us can remember how vulnerable we were when we were children surrounded by the giant adult world. In a way, our parents were our gods; they represented our only real protection against a confusing and dangerous world. It is damaging enough when a child is traumatized by any adult, but when a child is betrayed by his own father or mother, that betrayal has a tragic and lasting effect.

So, what does all this have to do with homosexuality? Everything. When talking about a child's reaction to trauma, it is important to understand that we are dealing with a scientific, repeatable phenomenon called conditioned response, discovered and made famous by the Russian psychologist Ivan Pavlov. In Pavlov's ground-breaking experiment, a dog learns to associate the ringing of the bell with food; soon he salivates at the sound of the bell even when there is no food. This associative technique can apply to anything; it is employed in just about any family situation. For this reason, almost any problem of compulsive behavior that a person might have can be clarified by understanding what went on in the homosexual's family. Once we realize that we have all gone through something very similar, we just manifest it differently, then we can have the compassion necessary to understand homosexuality.

Patterns

In many years of counseling, I have dealt with countless family situations conforming to the following pattern. Two boys are born into a dysfunctional family, composed of a cruel, confusing mother, and a brutal father (perhaps an alcoholic) who is rarely at home. Now, the anger and resentment which the (victim) mother feels for the father is unloaded on these boys. She unconsciously hates men, beginning with her own alcoholic father, but extending now to her husband—and becoming a cumulative traumatic experience for her sons. Because of the different dispositions and status of the two boys, one rebels from her control and one conforms. One way or the other, the boys have been traumatized away from their natural center, their true personhood.

Fathers and Sons

Homosexuality is a developmental problem that is almost always the result of problems in family relations, particularly between father and son. As a result of failure with father, the boy does not fully internalize male gender-identity, and develops homosexually. This is the most commonly seen clinical model.

Joseph Nicolosi, *Reparative Therapy of Male Homosexuality*, 1991.

There are many types of dysfunctional family disorders. One of them, of course, is overt homosexuality. The other is connected to the same pressures that cause homosexuality, but manifests in an entirely different way: "macho" behavior, a false masculinity that is a compensating overreaction to feelings of vulnerability and latent femininity. This compensation could well include any other traits of the child's father by association. So, for example, the boy could take on a veneer of religious values, picked up from his father by association, rather than by any true insight. This is the basic process by which one brother becomes homosexual while the other enjoys an apparently normal life.

Both boys carry a great deal of anger just beneath the surface—unconscious feelings of resentment toward the parents who failed them. As it is passed from generation to generation, this continuous flaw in the nature of the family structure itself can be cured only by overcoming denial barriers and facing hidden anger. Ironically, great political power can be derived by simply exploiting the existing rage that millions of people feel about their family experience. Radical Berkeley, California, is full of leftist posters that call for overthrowing "the patriarch." It is not hard to guess who is the intended target of that kind of message.

Abnormal Choices

In the case of the two boys, the mother's daily pressure on her rebellious son traumatizes him to side with his errant father. In such an emotional state, where common sense goes out of the window and there's more heat than light, there are only two lifestyle options available: rebel against your father and join your mother—or rebel against your mother and side with your father. Both are obviously abnormal choices, since the child wants and needs the balance of both parents.

So one errant son sides with his angry father rather than take the identity of his mother as his effeminate brother did. But again, just as his brother found a false femininity, he finds a false masculinity, laid on like a coat of paint rather than drawn naturally from within. This "macho" brother bonds falsely with various traits of his father's by association—like Pavlov's dog—perhaps his father lifts weights and talks tough. This bogus identity becomes the son's chief form of denial, and if that isn't enough of an escape from the thing he unconsciously fears the most—his latent femininity—he turns to other forms of addiction for comfort.

The question is, why is he in denial? Again, remember that the normal process is to have a loving mother/father unit, but when you are traumatized by anger at parental failure, a strange thing happens that affects you deep in your psyche. You don't actually "succeed" in your rebellion, but become slowly *transformed into the likeness of what you hate.* The reason for this is simple; you cannot hate without feeling guilt, hate being a destructive emotion—and you especially cannot hate your parents without guilt. You unconsciously relieve the guilt by bonding to the very thing you hated, by way of compensation.

But the main motivation compelling the macho son to escape is to avoid seeing what he has secretly become at the hands of his dominating mother. He is much more affected by his childhood bonding to her than he can ever admit to himself. Clinically, the rule of thumb is simply this: Reject your father and, no matter what, you will become overly influenced by your mother.

Sadly, there are many young men in America who are losing their grip on their true masculinity in this way. Simply put, it is the mother's instinctive responsibility to nurture the children, to protect them from the harsh realities of the world that they are too young to face. On the other hand, the father's instinctive responsibility is to bring the children into the reality of the world, to see to it that they are strong enough and independent enough to start another nuclear group—another family.

So therefore, there must be a healthy balance of these two types of love, one earthy and compassionate, the other a kindly but no-nonsense type—a tougher, masculine love without which the child is in danger of becoming spoiled and immorally wild, unable to make his way in the world. If the child becomes more interested in comfort than in challenge, more interested in "rights" than in responsibility, he will soon need a dictator in one form or another to govern him, his capacity for self-governance having been ruined. This is how nations fall.

Lack of Balance

Without this balance in the family, without a strong center, the macho, hard-drinking son is actually running away through drink and machismo activities from the fact that he has been and is evolving from a feminine, nurturing core. In this case, if he has enough women to mother him and make him warm and secure, that feminine "seed" tends to emerge, only to be further denied as the macho son immerses himself into more machismo behavior, hard drinking, and the like. This is an immutable law.

On the other hand, the weaker, conformist, effeminate son, is more directly mothered and loved for succumbing to his mother's will. As a result, he becomes the extension of her personality and thus comes under a compulsion to validate his mother identity by re-immersing himself in her approval. This is the classic denial process: We tend to reaffirm the wrong in us by identifying with the very people who corrupted us. Here, mother and son are "very close." This son is one of two types: If he retains his male behavior, he will be a weak and ineffective father, a womanizer, etc.—or else he will become an outright homosexual. The mother shows a kinder face to her approval-hungry, conformist son. She is very supportive of her identity in him. It must be clearly understood that the reason both parents treat their offspring so shamefully is that they too were victims of trauma in their own lives. They were hurt in much the same way as they are now doing the hurting—but they are not aware of it because of the denial of their own pain. By living in denial of what has gone wrong with them, they are, without realizing it, becoming the vehicle of destruction of innocence as a defense against realizing the truth.

Now, to the homosexual connection in all this! Here we have the rebel and the conformist, one who is homosexual or basically effeminate—the other who is rebelling against that same identity within him through machismo behavior and drink. One truth that the homosexual groups have always claimed is that there are two distinct types of homosexuals, one actual and one latent. As I said before, some men are transformed more directly into the female, early, directly from mother, while the rebel can also become a homosexual through a longer, more opposite course, in his struggle to deny his implanted feminine nature. The completely conformed homosexual simply takes on and accepts female characteristics and seeks acceptance for them, which is part and parcel of the denial process. He thinks and feels like a woman, looks at men through women's eyes.

Child Abuse and Lesbianism

There are special needs that little girls have that make them unique. When those needs are denied, ignored, or exploited, the future womanhood of that child is in jeopardy.

Just how are those needs denied, ignored, or exploited? Through abuse. . . . Abuse can be overt, as in physical or sexual abuse, or it may be more subtle. Of course, its more subtle versions wouldn't legally qualify as child abuse, but they are forms of abuse nonetheless, and they have far-reaching consequences. One of those consequences is a distorted sexual identity. I have seen, time and again, clear connections between early abuse and confusion in sexuality. And I cannot ignore the histories of the many women I've known who have survived one form of abuse or another and are also attracted to other women. Although abuse by itself does not cause lesbianism, it can certainly be found in the background of many lesbian women and has in many cases been a contributing factor to their orientation.

Carol Ahrens in *Desires in Conflict*, 1991.

The rebel goes on to lose himself in machismo behavior, boxing, body building, and the like, in an attempt to deny the implanted feminine identity which is gestating within him. He too, by virtue of his trauma, is very woman-fixated, often fearful of women, possibly even compensating for this fear through violence. (It is no coincidence that the incidence of rape has risen staggeringly in the last few decades, and that high school boys polled readily admit that they would rape if they knew they wouldn't get caught.)

Understand that in the normal growing-up process, the good parent weans the child away from needing excessive parental approval, but in this case, since the boy had a stunted relationship, he sadly goes through life looking for the motherly love he never really had. Logically, the macho male will suffer from this irresistible need and try to overcome it with further false manhood, when all along, real manhood, which has more to do with not needing outside reinforcement, escapes him. The trouble is that he doesn't come back to a woman as a man should in marriage—independent and ready to lead his own family. Rather, he comes back to the woman as a little boy needing his mom. And while he has the illusion, through the nurturing love he receives, that he is becoming more of a man (more powerful and in control), he is actually becoming emasculated like his brother. Sensing the loss of masculinity outrages him and throws him into fits of violence, verbal or physical, or he runs and hides in drinking and hanging out with "the boys."

So the macho son is drawn unwittingly to the kind of women his mother was—not to him (he was the rebellious one), but to his conformist, accommodating brother (now the homosexual). Since the macho rebel has the same secret nature that his brother does, the feminine nurturing he gets from his wife is actually evolving his feminine side to the surface. If the process is allowed to complete itself, he wakes up one morning and finds that his feminine identity is emerging from a chrysalis that can no longer contain him.

Emerging Homosexuality

This process breaks through all machismo compensations. That is why we so often see the muscle-bound, athletic man become a homosexual, after long and apparently normal relationships with women in which he tried to prove his manhood. The machismo compensator tries to deny the implanted femininity and may even succeed for many years, only to awaken one day because of some temptation as a full-fledged homosexual. He stops resisting the forces working within him. Now this newly emerged self, the "false self" discussed earlier, must be accepted as normal and the rebel who denied his feminine nature (rather than confronting and overcoming it) becomes a denier in a different way, in the same way as his homosexual brother. At first, the rebel denies his gay inclinations; in the end, he claims gay is normal. At that point, of course, the gay rights organizations rush in to "support" the poor fellow who deserved—but never got—his father's love.

There, in a nutshell, is the whole process. The violator (the abusive or weak parent implanting the original nature) and the compassionate supporter are one and the same in principle, and in spirit. Therein lies a terrible danger concerning the motives of all the "compassionate" nurturers of the liberal-left. The imbalance of too much mothering and not enough real fathering is what did both sons in. Even those abused and neglected sons who never become homosexuals live in deep conflict and torment their entire lives, having extremely difficult relationships with their wives—and sometimes even committing violence against women as a way of getting even with their mothers for the effect her false love had on them. However, the more typical reaction is that they use women sexually, often going from one relationship to another, never able to commit to a marital relationship based on respect and loyalty, because they fear the control that women have over them.

Problems with Masculinity

All in all, some American men have a problem with their own masculinity that often makes them more susceptible to "crossing the values line" and accepting homosexuality as a legitimate lifestyle. In a *Time* magazine cover article, "Onward Women" (December 4, 1989), the reporter made a startling admission: "Already, there are numerous signs that male attitudes and values are becoming 'feminized,' though most men might reject that description." She's right, of course, on two counts. Men *are* becoming feminized, especially the younger ones, and most men *would* object to the description. It comes too close to the truth. The chilling thing is that the *Time* reporter meant it positively.

Our nation is in great trouble because of the widespread lack of enlightened fathers. Where there is no real father, only a weak or violent one, or none at all, the mother inevitably fills the void. Thus the identity of the children springs dominantly from the feminine side of the family, resulting in great conflict. If, as a nation, we can get fathers to understand what is written here, we can return the hearts of the fathers to their children and the hearts of the children to their fathers where they belong. Women will not have to shoulder the burden of raising children alone which, as has been shown here, creates a devastating psychological imbalance in the offspring.

With the well-balanced American family unit back together again, the feminization of America will come to an end. Families can become strong and loving again—and the country can avoid the inevitable destruction that results when its men and women hate each other—and its children grow up hating their parents.

"There are neurotic family patterns and there are loving family patterns. Both types of families produce heterosexual and homosexual children."

Parent-Child Relationships Do Not Affect Homosexuality

Carolyn Welch Griffin, Marian J. Wirth, and Arthur G. Wirth

Many parents question whether their actions caused their child to become homosexual. The following viewpoint is by three such parents who are active members of Parents FLAG (Friends of Lesbians and Gays) in St. Louis, Missouri. Carolyn Welch Griffin, the mother of a gay son, is president of Parents FLAG and a teacher and counselor in Collinsville, Illinois. Marian J. Wirth is a center regional director for Parents FLAG. Arthur G. Wirth is a retired professor of education at Washington University in St. Louis. In the viewpoint, the authors criticize the notion that parents cause their children to be gay or that homosexuality can be traced to family upbringing.

As you read, consider the following questions:

1. What criticisms do the authors have of the Irving Bieber study of homosexuals? How are the studies they cite superior, in their view?
2. How do the authors interpret negative family experiences between parents and their homosexual children?
3. In what respects do the authors say they are biased concerning the question of homosexuality and its causes?

From Carolyn Welch Griffin, Marian J. Wirth, and Arthur G. Wirth, *Beyond Acceptance: Parents of Lesbians and Gays Talk About Their Experiences*. Englewood Cliffs, NJ: Prentice Hall, 1986. Reprinted with permission.

Since 1948 there have been only two comprehensive long-range studies that give hard facts about homosexuality. The earlier one was the famous Kinsey study published in two volumes in 1948 and 1952, entitled *Sexual Behavior in the Human Male* and *Sexual Behavior in the Human Female*. The more recent one was the Alan Bell, Martin Weinberg, and Susan Hammersmith study published in 1982, *Sexual Preference: Its Development in Men and Women*. Both of these studies were conducted under the auspices of the Alfred C. Kinsey Institute for Sex Research at the University of Indiana at Bloomington, Indiana. Both meet the criteria of carefully designed research. Consequently, we relied on these two studies extensively.

Myths About Homosexuality

We will examine [some] of the most commonly held myths, beginning with the ones that are the most difficult for parents—the myths concerning cause. Though there are numerous myths about cause, we chose four of the most common to report on. The cause myths are followed by a personal statement about cause which is based on our research and experience.

Myth #1—Neurotic Family Patterns Cause Homosexuality. Most parents have suffered in one way or another from being told that a gay child is produced by a neurotic family. Such a family is described as being the combination of a dominant or seductive mother and a weak or distant father There is a scientific ring to this falsehood which makes it difficult to ignore. We decided to find out the source of this myth.

Until the gay rights movement began in 1969, there was little research on homosexuality. The few studies that did exist tended to support the biases of the culture.

One work which was widely quoted was published in a book by Irving Bieber et al., *Homosexuality: A Psychoanalytic Study*. It stated that male homosexuality is caused by an engulfing mother and/or a weak, distant, or hostile father.

Critics have pointed out that this study was characterized by the following poor research methods: only people who were in psychoanalysis were studied, no attempt was made to have a representative sample, there was no comparative control group, and the researchers made no attempt to eliminate researcher bias. As a result, the opinions presented in the study were just that—opinions, with no basis of fact to back them up. The study revealed more about psychoanalytic patients than about gays.

Fortunately, the Alfred C. Kinsey Institute for Sex Research also decided to study the question of why some people are homosexual. The results of this work were published in the book, *Sexual Preference*, by Bell, Weinberg, and Hammersmith.

These authors used careful methods in order to ensure that

their conclusions would not be colored by old myths. Researchers Bell, Weinberg, and Hammersmith questioned 979 homosexuals and 477 heterosexuals who made up a representative and matched sample of the total population. Their meticulous study took ten years to complete—three years in which to collect the data, five years to analyze it, and another two years to check it. They found that family backgrounds had little or no effect on a person's eventual sexual orientation. One of the central passages in the book sums up a major finding that can help parents drop their guilt about cause.

For the benefit of readers who are concerned about what parents may do to influence their children's sexual preference, we would restate our findings another way. No particular phenomenon of family life can be singled out, on the basis of our

"Morris, you can take credit for his homosexuality, but I've got dibs on his chutzpah."

findings, as especially consequential for either homosexual or heterosexual development. You may supply your sons with footballs and your daughters with dolls, but no one can guarantee that they will enjoy them. *What we seem to have identified . . . is a pattern of feelings and reactions within the child that cannot be traced back to a single social or psychological root;* indeed, homosexuality may arise from a biological precursor (as do left-handedness and allergies, for example) that parents cannot control. In short, to concerned parents, we cannot recommend anything beyond the care, sympathy, and devotion that good parents presumably lavish on all their children anyway.

The accurate studies tell us there are neurotic family patterns and there are loving family patterns. Both types of families produce heterosexual and homosexual children.

Gender Nonconformity

Myth #2—Acting Like a Sissy or Tomboy Causes People to Be Gay. Some gay and lesbian children were at odds with their parents when they were growing up. A number of our parents reported that they were often left feeling frustrated and confused as they realized their child didn't follow the typical interest patterns of children their age; for example, a son who didn't enjoy competitive sports, such as baseball, or a daughter who did. Going outside of what our society considers typical—expected masculine or feminine behavior—is called by Bell, Weinberg, and Hammersmith "gender nonconformity." It often left parents feeling like failures as they wondered, "Why isn't he or she like the other boys or girls? Did I fail to provide a good role model?" The following excerpts show the problem:

Matt, my gay son, didn't fit the mold, the macho male mold, that his brother, John, did. Matt didn't have any interest in sports. His interests were along a different line. He tried baseball, but it was hard for him because he was a little bit on the stout side. He was the last one to be put into the game, and he was the strike-out king. Oh, I was in Boy Scouts with him, but as he got older, it seemed we communicated less and less. There was a big wall between us.

One time when Matt was in high school, I sat him down and told him that I felt this wall; that I wanted to break it down but that it had to be a two-way street. I asked him to help me. He said he would, but we were never successful. And that wall was there until he told us he was gay.

I suffered a great deal of guilt about the way I had related to Alex when he was growing up. When he was a baby, things were fine, but as soon as he got to where he could go outside and play, I failed him miserably. I feel I didn't do enough with him. I tried to play with him as I did with Joe and Vickie, but he wouldn't go by the rules. He always tried to change them.

He just wouldn't conform. I took him to things like Hi-Y and Cub Scouts and participated with him, but when it came to relating to each other every day, we just couldn't seem to hit it off.

By the time he was ten or twelve, he was very frustrated and dissatisfied. I think it was worse when he got old enough for competition. He could compete, but he didn't feel that he could. Sometime in there I think he put a name to his difference. He was very bright, and he read a lot.

I was frustrated because I didn't know what was wrong. I remember one time I told him I felt cheated because I never had the relationship with him that I wanted. I said, "You never let me do anything with you," which he didn't. He didn't fit the mold, my mold. I was probably terrified to bend enough to fit his mold, which is really terrible to say.

Homosexuality and Twins

Our own research has shown that male sexual orientation is substantially genetic. Over the last two years, we have studied the rates of homosexuality in identical and nonidentical twin brothers of gay men, as well as adoptive brothers of gay men. Fifty-two percent of the identical twin brothers were gay, as against 22 percent of nonidentical twins and 11 percent of the adoptive, genetically unrelated brothers.

In contrast, research on social factors has been fruitless. Despite many attempts, there has been no clear demonstration that parental behavior, even a parent's homosexuality, affects children's sexual orientation.

Michael Bailey and Richard Pillard, *The New York Times*, December 17, 1991.

These fathers and their sons suffered from their inability to understand each other. Neither side had the necessary information to help break down the wall, even though they wanted to. Mothers, too, recalled being concerned about the "gender nonconformity" of their sons. Many of our interviewed parents had trouble admitting that their sons acted in any way feminine.

From a very early age I could see that Mike was what you might call more feminine than the masculine "ideal." We had to decide as parents how we were going to deal with that. He enjoyed a lot of things that girls typically like. It wasn't extreme, but he liked music, art, quiet games, and that sort of thing. He didn't go for rough play or for athletics in general.

I decided that I didn't want to make Mike self-conscious about

40

his nature, but at the same time I did want to make "masculine" things available to him. So we went out of our way to teach him how to play ball. We did a lot of sports together as a family, which was fun because we all liked them. We went camping and did other rough-outdoor-activities. And from time to time we tried to interest him in things like Boy Scouts and Little League.

We would encourage him to take part in the usual "boy" activities, but we didn't want to make him feel uncomfortable if he didn't choose them. And he usually didn't choose them. He didn't like the rough-and-tumble. Although he did like camping and had some interest in certain sports, he didn't like contact sports. So we decided to keep off his back and let him do what appealed to him. Our goal was to make him comfortable with being whatever he was and not restrict him.

The nonconformity of a son tends to create more conflict than does such behavior in a daughter. Still, many parents reported that they noticed their daughter's lack of interest in traditionally "feminine" activities.

Thinking back over the years I remember there were several times when the possibility that Mary might be gay crossed my mind. But each time I brushed it from my mind and even felt guilty about having the thought.

Once when Mary was three years old she asked, "Do I always have to be a girl?" When she was growing up she liked the companionship of boys her age. She always enjoyed athletics even though she was not that good. She was never very interested in dolls. I can still picture her as a little girl with a softball in one hand, a bat in the other, and a toy gun in the holster on her hip.

When Melinda was little she was very much a tomboy, as I had been. I thought, "Well, she's a tomboy, but that's fine." She never did play with dolls. Neither did I. I had one doll in my whole life, and I hated it. I believed she was just behaving like I did.

I wondered if Melinda was gay when she was in high school, because her best friend was a tough-looking girl, and I didn't like that. I even asked Melinda if her friend was gay, but I never did ask Melinda if she was.

Even though we have many examples of parents who noticed nonconformity in their child, we also have examples from those who did not.

Jerry dated a little in high school. As I think back over it, there wasn't too much about his relationship with girls that would have led me to believe he was gay. He was a very good dancer, had a good personality and, if I say so myself, was very good-looking. Girls were always around here clamoring over him.

> I was never so surprised in my life as when Cathy told me she was a lesbian. She was just what you would expect a little girl to be. She played with dolls and had crushes on boys. She even dated a lot in high school. She chose to wear dresses and was very feminine.

> My son was "all boy" the whole time he was growing up. He liked sports and fishing. He was a good pitcher in Little League.

Usually, parents felt there was some lack in themselves that created the feminine actions of their sons or the masculine actions of their daughters, although parents were not as concerned about this kind of behavior on the part of the girls. They believed that such actions by boys indicated an unhappy and maladjusted child. They were also afraid that their sons would be subject to ridicule from classmates. As a result, some parents pressured their young children to change their natural behavior.

A Letter to Mother

Mother, I am gay. It took me a long time to admit that to myself, and a long time to get up enough courage to tell you. It is the way I am, and is something I realized way back in Jr. High School. It is not something I chose to be—anyone who would have you believe such a thing has not gone through the pain that such a realization can bring, or the bigotry and prejudice that exists for gay people in our society. If being gay were a matter of choice, there would be no gay people, as no one would choose it.

You also must not blame yourself. You no more caused my sexuality than you caused me to be five foot eight. I would never blame you, and you must not either. I can't stress this enough. No one really knows what causes someone to be homosexual, but it is known that an over-abundance, or lack of mothering does not cause homosexuality. You cannot blame yourself—even if this is your first instinct. There is nothing you could have done or did not do that would change my sexuality.

"Carl" in *Like Coming Home: Coming Out Letters*, 1988.

The authors of *Sexual Preference* believe that gender nonconformity may signal homosexuality for many gays and lesbians. But it is not a cause. Of course, it would have been better if we parents had known that we had little to do with the gender nonconformity of our children. Unfortunately for everyone concerned, we did not.

We hope that this information will clear away some of the

guilt that parents and children often feel when they look back over some of the parent-child conflicts of the early years together. As one father said so well, "Now I see that the problem in our relationship wasn't my fault, and it wasn't his. We were just caught up in something we couldn't understand."

Myth #3—Homosexual Seduction Causes Children to Be Gay. No other lie causes as much damage to our gay and lesbian children as does this one. People mount political hate campaigns in the name of saving the children. These campaigns have led to the denial of the basic democratic rights for gay and lesbian persons. Teachers lose their jobs if they are gay, even though there is absolutely no evidence that their being openly gay or otherwise will have any impact on their students' sexuality.

As with many of the ideas about cause, the authors of *Sexual Preference* found that neither gays nor lesbians were seduced into the homosexual life style. There was a significant period of time between becoming aware of being gay or lesbian and acting on that awareness. In fact, lesbian and gay adolescents often think they are alone. It is a frightening and sad time for them and can sometimes lead to tragic consequences.

Myth #4—A Traumatic Event with a Person of the Opposite Sex Can Cause Homosexuality. There was no evidence to support this idea in the study done by Bell, Weinberg, and Hammersmith. Traumatic events caused pain for both gay and nongay people. But it did not cause them to change their sexual orientation. Being gay or lesbian does not mean being angry with people of the opposite sex. It simply means being sexually attracted to people of the same sex.

A Personal Note from the Authors About Cause

Each time a new research theory comes out about cause, parents tend to look inside themselves, as well as at their total family life. They often say to themselves, "Did I do that? Was our family like that? Maybe someone has found out something that will indict me! Maybe I am guilty of a crime against my son or daughter!" After a while—when they are able to discriminate between fact and opinion—parents learn to reject the damage caused by their own negative thoughts and by the false opinions of others.

We wish we could say without question what the cause of homosexuality is. But as of this writing the cause is unknown. The scientific study of sexuality is in its infancy. Even the tools we use to investigate and measure with are primitive. The only statement we can make without hesitation is that parents should harbor no fears or guilt feelings that something in their parenting caused their child's homosexuality. These negative feelings can, and should, be dropped. . . .

We should explain our bias about this question. We lean toward a biological cause for two reasons. First, the latest and best research points that way. Second, it fits our experience.

We also want to see an end to the blame game that raises its ugly head with alarming regularity. When energy is spent on establishing blame, little is done to resolve issues. But, more than this, we believe that our society will accept gayness only if the vast majority of its citizens see it as a naturally occurring event. If most people understand that a certain percentage of society will be gay no matter what their family background is, or what their sexual experiences were, then gay people have a better chance of living their lives free from fears of retaliation.

"Social scientists have proposed many theories to explain sexual orientation, but none have been conclusively proven true."

The Causes of Homosexuality Are Uncertain

Deborah A. Miller and Alex Waigandt

Deborah A. Miller is an associate professor and health coordinator of the College of Charleston in South Carolina. She has published research articles and student workbooks on human sexuality. Alex Waigandt is an associate professor of health at the University of Missouri in Columbia, and has published numerous papers. The following viewpoint is taken from their book for young people titled *Coping with Your Sexual Orientation*. In it they summarize the various theories scientists have developed concerning the causes of sexual orientation, and conclude that scientists have yet to find the answer.

As you read, consider the following questions:

1. Why are the theories of causes of sexual orientation limited, according to Miller and Waigandt?
2. What is the main cause of heterosexuality, according to the authors?
3. According to Miller and Waigandt, what are the four main categories of theories concerning homosexuality?

Despite all the research into sexual orientation, we know very little about the development of heterosexuality, bisexuality, and homosexuality. Social scientists have proposed many theories to explain sexual orientation, but none have been conclusively proven true. We shall examine some of the more popular theories that have evolved since the development of "sexology," the scientific study of sexual relationships. . . .

The theories about sexual orientation that we are going to explore are just that, theories. No single theory is ever likely to explain how everyone's sexual orientation develops. No single theory will ever explain how your sexual orientation developed. As you read some of the best-known theories, notice that most of them try to explain why a person is bisexual or homosexual rather than heterosexual. Only a few current theories attempt to explain sexual orientation in general. Keep in mind that no one knows for sure what "causes" heterosexuality, bisexuality, and homosexuality.

Another word of caution is also needed. Any one of these theories may be correct and explain the sexual orientation of any one person, but not of everyone. It is important that you keep an open mind and continuously ask questions, just as a researcher does. Who knows, you may be the person, several years from now, who devises a new and better theory. Therefore, carefully analyze each of these theories as you read them and see if you can spot some of the flaws.

Heterosexuality

Have you ever sat in a busy mall or airport "people-watching"? If you have, you observed a wide variety of differences among people. Some were short, some spoke a different language, and a few may even have worn clothing associated with another country. But you probably also saw the most common sexual orientation in the United States, heterosexuality. If you talked to the average man on the street, he would say that heterosexuality is "natural" and something that you are born with. Therefore, why should we try to explain it?

Unfortunately, a person's sexual orientation cannot be so easily explained as by saying that it is "natural." Bisexual and homosexual people feel that their life-style is also something they are born with and feels "natural" to them. Now what can we say?

Researchers believe that people are heterosexual because they have been brought up to be heterosexual. From the moment you were born and the doctor said, "It's a boy" or "It's a girl," you have been directed toward activities appropriate to your sex. When you were younger, the toys you were given probably had a sexual orientation. Chances are that if you are a girl, people bought you dolls, miniature dishes, and pots and pans. Later you probably had to help your mother cook and clean while your brother was helping your father in the yard. If you are a boy, you probably received a baseball glove one Christmas. And although you may secretly have enjoyed playing with dolls, it was not considered the "masculine" thing to do. . . .

As you can see, your parents have been instrumental in forming a part of your sexual identity. But research has found that the attitudes you hold today have also been determined by another group, your peers. Young people want desperately to belong to a group, and they know that if they "step out of line" they run the risk of being ostracized. How often have you been out with a group of friends and someone has said, "Let's get something to eat"? Rather than say, "I'm not hungry," you went along with the crowd and got something to eat. That seems like a simple example, but consider how much pressure your friends can put on you. Needless to say, heterosexuality is expected of you by your friends and family. In fact, you were taught to be heterosexual, and any deviation from heterosexual behavior was probably treated in a harsh manner. . . .

Bisexuality

Sigmund Freud, called by many people the father of modern psychology, believed that all people had the capacity for both heterosexual and homosexual behavior. It was Freud's view that in the early stages of the infant's sexual development the contrast between masculine and feminine had no real significance. Instead, there was a contrast between active and passive sexual play which, depending upon circumstance, would result in final sexual orientation.

It would appear that Freud agreed with the theories proposed by Alfred Kinsey. . . . Kinsey theorized that people stabilize somewhere on a continuum between heterosexuality and homosexuality. The true bisexual stabilizes somewhere near the middle of that continuum. According to some Freudian psychologists, bisexuality is the result of mixed messages during sexual development.

Currently, social scientists are at a loss to explain bisexuality, let alone understand its origin. Bisexuals may like both sexes equally, they may prefer one sex over the other, or they may have no preference. They may have several partners of both sexes, or they may be sexually exclusive to one gender. According to some, bisexuality is transitory, and the bisexual eventually turns exclusively to the preferred gender. Some homosexuals believe that bisexuals engage in homosexual denial and therefore distrust them. A third group of people believe that bisexuals maintain an interest in both sexes.

Bisexuals now have organizations, clubs, and meeting places.

Although the number of people who consider themselves bisexual is not currently known, it is significant enough to create a trichotomy of sexual orientations (heterosexual, homosexual, and bisexual). Nevertheless, what constitutes a bisexual orientation remains ambiguous.

Homosexuality

Homosexuality remains a mystery to social scientists. In a society that provides just one script (heterosexuality) for sexual expression, while considering others abnormal, how do some people develop bisexual or homosexual orientations? Since Kinsey's work in the late 1940s, much research has been done on homosexual males, but the research on female homosexuality is still new and emerging. Even in light of all the new research, the experts disagree about the development of male and female sexual orientation. Our understanding of homosexual and bisexual orientations is limited by the complexity of the issue and the problems associated with conducting the research.

Different Kinds of Homosexuality

The biggest problem most people have in understanding homosexuality is that they think of it as a single way of feeling and acting, and therefore look for a single way of explaining it. But . . . there are a number of very different kinds of homosexuality. It doesn't make sense to think that they all have the same cause, that there is a single explanation for all of them. It makes much better sense to look for different explanations for the different kinds of homosexuality. The question to ask is: "Which of these explanations account for some kinds of homosexuality—and which kinds?" And the answer is that nearly all of them explain some kinds of homosexuality but not others—and that most homosexuality involves several of these explanations at once, several causes working together.

Morton Hunt, *Gay: What Teenagers Should Know About Homosexuality and the AIDS Crisis*, 1987.

It is not well understood how sexual orientation develops. Scientists have yet to find a single reason why some people develop heterosexual orientations and others develop homosexual orientations. Part of the confusion is because sex interest appears for different people at different times and under different circumstances. For some people, opposite and same-gender orientation appears in early childhood, whereas in others it emerges in adulthood.

Since heterosexuality is the orientation of most Americans,

and since from a biological standpoint heterosexual behavior is necessary for our species to reproduce, little qualitative research has been done on the development of heterosexuality. Many of the pioneers of psychological theory, such as Freud and Erik Erikson, turned their attention to the development of opposite-gender orientations. The contention of these and other researchers is that heterosexual orientation is the result of psychological reward and punishment experiences and various hormonal and social influences, and it develops in stages during prenatal life, infancy, and childhood.

As with many other socially accepted behavioral patterns, research is sketchy and dated. Alternative sexual orientations have been closely examined, and a number of theories (none of which fully explain the issue) have evolved. Let's examine these theories and see if we can understand why people believed them in the past.

Biological Theory

What are little boys made of?
Snips and snails, and puppy dogs' tails;
That's what little boys are made of.
What are little girls made of?
Sugar and spice, and everything nice;
That's what little girls are made of.
Anonymous

According to the verse above, there are differences between boys and girls. From early childhood to puberty a hormone called testosterone doubles in girls. In boys, testosterone levels increase as much as thirty times during the same time span. Testosterone is a chemical substance associated with physical aggressiveness, activity, competitiveness, and increased sex drive. Another hormone associated with the "aggressive" male is androgen. Female development is associated with the hormones estrogen and progesterone. According to sexologists J. Money and P. Tucker, it is because of the combinations of these and other hormones that the so-called biological differences between males and females can be assigned: "that men impregnate, and that women menstruate, gestate, and lactate."

Most of the biological explanations of sexual orientation suspect an imbalance of hormones that causes homosexuality. Some studies suggest that homosexuality is the result of a reduction of androgen (a male-oriented hormone) in some males. One researcher tested this assumption by giving extra androgen to some homosexual volunteers. All it did was to increase their desire for men. Other studies have found no clear relationship between androgen and homosexuality.

So far, those who have looked for biological explanations for homosexuality haven't found very much. Part of the problem is the normal tendency for hormone levels to fluctuate; another is that the interactions of various hormones are not well understood. All in all, findings have been contradictory and inconclusive. That does not mean that biological variables do not play a critical role in sexual orientation. They probably do, but scientists have not yet been able to prove it.

Social Theory

Another set of theories are social in nature. In some cultures males are expected to become involved in homosexual activities. For the Siwans of Africa, all males, including those married to women, are expected to engage in homosexual intercourse. Anyone who does not is considered "abnormal." Other societies consider it normal for females to engage in homosexual activity. In the United States, however, we learn early in life that physical contact with one's own gender is to be avoided. How then do some people develop bisexual and homosexual orientations?

Many Paths to Homosexuality

No one knows what "causes" homosexuality. For that matter, no one knows what "causes" heterosexuality either. Many theories have been proposed, but so far most have not held up under careful scrutiny and none have been proven. In fact, scientists probably have a clearer idea of what does *not* cause a homosexual orientation. Children raised by gay or lesbian parents or couples, for instance, are *no* more likely to grow up to be homosexual than are children raised by heterosexual parents. . . .

It also is not true that people become homosexuals because they were seduced by an older person of the same sex in their youth. The childhood and adolescent sexual experiences of both homosexuals and heterosexuals are fairly similar, except that homosexuals recall later that they found opposite-sex encounters less satisfying than did heterosexuals.

Current theory is that there probably are many different developmental paths by which a person can come to be homosexual, bisexual, or heterosexual.

June M. Reinisch, *The Kinsey Institute New Report on Sex*, 1990.

Some theorists believe that sex play with one's own gender as well as the opposite sex is normal. For some, sex play with someone of the same sex is found to feel good, and they may want to continue the activity. Although this play does not necessarily lead to homosexuality, it may later be incorporated into a same-sex orientation.

Learning Theory

Behaviorists emphasize the importance of learning in the development of sexual orientation and believe that homosexuality is the result of negative heterosexual experiences. They believe that we are all born sexual, not heterosexual or homosexual, and that we respond to anything that feels good, including people and objects. Young people who have had poor heterosexual relationships or heterosexual relationships that caused physical or mental pain may retreat, from all heterosexual experiences. Therefore, their natural response may be to turn their orientation to one of homosexuality or asexuality (no sexual interest regardless of gender). According to these behavioral theorists, homosexuality is normal sexual behavior attached to the stimulus of same-gender partners. The behavior is learned either by rewards stimulating the behavioral (homosexual) pattern or punishment associated with the opposite (heterosexual) behavioral pattern.

Psychodynamic Theory

A psychodynamic theory has proposed that the relationship between parents and children may have an effect on sexual orientation. Irving Bieber studied 106 homosexual males who were under psychiatric treatment. According to his findings, 73 percent had mothers who acted seductively toward them and were overprotective, to the point where they were never successful in developing the traditional "masculine" behaviors. He also found that none of the men studied had a "normal" relationship with his father. The fathers tended to be weak, hostile, or absent from the home. When looking at studies like Bieber's, it is important to realize that he was dealing with homosexuals who were seeking psychiatric help. The family patterns described do not necessarily describe the experiences of emotionally healthy homosexuals who were raised in a loving heterosexual family.

Psychodynamic theorists believe that we are all pansexual (arousable by both sexes) and that during the course of a lifetime we all go through stages both homoerotic and heteroerotic. Conflicts or fixations at key stages of development can result in a homosexual orientation, whereas conflicts or fixations at other stages can result in a heterosexual orientation.

As you can see, the causes of sexual orientation are not well understood. Scientists have not yet found a single cause why we are of the orientation that we are.

=====

"There is probably no essential heterosexual or homosexual nature."

=====

The Causes of Homosexuality Are Unimportant

Patricia Hersch

Some people have criticized the search for the causes of homosexuality and heterosexuality by questioning whether these two concepts really exist as a fundamental aspect of human nature. In the following viewpoint, free-lance writer Patricia Hersch asserts that dividing and labeling a person as simply homosexual or heterosexual is too simplistic. She cites research from the Kinsey Institute and other sources that reveals that sexuality is a broad spectrum of behaviors, all with different causes and characteristics.

As you read, consider the following questions:

1. What evidence does Hersch cite to demonstrate that there is no essential homosexual or heterosexual nature?
2. What theories of the causes of homosexuality does the author disparage?
3. Why does Hersch say sexual orientation is a kind of prison?

Patricia Hersch, "What Is Gay? What Is Straight?" *The Family Therapy Networker*, January/February 1991. Reprinted with permission.

It is widely assumed in our culture that people do not just engage in homosexual and/or heterosexual acts, they *are* homosexual or heterosexual, just as they *are* male or female. According to this logic, sexual orientation, whether gay or straight, is indistinguishable from core identity and reveals itself in every aspect of life—behavior, mannerisms, dress, choice of friends, career, interests. Ironically, this absolutist dichotomy—the division of humanity into two fundamentally different sorts of human beings—reinforces several contradictory points of view about the origins and meaning of homosexuality.

For some, the dichotomy sustains the belief that homosexuality is the natural, biological state of approximately 10 percent of the population, making it no more deserving of prejudice than left handedness or eye color. For others, however, the either/or universalism of sexual orientation fuels the conviction that homosexuality is a deeply engrained physical and psychological dysfunction, afflicting all aspects of personality and behavior.

On the other hand, if homosexuality is a choice, then, according to general opinion, the gay or lesbian has chosen to "be" completely homosexual—that is, to fulfill all society's stereotypes of what a homosexual is, and accept the consequences, including risk for AIDS, legal discrimination, exclusion from "normal" society, denial of family and children, and general harassment. Conversely, gays and lesbians who believe they have had no choice in the matter of their sexual inclinations very often choose to live a completely homosexual life-style in order to get the support, acceptance, and safety they are otherwise denied.

A False Division

But there is precious little evidence for the belief that strict heterosexuality and homosexuality are essential and fundamental attributes of human nature, inevitably reflected in lifelong patterns of sexual behavior and life-style. Indeed, according to the Kinsey Institute, approximately one-third of all males are thought to have had at least one same-sex experience leading to orgasm since puberty. For example, the married man who occasionally has sex with another man, or who has fantasies of doing so, probably considers himself "really" heterosexual, as do male prison inmates who have homosexual sex with each other for years, ostensibly because they are denied the company of women.

The Kinsey Institute also reported that around one-half of college-educated women and about 20 percent of non-college-educated women had at least one same-sex erotic contact since puberty. One woman may adopt a lesbian identity as a part of a feminist stance and keep it throughout life, or she may later resume her heterosexual orientation. Another woman may grow up with no conscious homosexual feelings at all, marry, have children, and then in mid-life fall in love with another woman and leave her husband.

On the other hand, many self-defined gays and lesbians have had heterosexual experiences. According to data collected by the Kinsey Institute, between 62 and 79 percent of men who call themselves homosexual have had sex with a woman. In a study of lesbians, the institute found that 43 percent of women who had always referred to themselves as lesbians had had sex at least once with a man since age 18. Of the whole group of lesbians interviewed, including those who had not always thought of themselves as lesbians, 74 to 81 percent had experienced heterosexual sex. However, many gays and lesbians may have engaged in heterosexual sex to conform to mainstream norms, or to test themselves—to see if they're "really" homosexual—or in an attempt to convert themselves to the "normal" orientation.

Does It Matter?

Does it make a difference to know what causes homosexuality in particular or sexual orientation in general? It seems to be more than simple scientific curiosity which motivates researchers working in this area. Certainly, this is not to deny that these are questions worth exploring, but it is important to note that any researcher is selecting one area of interest over another, and the ways in which the questions are formulated often reveal the bias. For example, might there be other sorts of questions which are of value to scientific research? Note how different the following questions sound: . . .

- Is heterosexuality the result of a fear of intimacy with members of one's own sex?

- Is heterosexuality caused by unpleasant early experiences with members of one's own sex?

- Is heterosexuality caused by an excess of hormones of one's own sex?

There is nothing intrinsically unscientific about the questions above, yet they probably seem peculiar to most of us. Few scientists, though, frame the questions in this way, even those who are more "sympathetic."

Warren J. Blumenfeld and Diane Raymond, *Looking at Gay and Lesbian Life*, 1988.

Like the division between male and female, the categorical division between heterosexuality and homosexuality once seemed as fixed as the planet Earth in its orbit, but, according to Kinsey's studies, actually shifts unsteadily back and forth like a leaky boat in high seas. In 1948, the Kinsey Institute published a homosexual-heterosexual rating scale, ranging from zero for exclusively heterosexual behavior to six for exclusively homosexual behavior. Drawing on an admittedly limited population of white, middle-class males between 16 and 55 during a three-year period, Kinsey determined that there were a few men falling at either end, but that most fell somewhere along the continuum—they had engaged, to varying degrees, in both heterosexual and homosexual activities.

Homosexualities

In 1986, the Kinsey Institute held a symposium for 50 eminent researchers from various fields, including anthropology, psychology, biology, history, medicine, psychiatry, and sociology, to reexamine the issue of sexual orientation and assess the usefulness of the scale. The symposium, published as the book *Homosexuality/ Heterosexuality: Concepts of Sexual Orientation*, was notable for the conclusions that were *not* drawn. The researchers unanimously challenged the idea, upon which the original scale had been based, that sex acts *per se* measured sexual orientation. Instead, they agreed that the behavioral scale—measuring the sexual acts a person engages in—had to be balanced with other scales measuring love, sexual attraction, fantasy, and self-identification—all of which could change over time. There is probably no essential heterosexual or homosexual nature, but many "homosexualities" and "heterosexualities" that characterize people. In other words, according to their report, sexual orientation is multidimensional, situational, changeable, contextual.

Nobody knows what "causes" homosexuality any more than they know what "causes" heterosexuality. (Of course, there is far less interest in what causes the latter.) Overtly, the old psychoanalytic bugaboos are dead: there is no evidence, according to the Kinsey Institute, that male homosexuality is caused by dominant mothers and/or weak fathers, or that female homosexuality is caused by girls having exclusively male role models. Furthermore, children who are raised by gay and lesbian couples are no more likely to be homosexual than children of heterosexual couples. Nor do people become adult homosexuals because they were seduced by older people or went to same-sex boarding schools. "We come into this world with a lot of things not determined but with some parameters laid out, and sexual orientation is probably like that," says psychobiologist Stephanie A. Sanders, an editor of the 1986 Kinsey book. "We are born with some potential range of possibilities and what happens to us is that each individual interaction with our environment determines where we are going to fall on that range."

Though the causes of sexual orientation are unknown and the

definitions fluid, the likelihood of converting a homosexual to a heterosexual orientation, or vice versa, is very slight. Some homosexual men and women voluntarily come for therapy to change from same-sex to opposite-sex partners, but it is not clear whether the limited "success" rate refers to a change in their feelings and the pattern of their desire, or just in their ability to consciously restrict their sexual contact to members of the opposite sex.

The Need for Understanding

Nature? Nurture? Perhaps the most appropriate answer comes from Evelyn Hooker, who showed in an important 1950s study that it is impossible to distinguish heterosexuals from homosexuals on psychological tests. Hooker takes the long view of the search for origins. "Why do we want to know the cause?" she asks. "It's a mistake to hope that we will be able to modify or change homosexuality. . . . If we understand its nature and accept it as a given, then we come much closer to the kind of attitudes which will make it possible for homosexuals to lead a decent life in society." The psychiatric profession heeded Hooker when it stopped calling homosexuality an illness. At 84, her voice has grown fainter, but the rest of us could do worse than listen to her now.

David Gelman, *Newsweek*, February 24, 1992.

Many sex researchers and therapists would like to loosen the stranglehold that beliefs about sexual orientation have on perceptions of personality. They want to see people develop an expanded definition of self that integrates sexuality rather than cling to a narrow sense of self held hostage to it.

Six Stages of Growth

Australian clinical psychologist Vivienne C. Cass, Department of Social Enquiry, Murdoch University, has identified a six-stage process of homosexual identity formation for gays and lesbians of all ages that sidesteps the social rigidities of sexual categorization. According to Cass, the process begins when a person recognizes that there is "something" about his or her behavior (including actions, feelings, thoughts) that could be called homosexual. After going through various stages of denial, confusion, self-realization, disclosure, and quest for approval, the gay or lesbian finally acquires a degree of mature self-acceptance in which sexual orientation is conceived as only part of a complex self—not the total identity. There is nothing inherent or inevitable within a person controlling the process, which grows out of a complex interaction between the individual and the environment. It can be set into motion at any time during the life cycle, and may be terminated at any stage along the way.

In itself, the great social divide between heterosexual and homosexual might not be so bad, even though the empirical link between sexual desire and identity is far from established. After all, people draw security and self-enhancement from all sorts of affiliations—from Republicanism to Trotskyite socialism, Episcopalianism to Tibetan Buddhism—that are not physiologically determined. But perhaps no distinction, with the exception of race, is used with such noxious and defamatory purposes as that of sexual preference. Nor does any other distinction comprise such a forceful weapon for social acquiescence. There is hardly an area of life—education, law, religion, housing, employment—that doesn't require, on some level, a show of the correct sexual orientation.

Many critics of these attitudes believe that sexual orientation should not be such a prison. "You have to discuss sexuality in the context of pleasure and intimacy irrespective of the gender of the other person," says anthropologist Michael Clatts. Mary Ziemba-Davis, researcher at the Kinsey Institute, likes to imagine a world without sexual boxes. "If we lived in a society that encouraged loving relationships and sexual expression regardless of sexual gender and orientation," says Ziemba-Davis, "people would be more free to choose partners consistent with their internal love map at various points in their lives without psychological conflict."

A Prison

Unfortunately, in the current climate of opinion, sexual orientation *is* a kind of prison, though perhaps it does not always have to be so. Just as men and women are learning that there is identity beyond strict gender definitions, perhaps they will one day be able to determine their sexual orientation without being determined by it. The real meaning of choice should not begin and end with a specific sexual act trailing behind it an entire life of prohibitions, obligations, and defensive maneuvers. Choice should extend to a whole range of human behaviors and life-styles, which are not necessarily determined by the gender of the person who turns you on. But if this expanded expression of human possibility is to become a reality, both heterosexuals and homosexuals need to focus less on sex acts and fantasies as the key to personality, and more on relationships that enrich their lives. All of us need friends and lovers of whatever orientation that allow us to be happy and most who we are.

Recognizing Statements That Are Provable

We are constantly confronted with statements and generalizations about social and moral problems. In order to think clearly about these problems, it is useful if one can make a basic distinction between statements for which evidence can be found and other statements that cannot be verified or proved because evidence is not available or the issue is so controversial that it cannot be definitely proved.

Readers should be aware that magazines, newspapers, and other sources often contain statements of a controversial nature. The following activity is designed to allow experimentation with statements that are provable and those that are not.

The following statements are taken from the viewpoints in this chapter. Consider each statement carefully. *Mark P for any statement you believe is provable. Mark U for any statement you feel is unprovable because of the lack of evidence. Mark C for any statement you think is too controversial to be proved to everyone's satisfaction.*

If you are doing this activity as a member of a class or group, compare your answers with those of other class or group members. Be able to defend your answers. You may discover that others come to different conclusions than you do. Listening to the reasons others present for their answers may give you valuable insights into recognizing statements that are provable.

P = provable
U = unprovable
C = too controversial

1. Dr. Simon LeVay examined the brains of nineteen homosexual men, sixteen men presumed to be heterosexual, and six women presumed to be heterosexual.
2. LeVay found that part of the anterior hypothalamus in homosexual men has the form usually found in women rather than the form found in heterosexual men.
3. The structural difference LeVay found may be a consequence of homosexual activity, not a cause.
4. It may be difficult ever to establish that any brain structure actually causes homosexuality.
5. An article in the December 4, 1989, issue of *Time* magazine claimed that male attitudes and values are becoming "feminized."
6. Until the gay rights movement began in 1969, homosexuality was little researched.
7. Scientists, in their haste to determine the "causes" of homosexuality, have been wrong before.
8. Homosexuality is probably caused by a combination of biological and environmental elements.
9. Sigmund Freud believed that all people had the capacity for both heterosexual and homosexual behavior.
10. Many self-defined gays and lesbians have had heterosexual experiences.
11. Homosexuality is a developmental problem that is almost always the result of problems in family relations, particularly between fathers and sons.
12. Parents are not the cause of their children's homosexuality.
13. The 1982 book *Sexual Preference* by Bell, Weinberg, and Hammersmith resulted from ten years of research.
14. For the Siwans of Africa, all males, including those married to women, are expected to engage in homosexual intercourse.
15. It is not true that people become homosexual because they were seduced in their youth by an older person of the same sex.
16. The homosexuals Irving Bieber studied in his research on causes of homosexuality were all under psychiatric treatment.
17. Scientists have not yet found a single, definitive cause of sexual orientation.
18. No single theory is ever likely to explain how sexual orientation develops.
19. God and sex are two subjects that cannot be reduced to scientific formulas.

Periodical Bibliography

The following articles have been selected to supplement the diverse views presented in this chapter.

Mona Charen   "My Brain Made Me Do It," *Conservative Chronicle*, September 18, 1991. Available from PO Box 11297, Des Moines, IA 50340-1297.

C. Bard Cole   "Homosexuality: Born or Bred?" *New York Native*, March 2, 1992. Available from PO Box 1475, Church Street Station, New York, NY 10008.

Joe Dallas   "Born Gay?" *Christianity Today*, June 22, 1992.

Albert Ellis   "Are Gays and Lesbians Emotionally Disturbed?" *The Humanist*, September/October 1992.

David Gelman et al.   "Born or Bred?" *Newsweek*, February 24, 1992.

Steven Goldberg   "What Is Normal?" *National Review*, February 3, 1992.

Denise Grady   "The Brains of Gay Men," *Discover*, January 1992.

Celia Hooper   "Biology, Brain Architecture, and Human Sexuality," *The Journal of NIH Research*, October 1992. Available from 1444 I St. NW, Suite 1000, Washington, DC 20005.

Stanton L. Jones   "Homosexuality According to Science," *Christianity Today*, August 18, 1989.

Simon LeVay   "A Difference in Hypothalamic Structure Between Heterosexual and Homosexual Men," *Science*, August 30, 1991.

Darrell Yates Rist   "Are Homosexuals Born That Way?" *The Nation*, October 19, 1992.

Marjorie Rosenberg   "Inventing the Homosexual," *Commentary*, December 1987.

Lindsy Van Gelder   "The 'Born That Way' Trap," *Ms.*, May/June 1991.

2 CHAPTER

Should Society Encourage Increased Acceptance of Homosexuality?

Chapter Preface

For most of American history, homosexuality has been condemned. Churches have called it immoral; state laws have outlawed its practice. Despite the rise of an activist gay movement in recent decades and the decriminalization of homosexual acts in some states, many Americans still view homosexuality with disapproval. In fact, a 1992 poll revealed that 54 percent of Americans believe homosexual relationships between consenting adults are morally wrong.

Gay authors Marshall Kirk and Hunter Madsen, in their book *After the Ball: How America Will Conquer Its Fear and Hatred of Gays in the 90s*, argue that such attitudes cause hardship for America's lesbians and gays. Kirk and Madsen paint a harsh picture of American society:

> Gays are still hounded from pillar to post by the watchdogs of American society. As children they are humiliated, beaten, even turned out of their homes. As adults, insult and injury are added to insult and injury: exposed gays lose their jobs, their homes, their churches, their children, and, not infrequently, their very lives.

Kirk and Madsen believe that America, to fulfill its vision of itself as a just and open nation, must accept gays and lesbians and acknowledge them as full-fledged members of society. These goals remain controversial to many who argue that the heart of the issue is not the treatment of lesbians and gays, but whether American society should condone or encourage homosexual behavior. Many people, like conservative writer and theologian Michael Novak, believe homosexuality is in fundamental conflict with traditional family life. Novak writes:

> There are three features in the very structure of homosexual life that tell against it. The first is a preoccupation with one's own sex. Half the human mystery is evaded. The second is the instability of homosexual relationships, an instability that arises from the lack of the full dimension of raising a family. . . . Thirdly, . . . homosexual love is somehow apart from the fundamental mystery of bringing life into the world, and sharing in the birth and death of the generations.

Novak and others conclude that "society has a strong interest, in private and in public, in encouraging heterosexuality and discouraging homosexuality."

Many people disagree with Novak's assessment of homosexuality and argue that the problem America faces is bigotry, not homosexuality. Some of the most prominent debates concerning society's attitudes toward homosexuality are covered in this chapter.

"Society imposes an image that being a homosexual is somehow wrong, or bad, and disgraceful. These attitudes are senselessly hurting a great many people throughout this nation."

Society Should Accept Homosexuality

Jeff Peters

Jeff Peters is a senior attorney with the Florida attorney general's environmental law section. In the following viewpoint, he argues that gays and lesbians in the United States face numerous obstacles and difficulties, including violent attacks, because of prejudice against their sexual orientation. He describes how social prejudice has caused difficulties in coming to terms with his own sexual orientation, and calls for the end of all discrimination against homosexuals.

As you read, consider the following questions:

1. What examples of violence against gays and lesbians does Peters give? How common are such incidents?
2. How has AIDS affected prejudice against homosexuals, according to the author?
3. What steps does Peters recommend people take to fight anti-gay discrimination?

From Jeff Peters, "When Fear Turns to Hate and Hate to Violence," *Human Rights* 18:1 (Spring 1991). Reprinted with permission of the American Bar Association.

This is what being gay in America increasingly means:

• The windows of one man's car were broken, the tires slashed, and the word "fag" was spray-painted on the hood and the driver's side of the automobile.

• A woman was attacked walking on a street near the home she shared with her lover of 12 years. She was called a "dyke" and taunted for not wanting to have sex with "a real man." She suffered several broken bones and bruises at the hands of her attackers—three 15-year-olds.

• A man had just learned that he had tested positive for HIV. The news hit him hard. He decided to get a little drunk in the privacy of his own apartment. Unfortunately, some local teenagers had gathered outside his apartment, shouting "fag" and "AIDS carrier," among other equally ugly epithets.

He feared for his life, so he called the police; they refused to respond. He placed another call as rocks and other objects were aimed at his windows. The police finally arrived; they scolded him and told the teens, "If the fag comes out, beat the crap out of him." He did come out, they did attack, and he spent several days in the hospital.

An article in the February 28, 1990, edition of the *Miami Herald* reported that two mysterious murders had been solved with the arrest of a 15-year-old high school dropout, who was described by the police as a street hustler who preyed on gay men. He was charged with the beating deaths of a hospital radiology worker and a retired computer programmer.

Hate Crimes Increasing

Hate crimes motivated by the sexual orientation of the victim reflect a growing trend nationally. More than 7,000 hate-motivated incidents have been reported to the National Gay and Lesbian Task Force. These numbers only reflect those individuals who called to report the crime. Many more have gone undetected. Some people are afraid to come forward; others believe the government isn't interested in solving gay- and lesbian-related hate crimes.

Murders, shootings, serious bodily injuries, property damages, verbal insults, and hate mail have increased to a level never experienced before. The press has been slow to recognize and report on the increasing number of hate crimes motivated by sexual orientation. The little that is reported confirms the seriousness of this problem.

Kevin Berrill of the National Gay and Lesbian Task Force keeps track of the figures that are reported to the organization. On television and in the press, he bemoans the attacks on the lesbian and gay community and the general lack of response from law enforcement to most of these crimes.

Urvashi Vaid, task force executive director and champion of the lesbian and gay community, makes the crucial point that these figures sharply underestimate the actual extent of antigay harassment and violence in the United States. Berrill maintains that the vast majority of antigay episodes in U.S. towns and cities are never reported. The impact of that statement is enormous: We essentially have an epidemic in this country.

AIDS and Prejudice

AIDS has become a factor in hate crimes as some people use the illness as an excuse to express their homophobia. HIV-related discrimination reports increased nationwide by 50 percent from 1987 to 1988, according to the latest report published by the ACLU AIDS Project, which examines national trends in HIV-related discrimination.

This followed an 88 percent increase in discrimination complaints from 1986 to 1987. The study found that in 1987, discrimination reports rose 141 percent faster than AIDS cases. In 1988, discrimination reports rose 35 percent faster than newly diagnosed AIDS cases reported to the Centers for Disease Control.

Joel Pett/*Lexington Herald-Leader*. Reprinted with permission.

People who are HIV-positive or who have AIDS-related complex face discrimination in a number of areas, including insurance, employment, housing, health care, and government services. To have to endure hate crimes in addition to these other problems is simply untenable.

The figures released in the ACLU study are reflected in an ongoing study being conducted by the Florida AIDS Legal Defense and Education Fund, which has found an equally alarming increase in the number of hate crimes. That finding has led to its call for the inclusion of HIV- and AIDS-related hate crimes, along with sexual-orientation-related crimes, in Florida's Hate Crimes Act. . . .

In April 1990, President George Bush signed into law the Federal Hate Crimes Statistics Act, which includes sexual orientation among the hate crimes for which data must be collected. Lack of similar hate crime provisions on the state level continues to hamper the effectiveness of the act.

Homophobic Attitudes

Society imposes an image that being a homosexual is somehow wrong, or bad, and disgraceful. These attitudes are senselessly hurting a great many people throughout this nation.

Just as society has worked toward changing discriminatory racial attitudes and conduct, the same must be done by each individual to turn around the society's homophobic attitudes; only then will each American be able to realize the right to the pursuit of happiness, so cherished by all of us. This is especially appropriate now as we celebrate with people around the world the new freedom emerging in Eastern Europe, and witness the creation of a European market that has the potential to bring people together as never before.

On radio stations across America, lesbians and gay men are the subject of ugly jokes. Hatred of the lesbian and gay community is splashed across editorials and in letters to the editors in newspapers throughout the nation. The *Tallahassee Democrat* recently ran its first in-depth story on the lesbian and gay community residing in the capital. Readers wrote to the *Democrat* expressing outrage at the attempted depiction of "these people" as normal, decent citizens.

Television programs and movies often depict lesbians and gay men as the villains or as unhappy, lost souls to be pitied. National groups such as the Gay and Lesbian Alliance Against Defamation have begun to fight back, demanding the same respect and concern for the lesbian and gay community afforded to others.

Lesbians and gay men find it increasingly difficult to lead their lives without facing acts of discrimination and violence. Society should not be allowed to drive lesbians and gay men into a life of self-hatred. Everyone in this country has a right to dignity, to the essence of being. We should all be free to pursue our hopes and dreams without the interference of people with so little happening in their lives that they feel they must attack another human being.

Too many people are forced to live a closeted life without the love and support that each human being deserves—in large part because of the society's homophobic attitudes. These antiquated views help foster a negative self-image, which ultimately can lead to tragedy.

A Personal Struggle

Like many people, I had a difficult time coming to grips with my sexual orientation. It wasn't until my third year of law school that I was finally able to look inside myself and be honest about my sexual orientation. I was afraid to deal with this aspect of my life. Up until that point I had simply ignored my feelings, even though I always knew the truth. I excelled in school, politics, and civic endeavors and had some good friends, yet I was unhappy. The pain and anguish I was feeling is familiar to many in our community. It should not have been so.

Personal Discomfort

Many heterosexual Americans reject gay people at the personal level. In 1987, a *Roper* poll found that 25% of the respondents to a national survey would strongly object to working around people who are homosexual, and another 27% would prefer not to do so; only 45% "wouldn't mind.". . .

Negative attitudes often are expressed behaviorally. Of 113 lesbians and 287 gay men in a national telephone survey, for example, 5% of the men and 10% of the women reported having been physically abused or assaulted in the previous year because they were gay. Nearly half (47%) reported experiencing some form of discrimination (job, housing, health care, or social) at some time in their life based on their sexual orientation. Other research similarly has found that significant numbers of gay men and lesbians have been the targets of verbal abuse, discrimination, or physical assault because of their sexual orientation.

Gregory M. Herek in *Homosexuality*, 1991.

I was really struggling with my sexual orientation when I began my first job as an attorney nearly four years ago. Right out of law school I had begun to work with the special projects section of the Florida Attorney General's Office. The section's focus was on complex environmental litigation, a favorite area of mine. I was ecstatic to be working for an attorney general whom I knew to be a strong environmentalist who cared deeply about public service.

My excitement was tempered with a certain element of fear, since I was uncertain how my friends, family, and coworkers would treat me once they became aware of my sexual orientation. The rampant homophobia made me feel alone and concerned about the adverse consequences I might face. Coming out to identify yourself as a lesbian or gay man is a long and often painful process, thanks in large part to the ignorance and prejudice in our society.

The pivotal moment for me was when I determined that I had just as much of a right to happiness as every other citizen of this country. Once that very basic fact sunk into my mind, there was nothing the bigots could do to make me feel less of myself. I would no longer accept the lies and ignorance I had been subjected to by society.

In 1989, Vanderbilt University completed a report on antigay discrimination. It found that the health of lesbians and gay men is affected when day after day they are forced to say the opposite of what they feel. Is it any wonder the teen suicide rate is three times higher among lesbians and gay men? . . .

The American Bar Association Section of Individual Rights & Responsibilities has a committee actively working on issues of interest to the lesbian and gay community. That committee under the direction of its chair, Mark Agrast, is working with bar associations and groups around the country to secure passage of policies in states and municipalities which would prohibit discrimination based on sexual orientation.

When a person is attacked because of color, religion, race, sex, or sexual orientation, the rights and liberties of all of us are threatened. Bigotry and prejudice must not be tacitly approved by silence. It must be challenged. Let us join together as one nation, and call for an end to discrimination against lesbians and gay men. We must provide a safe and nurturing environment for everyone.

What Can Be Done

There are a number of things that can be done immediately. The easiest thing for everyone to do is to correct people when antigay remarks are made. Write to your state legislators and encourage them to support passage of a hate crimes act that includes sexual orientation- and HIV/AIDS-related attacks.

Support efforts by state and national groups to strike down the "sodomy" statutes. Support antidiscrimination provisions throughout the nation.

I encourage you to march regardless of whether you are a member of the lesbian and gay community. Contact the National Gay and Lesbian Task Force for additional information. It's time we secured the rights of all Americans.

"Gay bashing . . . is in some measure a product of the very laws designed to punish it. "

Society Does Not Need to Accept Homosexuality

Carl F. Horowitz

Many people argue that gays, lesbians, and bisexuals are treated unfairly in the United States and are being denied basic civil rights because of their sexual orientation. In the following viewpoint, Carl F. Horowitz offers an alternative explanation for prejudice against homosexuals. He argues that many acts of prejudice and discrimination against gays and lesbians are a result of the gay rights movement's attempts to force its views on the rest of America. Changes in civil rights laws, he asserts, would result in affirmative action laws in favor of homosexuals, and would ultimately cause a backlash of resentment and unrest against gays and lesbians. Horowitz is a policy analyst at the Heritage Foundation, a conservative think tank in Washington, D.C.

As you read, consider the following questions:

1. What examples of objectionable behavior by homosexual activists does Horowitz provide?
2. What are the goals of the homosexual rights movement, according to the author?
3. According to Horowitz, what are the causes of violence against gays and lesbians?

Carl F. Horowitz, "Homosexuality's Legal Revolution," *The Freeman*, May 1991.

In April 1990, a brief series of events occurred in a Madison, Wisconsin, restaurant that spoke volumes about the current character of the homosexual rights movement. An employee of the Espresso Royal Cafe asked two women—presumably lesbians—to refrain from passionately kissing as they sat at a window table. Madison's gay community was not amused. The very next day, about 125 homosexual demonstrators showed up on the premises, and conducted a "kiss-in" for several minutes. A spokeswoman for the protesters, Malvene Collins, demanded, "You say gays and lesbians cannot show affection here? Why not here but in every other restaurant in Madison?" The establishment's chastised owner, Donald Hanigan, assured the crowd, "I regret that this incident ever happened. I want all of you to come in here every day."

In October 1990, several dozen homosexual males, many of them dressed in women's clothing, openly hugged and kissed in a terminal of Seattle-Tacoma Airport, and handed out condoms and leaflets to travelers. Matt Nagel, spokesman for the Seattle chapter of a new homosexual organization, Queer Nation, seemed to sum up the feeling among militants in the local homosexual community. "We're going to homophobic bars, we're going to pack them, we're going to be openly affectionate, we're going to dance together and make it uncomfortable for all the straight people there."

At the same time in Chicago, six homosexual couples staged a "kiss-in" at the cosmetics counter of a Bloomingdale's department store until they were escorted out by security guards. Far from being deterred, the couples shortly went down to the cafeteria of a nearby office building, where they resumed their public display of affection.

A Bid for Legitimacy

After some two decades of confrontation, the homosexual rights movement is consolidating its bid for legitimacy. The phrase, "Out of the closet, and into the streets," sounds quaint. That battle has already been won. Openly homosexual adults are certainly in the streets—and in stores, airports, and "homophobic" bars. Openly gay television characters, each with handsome, well-scrubbed looks, populate daytime and evening drama. Gay-oriented news programming is available on radio and television. Homosexual activists have all but completed their campaign to persuade the nation's educational establishment that homosexuality is normal "alternative" behavior, and thus any adverse reaction to it is akin to a phobia, such as fear of heights, or an ethnic prejudice, such as anti-Semitism.

The movement now stands on the verge of fully realizing its use of law to create a separate homosexual society paralleling

that of the larger society in every way, and to intimidate heterosexuals uncomfortable about coming into contact with it.
Through aggressive lobbying by such gay organizations as the
Human Rights Campaign Fund, the Lambda Legal Defense and
Education Fund, and the National Gay and Lesbian Task Force,
the first part of that mission has enjoyed enormous success.
About 90 counties and municipalities now have ordinances banning discrimination on the basis of gender orientation. There
are roughly 50 openly gay public officials, up from less than a
half-dozen in 1980.

Asay, by permission of the *Colorado Springs Gazette Telegraph*.

Gay couples are increasingly receiving the full benefits of
marriage, if not through state recognition of homosexual marriage ceremonies, then through enactment of domestic partnership laws. The State of California took a big step toward legalization of such marriages: in December 1990 it announced that
"non-traditional" families, including homosexual couples, could
formally register their unions as "unincorporated non-profit associations." Divorced gay parents are receiving with increasing
frequency the right to custody of natural children. Gay adults
without children are increasingly receiving the right to adopt
them. Aspiring homosexual clergy are demanding—and receiving—the right to be ordained. Openly gay teachers are teaching

in public schools. Homosexual soldiers, aware that their sexual orientation is grounds for expulsion from the military, openly declare their proclivities.

A federal gay rights bill is the ultimate prize, and homosexual activists are blunt and resolute in pursuing such legislation. For example, Jeff Levi, spokesman for the National Gay and Lesbian Task Force, remarked at a press conference coinciding with the national gay march on Washington in October 1987:

> . . . we are no longer seeking just a right to privacy and a protection from wrong. We also have a right—as heterosexual Americans already have—to see government and society affirm our lives. . . . until our relationships are recognized in the law—through domestic partner legislation or the definition of beneficiaries, for example—until we are provided with the same financial incentives in tax law and government programs to affirm our family relationships, then we will not have achieved equality in American society.

Yet, homosexual activists know that this legal revolution will never succeed without the unpleasant task of coercing heterosexuals into masking their displeasure with homosexuality. It is thus not enough merely to break down all existing barriers to homosexual affection being expressed through marriage, child-rearing, or employment. The law must additionally be rewritten to make it as difficult as possible for heterosexuals to avoid contact with such displays, or to show discomfort toward them.

This two-edged approach would create a world in which stringent laws at all levels, aggressively enforced and strictly interpreted, force business owners to refuse to discriminate against the openly homosexual in patronage, leasing, and hiring. Removing overtly homosexual patrons from a bar, an airport, or any other public space would result in heavy fines and even jail sentences against property owners or their employees (or in lieu of these sanctions, mandatory purgation). Derogatory remarks directed at homosexuals, even with sexuality only incidental, would likewise result in criminal penalties. . . .

Civil Rights

The homosexual lobby speaks of itself as struggling for "civil rights." "The gay community's goal is integration—just as it was with Martin Luther King," argues homosexual activist and San Francisco Board of Supervisors President Harry Britt. Yet, underneath the surface, gay civil rights seems analogous to black "civil rights" *after* Reverend King's death. Far from seeking integration with the heterosexual world, it vehemently avoids it. More important, the movement seeks to win sinecures through the state, and over any objections by "homophobic" opposition. With a cloud of a heavy fine or even a jail sentence hanging over a mortgage lender, a rental agent, or a job interviewer who might be discomforted by them, homosexuals under these laws can win employment, credit, housing, and other economic entitlements. Heterosexuals would have no right to discriminate against homosexuals, but apparently, not vice versa. . . .

Argument by Insult

Both Judaism and Christianity insist that there is a divinely ordained right order of things, and that our sexual drives find appropriate expression within that order in monogamous heterosexual unions. Only in the quite recent past has that millennia-old understanding come into question. It takes no extraordinary perception to see that God made men and women for each other; indeed, it requires remarkable perversity of mind to get around that obvious intent. Homosexuals have the right to expect of the rest of us decent and respectful treatment as human beings and citizens; they have no right to insist that we surrender our fundamental moral and religious beliefs in order that they might feel comfortable with their sexual behavior. When the militants among them choose to conduct argument by insult—such as labelling all opposition to their agenda as homophobia—they consign themselves to the same moral category as the gay-baiters of the heterosexual world.

First Things, November 1990.

For gay activists, therein lies the payoff. By codifying into law "protection" of homosexual mannerisms, they can intimidate gatekeepers into providing job security and housing for the openly homosexual. Thus, without necessarily mentioning anything about quotas or, for that matter, homosexuality, law in the U.S. is increasingly mandating *homosexual affirmative action*. Such law has the same intent as the vetoed Kennedy-Hawkins Civil Rights Act.

Sexual Schism

If the homosexual rights movement is in large measure an affirmative action strategy, certain consequences should be evident, all of which already are on their way to being entrenched. Most obviously, American culture is experiencing a sexual schism as deep as any racial one. There are other damaging ramifications.

First, wherever such laws exist, they will attract homosexuals to the jurisdictions enacting them. Common sense dictates that any community laying out the welcome mat for homosexuality lays it for homosexuals, implicitly telling others to kindly step aside. Aside from legal protection, there is political strength in concentrated numbers. Most aspiring elected officials in San Francisco, for example, must now pay homage to the achievement of local gays, and show up at gay events. As Proposition K coordinator Jean Harris remarked, "We've shocked the world and made history with this lavender sweep. . . . It's clear that if you don't get the support of the gay-lesbian community you're going to be in trouble." While the homosexual voting bloc will never be a majority in any city, even San Francisco, it can wield enormous veto power over the objections of all other blocs.

Second, having learned the power of the gatekeeper role, many homosexuals will seek to become gatekeepers themselves. It takes no great stretch of imagination, for example, to understand that the growing number of college administrations severely punishing anti-gay harassment (even if such "harassment" takes no more sinister a form than a satirical campus newspaper editorial or cartoon) has much to do with the growing number of college administrators and faculty who are themselves homosexual (and possibly were hired on that very basis). Nor does it take much imagination to understand that gay employers have more reason than ever to favor homosexuals in their hiring and promotion practices.

Third, these laws will create market bottlenecks. Heterosexuals and even "closeted" homosexuals will be at a competitive disadvantage for jobs and housing. For them, prices will be higher and wages lower than in the absence of such "safeguards." This is especially significant since gay culture is visible in high-cost cities such as New York and San Francisco. . . .

Fourth, the new legalism will increase heterosexual anger—and even violence—toward homosexuals. Reports of "gay bashing" (the real kind) simultaneous with increased homosexual visibility cannot be a coincidence. What economist Thomas Sowell and psychologist Stephen Johnson have each revealed about racial affirmative action can apply to sexual affirmative action as well; unprotected groups, lacking recourse through rule of law, may resort to violence against innocent members of protected groups. Those who make it their bailiwick to monitor every incident of petty harassment of gays are impervious to any possibility that when laws force heterosexuals to bottle up dialogue, their feelings may erupt in more destructive ways. *Gay bashing, then, is in some measure a product of the very laws designed to punish it. . . .*

The Growing Threat of Violence

There is something about encountering homosexuality in its militant and pugnacious form that touches a deep, almost reflexive anger, even among most heterosexual liberals. That is why attempts at "mainstreaming" gay culture, even when holding an olive branch, are bound to fail. One of the saddest books to appear in recent years is *After the Ball: How America Will Conquer Its Fear and Hatred of Gays in the 90s.* The authors, Marshall Kirk and Hunter Madsen, both homosexual, advocate a national campaign to cheerfully "sell" gay culture. They suggest, for example, that gay organizations buy up advertising space in "straight" newspapers with pictures of historical figures such as Alexander the Great, asking: "Did you know he was gay?"

Losing Patience

Under the combined pressures of fear and pity, I've been forced to confront my own tangled notions about gays. I cherish my gay friends, and want them to live long and productive lives. But while AIDS has made many millions even more sympathetic to and understanding of gay lives, I find myself struggling with the powerful undertow of the primitive codes of my youth. I've lost all patience with much of the paranoid oratory of gay radicals. I can't abide the self-pitying aura of victimhood that permeates so much of their discussion. Their leaders irritate me with their insistence on seeing AIDS as if it were some tragic medieval plague of unknown origin instead of the result of personal behavior. . . .

I'm not among those who believe there is some all-powerful "Homintern" that manipulates the media while filling the museums with Robert Mapplethorpe photographs. But I don't feel I'm lining up with the unspeakable Jesse Helms when I say that I'm also fed up with the ranting of those gays who believe that all straights are part of some Monstrous Conspiracy to end homosexual life. One lie is not countered with another.

Pete Hamill, *Esquire*, August 1990.

Kirk and Madsen, like their surlier compatriots, fail to grasp that public homosexuality strikes at both a heterosexual's fear of loss of sexual identity and sense of belonging to a family. For even in this age of artificial insemination, families are not sustainable without heterosexuality. No matter how much the homosexual activist naively protests, "Gays are people, too," such a plea will receive in return grudging respect, and little else.

In a summary piece for *Newsweek*'s March 12, 1990, cover story, "The Future of Gay America," Jonathan Alter revealed a rare understanding of this dynamic. He notes, "'Acting gay' often involves more than sexual behavior itself. Much of the dislike for homosexuals centers not on who they are or what they do in private, but on so-called affectations—'swishiness' in men, the 'butch' look for women—not directly related to the more private sex act." Quite rightly so—one doubts if more than a tiny fraction of heterosexuals have even *inadvertently* witnessed a homosexual act. Alter then gets to the core of the issue. "Heterosexuals," he writes, "tend to argue that gays can downplay these characteristics and 'pass' more easily in the straight world than blacks can in a white world. . . . This may be true, but it's also irrelevant. For most gays those traits aren't affectations but part of their identities; attacking their swishiness is the same as attacking *them*."

Antagonizing Heterosexuals

Yet if gays, through their carefully practiced "gay" mannerisms, know fully well they are antagonizing many heterosexuals, then why do they display them? Is it not in part to make heterosexuals sweat? By aggressively politicizing these traits, and demanding that those objecting must grin and bear it, they are in a sense restricting heterosexual freedom of speech. Male and even female opposition to persons with these traits is slowly taking a nasty turn, moving from violence of language to violence of fists. And yet, given the emerging legal climate, one discovers within oneself a disquieting empathy with the inchoate rage behind such acts.

Most heterosexuals are reasonably libertarian; an October 1989 Gallup Poll indicated that by a 47-to-36 margin (with the remainder undecided) Americans prefer legalization of homosexual relations between consenting adults. This is all to the good. Anti-sodomy laws serve no purpose but to intimidate people out of private, consensual acts. On the other hand, the brazen, *open* display of homosexuality—as if to taunt, to tease, to maliciously sow confusion into sexual identities—is something most heterosexuals do not handle gracefully. With an unofficial government mandate for preferential treatment, it is not difficult to imagine a backlash. When homosexual lawyer-artist William Dobbs plastered explicit homosexual artwork throughout the Yale University campus back in 1989, he was not simply making a homoerotic statement; he was daring "homophobes" to remove the art, and risk suspension or expulsion from the university. Those having little to lose may accept his dare—and it may be people like Dobbs as well as such art that gets torn up.

Should a sober discussion of the possibilities for heterosexual violence be forbidden? Nobody in a *rational* state of mind would seek to emulate the exploits of "skinheads" or the late San Francisco Supervisor Dan White. Yet let readers here imagine themselves in that Madison restaurant or Seattle airport, being witness to mass displays of homosexual kissing, and feeling utterly helpless to evince the slightest disapproval. Would not such a scenario provoke an impulse, however fleeting and irrational, to do bodily harm? Does not the knowledge that the law is now stacked against even nonviolent disapproval ("hate crimes") merely add to the likelihood of a conflagration?

The principal motive of the gay movement is coming into focus with each passing month: to bait heterosexuals' less morally sturdy side, goading them into verbal or (better) physical assaults against the openly homosexual. That way, cries of homosexual victimhood would carry even more self-fulfilling prophecy, so much the better to vilify heterosexuals.

Gay militants aren't hesitant about admitting to such motives. Some want nothing less than war in the streets. Homosexual playwright and ACT-UP founder, Larry Kramer, called upon a gay audience to take gun practice for use in eventual combat against police and gay-bashers. "They hate us anyway," he rationalized. A cover of a recent issue of *Outweek* displayed a lesbian pointing a gun at the reader, with the headline, "Taking Aim at Bashers," while another cover announced, "We Hate Straights." Even "mainstream" gay leaders, such as Urvashi Vaid, executive director of the National Gay and Lesbian Task Force, endorse such tactics, whatever the loss of potential supporters.

The crowning legacy of the new gay legalism may yet be widespread violence, a violence brought on by state inhibition of rational dialogue at the behest of gay radicals, and in the name of "sensitivity." That alone is enough reason to oppose it.

"Since gay people have been, and continue to be, the victims of irrational discrimination, they ought to be protected by civil rights law."

Homosexuals Need Civil Rights Protection

Matthew A. Coles

Civil rights laws are made in the United States to protect members of minority groups from discrimination in employment, housing, and other areas. In recent years many localities and states have passed laws prohibiting discrimination on the basis of sexual orientation. In the following viewpoint, Matthew A. Coles argues that more such laws are needed on the national level. He asserts that gays and lesbians face severe discrimination in American society because of misguided prejudices against homosexuality, and that they need civil rights protection in order to ensure fair treatment. Coles teaches law at the University of California, Hastings College of Law, in San Francisco, and is a staff attorney for the American Civil Liberties Union of Northern California.

As you read, consider the following questions:

1. What are the hallmarks of a group that needs civil rights protection, according to Coles?
2. How does the author counter arguments favoring discrimination against homosexuals?
3. How does AIDS affect the question of gay rights, according to Coles?

From Matthew A. Coles, "The Case for Gay Rights," *Hamline Journal of Public Law and Policy* 9:2 (Fall 1989). Reprinted with permission.

The United States should have laws protecting the civil rights of lesbians and gay men because the social structures which are supposed to make sure that people are treated fairly do not protect gay people.

For the most part, America relies on social norms, not law, to ensure that people are treated fairly. The idea is not simply that people should be committed to fairness (although that is an important part of the theory), but that those people who are consistently unfair will fail. Business people, for example, who base employment decisions on something other than merit will suffer inasmuch as they will be less efficient than others. A similar fate will befall landlords who are arbitrary about tenants and business people who are arbitrary about customers. America, generally, does not have laws requiring "good cause" in employment, housing, etc. because such laws are thought to be unnecessary.

This may or may not be a wise theory; it may or may not be a relatively accurate description of how American society actually works. Sometimes at least, this model of society is neither wise in theory nor accurate in reality. Sometimes, groups of people suffer for reasons that have nothing to do with merit or ability, and the system does not correct that.

The purpose of civil rights law is to step in where society fails. Civil rights laws are appropriate whenever society consistently disadvantages a group of people for reasons that are not related to ability. Since gay people have been, and continue to be, the victims of irrational discrimination, they ought to be protected by civil rights law. . . .

The hallmarks of a group in need of civil rights protection are the following:

1. a history of having been disadvantaged by society; and
2. evidence that when society disadvantages the group, it is not because of the group's incapability or because the group is dangerous.

Lesbians and gay men meet both of these criteria.

Employment Discrimination

A job is one of the single most important things a person can have in this society. It is not just the way people support themselves; it is critical to the way people define themselves and the way they are defined by society.

Lesbians and gay men have lost or been denied jobs as librarians, telephone operators, budget analysts, and police officers. Until relatively recently, they were barred from federal employment. They remain barred from the military, and while not denied security clearances outright, lesbians and gay men are subjected to lengthy special investigations that make employment in many high technology jobs impossible. Gay people have even been denied admission to the bar.

Gay teachers have had a particularly difficult time. They have been fired for being open about their sexuality with co-workers, and for concealing their sexuality from their employers. They have also been fired for "socializing" with other gay people away from work.

The teacher cases illustrate a startling fact about gay people who get fired: employers almost never claim that gay people cannot do the job. Instead, they try to justify discriminating against people by claiming:

1. that gay people are immoral and thus unfit to work;
2. that gay people are mentally unbalanced; and
3. that gay people disturb the workplace because co-workers and others do not like them.

Immorality

The "immorality" argument usually covers two distinct ideas:

1. that being gay goes against some basic natural law of life on earth; or
2. that being gay goes against God's law.

A. *The "laws of nature" argument.* The first strand of this argument says that it is unnatural to be gay because same sex sexual behavior does not occur among non-human species. This is simply wrong. Same sex sexual activity, including the formation of same gender "couples," exists in countless other species, both in the wild and in captivity. . . .

The best answer to this argument is that if the historic agreement of most moral and social leaders is proof of immorality then it is (or at least it was) immoral to think that the earth is round, that it revolves around the sun, that blacks are human and that women are capable of work that requires thought.

Sometimes, this argument simply comes down to the notion that being gay is wrong because society as a whole disapproves of it. All this really says is that gay people are unpopular. It has nothing to do with whether a gay person is capable of doing a job, or whether she or he represents some real threat to the personal integrity of others. . . .

B. *God's Law.* Put aside the fact that those who think they know God's law are far from agreement on the morality of being gay. Put aside the fact that even in those parts of the Christian church which find being gay immoral the idea is, in the Christian scheme of things, relatively recent. That a group of people believe that God disapproves of another group of people is simply not a sufficient proof that the second group of people is a danger to the first. If it were, we would have to accept the idea that slavery was justified by the threat blacks posed to whites. Absent some evidence of incapacity or potential harm, the invocation of God's law, no matter how devout the belief in it, is no different than the invocation of historic consensuses or current unpopularity. It is an attempt to deflect the inquiry from the tangible to the nonexaminable.

Mental Instability

The fascinating thing about this argument is that typically, those against whom it is used have shown no instability at all; on the contrary, they are often recognized as model workers. Furthermore, virtually every respectable mental health professional has rejected the claim that as a rule, gay people are less mentally stable than others.

Peace in the workplace is the theme of this justification. If gay people are present, so the argument goes, co-workers will become uncomfortable and efficiency will suffer.

'We don't discriminate against homosexuals in this company. As a matter of fact, we've already set up an office for you.'

Like the argument about mental instability, this claim is rarely supported with real evidence of controversy in the workplace. However, even if the argument was supported by evidence, the dislike of co-workers is simply an employer-specific version of the argument that discrimination is justified because people do not like lesbians and gay men. The argument has nothing to do with the capabilities of gay people.

Personal Relationships

Personal relationships are every bit as important as work. However, America makes personal relationships of all kinds very difficult for lesbians and gay men.

For example, in many states it is illegal for two persons of the same gender to have sexual relations, while at the same time, the same conduct is legal if done by heterosexuals.

Gay people cannot marry. They cannot form common law marriages. Attempts by gay people to formalize relationships privately are apt to get less respect from the law than similar heterosexual relationships. While the law sometimes allows unmarried heterosexual couples the benefits of marriage, those benefits are almost never extended to gay couples.

Courts have forced gay parents to choose between their lovers and their children, conditioning custody and visitation on the absence of a lover from the parent's home—and in some cases, on the absence of anyone of the same gender. While the law says that child custody and visitation are always to be controlled by the "best interests of the child," gay parents have lost custody even though all the evidence showed separation was not in the child's interest.

Most of these policies are justified with the same "morality" arguments described above. Bans on formalizing gay relationships are also justified with these arguments:

1. gay people are unable to form meaningful relationships;

2. gay relationships are a threat to the traditional family. Orders separating gay people from their children use all of these and two more:

    a. the children of gay parents will turn out to be gay;

    b. the children of gay parents will be psychologically damaged by the stigma society attaches to the parents. Like the "morality" arguments, none of these will stand a close look.

1. Inability to Form Relationships.

It is simply not true. Lesbians and gay men do form strong, enduring relationships.

It would hardly be necessary to keep gay people from formalizing long term relationships if they were incapable of forming them. The bans on same sex marriage are "needed" only because this argument is simply wrong.

2. Threat to the Family.

If the idea is that people will not enter traditional families if the option to live in a gay relationship is open, the family is indeed in trouble; nothing will save it. Occasionally, it is said that gay people will "recruit" children, or subject them to sexual assault, and are a threat to the family in that sense. Almost all adults who become sexually involved with minors are heterosexual men.

Sometimes people say that since gay people do not conform to traditional gender "roles," they are a threat to the family. Apparently, this idea begins with the notion that gay men are in general "feminine" and lesbians are "masculine." The presence of masculine women and feminine men in families, or even in the same society with families will destroy the family, the argument goes, *because* children who see feminine men and masculine women will not learn how to be feminine women and masculine men. Since they will not learn that, they will be unable to learn how to be good mothers and good fathers, therefore the family will collapse.

This is nonsense on a grand scale. To begin with, it is not true that gay women tend to be any less feminine than heterosexual women, or that gay men tend to be less masculine. But more important, there is not a shred of evidence that growing up in the company of "strong" women or "gentle" men makes it more likely that girls will be strong and boys gentle. And, perhaps most important of all, there is no evidence that strong women make bad mothers or that gentle men make bad fathers. Indeed, I suspect the experience of most people is to the contrary.

3. The Children of Gay People Will Tend to Be Gay.

This argument starts off by assuming what it is used to prove: that it is not good to be gay. In any event, the evidence shows that it is quite false; children of gay parents are no different than the children of heterosexual parents. . . .

Double Standards

Gay people are told not to dance with each other, not to eat together in private booths, not to "hangout" in bars, not to hug each other, and not to go to the prom together. Gay men have been arrested for making passes at men and convicted by courts which said (incredibly) that straight men do not make passes at women and by courts which went on to rule public sex is legal when it involves heterosexuals.

Gay people have lost their homes, as have straight people who associated with gay people. Gay organizations have been told that they cannot incorporate. Gay groups have been told, in the finest tradition of unintentional government irony, not to take part in the bicentennial of the American Revolution. The arguments for all of these are the same: morality and general social dislike for gay people.

Discrimination against lesbians and gay men runs throughout American society. It has a long history. The explanations offered to justify it rely on things everybody "knows" but which nobody ever tries to prove—things which, when tested, never prove to be true. There ought to be a body of civil rights law protecting lesbians and gay men.

Three Arguments Against Civil Rights for Gays

A. Sexual Orientation Is Neither Immutable nor Uncontrollable.

There is no point in getting into the argument about whether sexual orientation is "inborn," "set at an early age," or a matter of "choice." It is simply not true that in America, civil rights law protects only groups defined by conditions which cannot be changed. We have a body of law forbidding discrimination against illegitimate children and one protecting noncitizens. Both of those conditions can be changed. It is not true that civil rights law only protects groups defined by conditions they are born with. We have laws banning discrimination based on marital status, a choice made long after birth. It is not true that civil rights law protects only conditions which, if changeable, need to be changed by someone other than a member of the group in question (the "uncontrollable" trait). We do not allow discrimination on the basis of the most basic philosophical choice, religious preference.

Hostility Toward Gays

Institutional and personal hostility toward lesbians and gay men is a fact of life in the United States today. At the cultural level, homosexuality remains stigmatized through institutional policies. Statutes prohibiting antigay discrimination in employment, housing, and services are in force in only two states (Wisconsin and Massachusetts), the District of Columbia, and a few dozen municipalities and local jurisdictions (for example, San Francisco, New York, Chicago). Lesbian and gay military personnel are subject to discharge if their sexual orientation is discovered, no matter how exemplary their service records. Gay civilians routinely are denied government security clearances, or are subjected to more intensive investigation than are heterosexual applicants. Lesbian and gay relationships generally are not legally recognized and, in 24 states and the District of Columbia, the partners in same-sex relationships are forbidden by law from private sexual contact.

Gregory M. Herek, *Homosexuality*, 1991.

B. AIDS.

There are two distinct arguments: first, that civil rights laws which protect gay people will encourage the spread of the AIDS

84

epidemic; second, that AIDS proves that gay people are not worthy of protection by civil rights law.

Both arguments wrongly assume that all or most gay people have AIDS. This simply is not true. In fact, some gay people (lesbians) are at a lower risk than anyone else in society. The first argument then compounds its error by assuming that all same sex sexual behavior spreads AIDS. That of course is not true; anal intercourse without the use of condoms by persons already infected with the virus which causes AIDS is not the only sexual activity of which gay people are capable. On the other hand, it is true that heterosexual activities (including vaginal intercourse by an infected person without a condom) can spread the disease and that nonsexual behavior (inoculation with infected blood) can spread it as well. The argument's final assumption—that gay people who know about the risks of AIDS will nonetheless continue to spread it—is quite wrong. There are virtually no new AIDS infections among gay men in San Francisco. When people learn about the disease and how to stop it from spreading they do what is necessary. Civil rights protection for members of the community most hurt by the disease will not change that.

Both of these arguments are really based on an unattractive desire to punish the victims of this disease. Only a fool would think that being ravaged by an epidemic is evidence of a person's collective worth. It makes as much sense to say that we should condemn all those who live on the gulf coast for allowing themselves to be devastated by a hurricane.

C: The Right to Discriminate.

Along with its philosophy of civil rights, America has a philosophy of individual freedom. People ought to be free to associate with whomever they wish, and free not to associate with whomever they wish to be apart from.

Civil Rights Laws and Individual Freedom

Observing that many Americans believe in that kind of individual freedom does not help answer the question of whether there ought to be a body of civil rights law protecting lesbians and gay men. All civil rights law clashes with the notion of individual freedom. An employer may not refuse to hire black people even though he or she wants nothing to do with them. Landlords cannot refuse to rent to religious fundamentalists, no matter how much they would prefer not to deal with them.

The issue is not whether Americans believe in a strong individual freedom to choose one's associates. The issue is when and where that value must give way to the values represented by civil rights law. That "freedom to choose" must give when it is directed against a group so victimized by prejudice that its members cannot participate on the basis of merit in what is supposed to be a merit system.

But the freedom to choose does not give way completely. No civil rights law dictates who one might have to dinner, who one might marry, or who one might share a beer with. Civil rights laws go no further than those essentials of life: jobs, housing, businesses and political participation.

A Final Word

Civil rights law will not end prejudice against lesbians and gay men; it will not even end discrimination. It will begin moving America a little closer to what it aspires to be: a society committed to human rights and devoted to justice.

Today we are ashamed of court decisions and laws which supported slavery, which kept women away from the workplace, and which put Japanese Americans in concentration camps. We ought to be frightened, as well as ashamed, for those laws and decisions which show how fragile our commitment to fairness is. We are often comforted by the thought that those were mistakes of the past.

But, just as it is a mistake to ascribe to the framers of the Constitution a wisdom far beyond our own, it is a mistake to ascribe to the lawmakers of the last two centuries an ignorance which we have outgrown. The blindness which was ours in 1789, in the 1840's and in the 1940's is still with us today.

Every day that we allow lesbians and gay men to remain unprotected by civil rights laws, we postpone any change of progress to greatness. We should not wait another moment.

> *"Gay rights laws meet none of the traditional requirements for human rights protection."*

Homosexuals Do Not Need Civil Rights Protection

Roger J. Magnuson

Roger J. Magnuson is a trial lawyer in Minneapolis. In the following viewpoint, taken from his book *Are Gay Rights Right?*, he argues that homosexuals should not be entitled to special civil rights protection as a group. He asserts that gays and lesbians already have the basic civil rights and liberties all Americans enjoy, and that additional civil rights laws are attempts to force the government to legitimize and sanction the homosexual life-style. People should retain the right to discriminate against those whose behavior they believe is immoral, Magnuson concludes.

As you read, consider the following questions:

1. What is the real agenda behind efforts to give homosexuals civil rights protections, according to Magnuson?
2. In what cases does the author believe discrimination against gays and lesbians is justified?
3. Why does Magnuson object to equating civil rights for minorities with civil rights for homosexuals?

From Roger J. Magnuson, *Are Gay Rights Right?* © 1990 by The Berean League Fund. Reprinted by permission of the publisher, Multnomah Press.

In the last two decades, gay rights activists have begun to press a new, radically different set of claims to civil rights protection. Human rights statutes historically have granted special legal standing to those "discrete and insular minorities" who share an immutable *status*. That status was generally unrelated to behavior, traditional perceptions of moral character, or public health. One's racial inheritance, for example, creates a true *status*. Race tells us nothing about a person's life-style or behavior. Removing race as a criterion of social decision making therefore makes sense to all but the most arbitrary decision maker.

Gay rights proposals redefine status without ever saying so. Rather than acknowledge that such laws protect a social behavior (say, the commission of anal sodomy) whose benefits or detriments to society must be objectively evaluated before the protection is given, proponents create a new minority status. An uncritical acceptance of that new status derails a rational inquiry into the underlying behavior and disguises the fact that this minority is bound together by sexual activity—a common inclination to commit sodomy with members of the same sex. This new status group, given a new name ("gay") which itself begs the question of whether the group shares a common nature or a common behavior, has been proposed as worthy of legal protection under human rights laws extended to include "sexual preference" or "sexual orientation.". . .

The Rationale of Gay Rights Explored

The real issue underlying the gay rights controversy is whether the law should give special protection for homosexual behavior. Does the inclination to practice anal or oral sodomy (or related sexual practices) with members of the same sex merit special legal safeguards?

The public policy issue is straightforward. A group of citizens, bound together by common sexual taste, comes seeking insulation of their sexual behavior from scrutiny by other members of society; they want, in short, to debar others from taking sexual orientation or behavior into account in making social decisions. They seek the privilege of having one aspect of their personality or behavior eliminated as a criterion for exercising a general right to associate, or dissociate, with others.

It is important that the issue be correctly stated. Much of the discourse about such political claims leaves underlying presuppositions unanalyzed. Among them is the presupposition that everyone has a preexisting right to protect his preferences and predispositions from being taken into account by other people. Referring to "gay rights" as "civil rights" is begging the question. It assumes such rights exist. With that assumption in place, the only question that remains is, have those rights been infringed?

Has there been discrimination? Once discrimination has been shown, it follows that wrong should give rise to remedy. The remedy is explicit civil rights protections for homosexuals.

That model is defective. Civil rights protections have always required a sensitive balancing of social interests. On the one hand, a substantial social benefit is derived in continuing the historic deference given to human choices and discretion. The freedom of association valued by all Americans includes a corollary right to nonassociation. On the other hand, there is also a strong social benefit in discouraging arbitrary decisions that cause widespread injury to innocent parties. Human rights laws have struck a delicate balance that accommodates both interests. They give substantial relief to those who have been the victims of prejudice, but they do so without limiting the right of anyone to make decisions based on any reasonable criteria. By forbidding arbitrary or irrational decisions that cause substantial harm to innocent parties, human rights laws preserve intact discretionary decision making based on reason and common sense.

Looked at in an alternative way, homosexuals have all the same rights heterosexuals do. They are protected by the Bill of Rights, by federal and state statutes, and by common-law decisions. They have the same status before the law as do other citizens. Yet through gay rights ordinances, they demand to join the few classes of citizens having characteristics immune from scrutiny. The issue is not whether rights have been infringed. The issue is whether new rights, not previously recognized, should be created.

Are Gay Rights Laws Necessary?

The legislative history of gay rights ordinances is typically long on emotion and short on evidence. There are no rigorous studies, and no substantial testimony, that prove homosexuals are routinely discriminated against. The legislative history underlying past battles over civil rights was filled with evidence that blacks suffered systematic discrimination against them in the South and structural forms of deprivation, such as isolation, in the North. Disparities in income, housing, employment, cultural opportunities, and education were not merely suspected, they were demonstrated by statistics, sociological studies, and voluminous testimony.

Lack of such proof here is no accident. As one observer has pointed out, "One of the most striking phenomena of the past few years is what appears to be a massive increase in the acceptability of homosexual behavior in America." Aside from social pressure on those flaunting personality traits that would make heterosexuals equally unpopular, people do not routinely discriminate against homosexuals. Homosexuals live in nice neighborhoods, in well-furnished homes and apartments with expensive accouterments. They are popular in athletics (Billy Jean King, Martina Navratilova), in the arts (Rock Hudson, Boy George, Liberace, Truman Capote, and a long list of others), in Congress (Congressman Barney Frank), and in the professions.

Indeed, homosexuals have become so strong in the marketplace that nearly every major manufacturer of consumer goods has a marketing plan directed specifically to them. Homosexuals have become a new "power bloc" that has both "votes and money." One writer estimated that homosexuals control one-third of the buying power in California. The estimate is inflated, but there is no doubt about homosexual influence. . . .

Asay, by permission of the *Colorado Springs Gazette Telegraph*.

Gay rights laws are also unnecessary when one considers the extensive rights the homosexual already has under existing law. These rights supplement the routine constitutional privileges the homosexual has in common with all Americans: the Bill of Rights' protections, encompassing such things as freedom of speech, association, religious practice, due process of law; enforcement of contracts; use of the courts; equal protection of the law. In addition to such protections of law shared with all citizens, a homosexual can

- form organizations to lobby for his political rights.
- incorporate under state incorporation laws.
- form student organizations on state-supported campuses, including rights to the same benefits received by any other campus organizations, such as organized social functions and homosexual dances on campus.
- obtain tax-exempt and tax-deductible status.
- publicly assemble, rally, petition, and carry out all forms of political activism in support of his political ideas.
- wear badges and buttons in public schools and colleges without fear of disciplinary action by the school. . . .

This litany of rights is by no means exhaustive. The homosexual has all the rights the heterosexual does, but he wants a right the heterosexual does not have. He wants to coerce others not to take into account his inclination to practice sodomy, his prevailing preference, even when those others, including parents, employers, or landlords, have contrary convictions. The result expands the privileges given to homosexuals and shrinks the rights of other citizens. . . .

Even if homosexuals believe gay rights laws are necessary, such laws would still be undesirable for society as a whole, for a number of reasons.

An Inappropriate Addition to Human Rights Laws

As we have already seen, proponents of gay rights laws rely heavily on an analogy to other human rights legislation. If human rights laws have provided protection to other minorities, why should society not add one more group to those protected from discrimination? Hitching their wagon to the broadly based support Americans have traditionally given civil rights laws, gay rights advocates have made surprising progress in the past decade.

The human rights analogy, though popular and politically understandable, cannot withstand careful analysis. Adding homosexual behavior to a list of classes that includes racial and religious minorities makes no sense. The tenuous balance of social interests represented by these laws is reflected in the few, and carefully chosen, classes they protect. Relief has been given only in extraordinary circumstances. To add another protected class, at least five requirements have had to be shown: *(1) A demonstrable pattern of discrimination (2) based on criteria that are arbitrary and irrational (3) causing substantial injury (4) to a class of people with an unchangeable or immutable status (5) which has no element of moral fault.* Each of these requirements needs to be examined in some detail.

1. A demonstrable pattern of discrimination. The discrimination alleged must be more than a collection of isolated instances.

There must be a clear pattern. At some time or other, everyone has been a victim of discrimination. A nervous applicant has lost a job opportunity because someone didn't like his tie or handshake or hairstyle. The beef-eater has been snubbed by the animal rights militant; the vegetarian has suffered the insults of the red-meat enthusiast. Everyone has an anecdote of some opportunity lost unfairly. The coercive power of law will only intervene, however, where there is a pervasive practice of discrimination throughout society. As was shown in the previous section, however, evidence of such a pattern of discrimination against homosexuals is almost totally lacking.

2. Based on criteria that are arbitrary and irrational. Civil rights laws do not limit anyone's freedom to make rational choices. They simply cancel a license to be prejudiced and to indulge irrational whims. Suppose a supervisor has been given the responsibility of hiring an employee for a day-care center. Who will be a better employee, a person whose skin is pigmented black, brown, white, yellow, or red? Would it be preferable to choose a Methodist over a Presbyterian? Is a Swiss a better diaper-changer than an Austrian? If one chooses to answer such silly questions at all, the only reasonable response would be, "It depends." It depends, of course, on the character of the individual. The status—black, Presbyterian, Swiss—is of no consequence to the rational decision maker. . . .

The Homosexual Agenda

Their social agenda is clear: destigmatize, legitimize, and gain privilege. They say they seek equality, but the very nature of their existence only lends itself to contention as they move their way into the value system of middle America. They ask for something they can only achieve through despotism—forcing Americans to accept homosexual sodomy as they do their own heterosexuality. What begins as a call for equality will naturally lead to a call for privilege.

William Dannemeyer, *New Dimensions*, January 1990.

When it comes to making choices among people, however, deviant sexual behavior tells significantly more about a person's character, or at least his characteristics, than does race, color, or religion. Even when done consensually and in private, homosexual behavior has spillover effects with public dimensions because it is a self-destructive, disproportionately disease-ridden behavior.

Taking into account a person's perverted sexual orientation is neither arbitrary nor irrational. If the operator of a day-care center knows that a homosexual applicant statistically is a significant health risk, that he is peculiarly susceptible to infections especially dangerous for young children, that his promiscuity makes him anything but an appropriate role model for the children, is it socially responsible to make it illegal to take such relevant factors into consideration? Already some doctors are calling for more discriminating standards on who can give blood or work as food handlers or care for the physically weak—all as a result of shocking discoveries of homosexual health hazards. Is the law prepared to coerce people into ignoring facts that their common sense, moral convictions, and increasing medical knowledge tell them are relevant? If so, there may emerge a disrespect for the very laws in which many deserving minority groups have found refuge.

3. *Causing substantial injury.* Another element is whether or not there has been a demonstrable pattern of discrimination resulting in substantial injury. Public policy suggests that the creation of far-reaching rights ought not to be done in the absence of extensive wrongs and injuries. A substantial rationale for civil rights protection for blacks was, of course, a century of disproportionate access to wealth and other social benefits. Economists might differ on the reasons for this disproportionate sharing in social benefits, but the fact of disparate social status was clear.

The Need for Mutual Tolerance

Living with human beings in an imperfect world requires mutual tolerance. Society does not want to encourage people to run to the courts with every complaint, to guard tender egos from every slight, to seek damages for every insult. Laws give protection where the damage is demonstrably substantial. As the arguments of the previous section make clear, no such damage to homosexuals has been demonstrated.

4. *To a class of people with an unchangeable or immutable status.* Since the prophet Jeremiah observed that the Ethiopian could not change his color nor a leopard his spots, no one has questioned that everyone has, from the moment of birth, certain unchangeable features. Race, color, and national origin never change. . . .

Some have perceived the homosexuals' claim that they have an immutable nature, a fixed orientation that draws them to commit sodomy with each other, as an important rationale for the creation of gay rights laws. The key element is volition. If homosexuals cannot help being what they are, their argument for special protection in public accommodations and distribution of other social benefits seems more analogous to other civil rights claims.

Although immutability is one reason for special civil rights privileges, it alone is not a sufficient reason to give such protections. Many characteristics are immutable but not protected. The

Sermon on the Mount asks, "Who of you by worrying can add a single cubit to his height?" Height is, at least without radical surgery, immutable, but height (or lack of it) is not protected. . . .

Even if immutability were a sufficient reason, those who advance gay rights measures ignore substantial evidence that homosexual behavior is not innate or immutable. Most psychiatrists view the innate or genetic explanation of homosexual behavior as a "myth" or "fallacy." If homosexual behavior is not innate, it is therefore learned or acquired. It is not, as Dr. Charles Socarides points out, "inevitable."

5. *Which has no element of moral fault.* Human rights laws were never intended to give a social blessing to immorality. The classes they protect are all morally neutral. No moral fault is attached to being black or white, a native or an immigrant, a male or a female. The moral innocence of the victim of discrimination has made the need for such laws compelling. . . .

Discrimination Sometimes Justified

"Sexual orientation" does not constitute a quality comparable to race, ethnic background, etc., in respect to non-discrimination. Unlike these, homosexual orientation is an objective disorder and evokes moral concern.

There are areas in which it is not unjust discrimination to take sexual orientation into account, for example, in the placement of children for adoption or foster care, in employment of teachers or athletic coaches, and in military recruitment.

Vatican Congregation for the Doctrine of the Faith, *Origins*, August 6, 1992.

No one can seriously argue that there is moral fault in being black or female, German or Chinese. But as the Supreme Court has stated, "To hold that the act of homosexual sodomy is somehow protected as a fundamental right would be to cast aside millennia of moral teaching." To prohibit the use of such a criterion is, therefore, to take away a fundamental right of association, based on a good faith perception of moral character.

In short, gay rights laws meet none of the traditional requirements for human rights protection. Homosexuals have never been able to demonstrate a convincing pattern of discrimination that causes them substantial socioeconomic injury. They are a class of people linked together through behavior, not unchangeable status. Their actions are not morally neutral. Reasonable people—for reasons of deep-seated moral conviction, of health, of psychological stability, or of common sense—may wish to take a person's homosexual life-style into account in their decision making, all without the slightest tinge of bigotry or irrationality. . . .

Conventional wisdom tells us that to tolerate weakness is often a virtue; to encourage immorality is always a vice. Gay rights laws that give special protections and privileges to people who practice sexual perversion are little more than a reward for immorality. . . .

Gay rights, therefore, pose a paradox for society. The creation of novel rights will inevitably create new wrongs: wrongs to religious institutions that seek to use their facilities or hire their employees in accordance with their historic beliefs; wrongs to society by proliferation of a now-accepted behavior that is demonstrably costly to society; wrongs to individuals injured directly or indirectly by homosexual behavior; wrongs to the family structure which is the chief building block of society. Civil rights statutes should continue to prohibit judgments based on color and true status, and to encourage judgments based on character.

conclusion

"The strongest argument for gays in the military is quietly made elsewhere—in countries . . . where gays have already been integrated into the armed forces."

The Military Should Accept Homosexuals

Eric Konigsberg

The U.S. military officially bars gays and lesbians from military service, investigating suspected gays and lesbians and discharging them if they are found to be homosexual. Despite the policy, Allan Berube, author of *Coming Out Under Fire*, estimates that there may be as many as 100,000 to 200,000 homosexuals in the military. In the following viewpoint, Eric Konigsberg, a reporter for the *New Republic*, rebuts arguments that allowing homosexuals to serve in the military would destroy troop morale and effectiveness. He examines the military forces in other countries, such as Denmark and Holland, which have successfully integrated gays and lesbians within the armed forces, and concludes that, with proper education, the United States can do the same.

As you read, consider the following questions:

1. How have other countries successfully integrated homosexuals into their military forces, according to Konigsberg?
2. How does the author respond to the argument that homosexuals are vulnerable to blackmail?
3. How does the military ban on homosexuals cost the United States money, according to Konigsberg?

From Eric Konigsberg, "Gays in Arms," *The Washington Monthly*, November 1992. Reprinted with permission from *The Washington Monthly*. Copyright by The Washington Monthly Company, 1611 Connecticut Ave., NW, Washington, DC 20009. (202) 462-0128.

Maybe Fort Bragg cadet Hallie Weinstein would have been better off if she had agreed to date the captain who asked her out. Once spurned, he began snooping into Weinstein's private life and reported to her superiors that she was a lesbian, a revelation that got her and her lover thrown out of the military. Surely Weinstein would have been better off had she been a soldier in the Dutch army.

A Wasteful Policy

In the United States, the debate over gays in the military remains a war of abstracts: Defenders of the status quo rehash fears about unwelcome advances in the showers and warn darkly of morale problems, while critics of the gay ban continue to lob rocks at the policy from the moral high ground of human rights. But with our policy stuck in hypotheticals, the strongest argument for gays in the military is quietly made elsewhere—in countries such as Holland, Denmark, Sweden, Israel, and to a lesser extent France, where gays have already been integrated into the armed forces. While the Pentagon pursues a policy that every year hounds 1,000 able-bodied gay men and women out of the service—wasting $27 million in training costs annually—other countries demonstrate that with the right mix of education and cajoling, a military with gays can work.

Take Holland, where an estimated 12,000 soldiers—10 percent of the total force—are gay. Holland's government considered homosexuality grounds for dismissal until 1974, when the Association of Dutch Homosexuals convinced the minister of defense that gays posed no threat to national security. Nevertheless, gays could still legally be passed over for promotion simply because of their sexual orientation. But in 1986, Réné Holtel, then a major, was told by his commander that though he was an excellent officer, "he wouldn't want me to rise in rank because I was gay." Holtel went to his superiors and fought the camouflage ceiling, which was abolished in 1987, leading to the birth of the Foundation for Homosexuality in the Military, which Holtel, now elevated to lieutenant colonel, chairs.

Holland's success stems from its effort to educate soldiers. Already required of officers and noncommissioned officers in the air force, and soon to be mandatory in the army and navy, is a four-day course known as *Aeen Kwastie van Kyken*, which roughly translates to "It's in the eye of the beholder." The seminar is designed to teach sensitivity toward minorities in the military, in particular women, blacks, and gays. Apparently it works. Rob Segaar, a 29-year-old veteran of the navy, summed up the Dutch attitude this way: "Suppose you're on the beach in a skimpy bathing suit. The guy next to you might be gay. Does that harm your morale? Is that dangerous?" Army doctors,

97

priests, and psychiatrists will soon be required to complete coursework that will enable them to offer guidance to soldiers struggling with the decision to "come out." The Dutch department of defense recently published a booklet on homosexuality containing pictures of a lesbian couple embracing near a ship and a young man greeting his boyfriend in Amsterdam's Schiphol Airport after a stint in Lebanon.

Reprinted with special permission of North America Syndicate.

Denmark is another success story. There, success with gays in the military is the product of necessity: Service is mandatory and the country needs all the warm bodies it can muster. Discrimination and harassment have been outlawed in the Danish army since 1981, and are grounds for expulsion. The result: Danish gay-rights advocates boast of prominent and openly gay military leaders and the armed services report no cases of threats to gays, morale, or national security since the policy was initiated. "It's not something you think about," says Stephen Arynczuk, a second lieutenant in the Danish air force. "Homosexuality, we know it's legal and it's not an issue." Asked what kinds of problems were encountered with gays among their ranks, Danish Brig. General Kristian Anderson responded, "Problems? No, should there be? I've been in the air force since

1954, and I can't remember one problem caused by someone being a homosexual."

Who else doesn't discriminate? Sweden has no ban, and Norway's government states that "Anyone who in written or oral form is threatening, scorning, persecuting, or spiting a gay or lesbian person will be punished with fines or prison for up to two years." The Swiss don't discriminate, though gay soldiers, according to their regulations, are prohibited from forming cliques, whatever that means. And it's not just in progressive Nordic climes that gays have gained entry into the army. Only five out of the sixteen NATO [North Atlantic Treaty Organization] countries have policies specifically restricting homosexuals and two of the five—Canada and Australia—are expected to lift their bans on gays in the military in the near future. . . .

Israel

Critics will answer that none of these countries offers a legitimate example of a working army with gays. After all, Sweden, Denmark, and Holland haven't had top-notch armies since the days of Beowulf. . . . But look at Israel, a nation surrounded by enemies and the possessor of one of the world's most battle-tested, successful armies. Uncloseted gays in the Jewish state are treated no differently than straights. Mandatory service draws every 18-year-old man and woman into the military, without exception. Said a recently Americanized Israeli soldier: "I had thought Israel was less tolerant than the United States, but when I enlisted, I never witnessed any morale problems caused by homosexuals and didn't really hear any homophobic talk—nothing along the lines of 'He shouldn't be serving.' There were openly gay soldiers I encountered, but no one seemed to resent it. It's not even an issue. I don't know why it is in America."

If this ex-Israeli soldier wanted to find out, he could read the hairy-chested alarms of writers like *Newsweek* contributing editor David Hackworth, who writes, "Civilian standards of fairness and equality don't apply down where the body bags are filled. Ask Marine gunnery sergeants and army platoon sergeants what a few gays would do to the fighting spirit of units."

Why not ask a soldier, like Johan Bierkus, a Swedish corporal stationed in the coastal town of Musko who *has* trained and lived with gays? "I didn't think that there should be any gays in the military. I thought homosexuality was a bit crazy," he admits. "It scared me in the army, like you just don't know what someone like that is thinking when he's with you." But when Bierkus found himself sharing a small house with eleven other boat chiefs, one of whom was gay, he was unbothered. "He was a good leader and one of my best friends in the whole group," he says. "It wasn't such a big deal that he was gay."

Next to the disintegration of the "spirit of the unit" that people like Hackworth fear, the most common excuse for bias against gays in the U.S. military has been fear of blackmail. Of course, the most recent instance of a gay soldier being blackmailed is generally believed to be in 1912, when Austrian Colonel Alfred Redl betrayed his country's secrets to the Russians. Israel takes the saner position that gays in the closet (those who, for example, may have informed their superiors of their sexual orientation, but on a confidential basis) can't get security-sensitive jobs while those who are out can work anywhere. But even some U.S. military brass seem ready to abandon this perennial cornerstone of the gay ban. As Secretary of Defense Dick Cheney reported to Congress in July 1991, "I think there have been times in the past when [opposition to gays in the military] has been generated on the notion that somehow there was a security risk involved, although I must say I think that is a bit of an old chestnut." The next step will be for the United States to realize that gays can only be blackmailed if public knowledge of their sexual appetites will get them in trouble, which is possible for as long as homosexuality remains grounds for dismissal.

Education is too often offered as a pat remedy for changing attitudes and fighting discrimination. Reeducating soldiers would have to be more sophisticated than, for instance, the superficial efforts to change the minds of high schoolers about drugs with "Just Say No" buttons. An aggressive army training and indoctrination program would have to be aimed at both officers and enlisted men. Because American recruiters in the post-Soviet world enjoy a buyer's market for new talent, inveterate gay-bashers could be weeded out before they get into uniform. For soldiers who have already been through boot camp, the Holland example suggests that if the Pentagon was willing to supply the effort, gays could be integrated with no more upheaval than when blacks were integrated decades ago. As for costs, if any new education efforts cost taxpayers less than the $27 million we lose every year training soldiers and then throwing them out because they're discovered to be gay, letting gays into the army will save us money.

The Public Wish

In the meantime, the American public is slowly producing another compelling reason to drop the gay ban: The people *want* it dropped. Sixty-nine percent of all Americans, according to a 1991 Gallup poll, believe gays should be hired as armed forces members—that's up from 51 percent in 1977.

With racial integration of the military, America's generals already proved that bigotry can be fought by fiat and force of will. The Tailhook incident behind it, the navy is again about to show that it can alter the behavior of its underlings, this time with a top-down campaign to fight sexual harassment. The experience of other nations' armies with gays reinforces what has always been true here: Soldiers take their cues from above. If history is any way to tell, gays will be unwelcome in U.S. forces for as long as the military's high ranks cling to unreasonable rationales for excluding them. If conservatives are really interested in creating the most effective military possible—one with the fittest, sharpest soldiers—then a lieutenant who protested the expulsion of Hallie Weinstein's lover in a formal letter to Fort Bragg commanders has a simple, overdue suggestion: "The army cannot afford to lose soldiers like her but instead should be concentrating on efforts to eliminate the multitude of mediocre nonperformers."

"Sure, banning gays from defending their country is discriminatory. But discrimination is necessary when a larger public purpose is served."

The Military Should Not Accept Homosexuals

David Hackworth

One of the most prominent institutions in which homosexuals have faced systematic discrimination is the U.S. military. According to Department of Defense rules revised and strengthened in 1980, gays and lesbians are barred from military service. The following viewpoint by David Hackworth defends military rules. Responding in part to 1992 legislation introduced by Congresswoman Pat Schroeder of Colorado repealing the military ban, Hackworth states that allowing homosexuals to serve in military units would have detrimental effects on troop morale and military readiness. Hackworth is a contributing editor on defense issues for *Newsweek*. He served in the U.S. Army during the Korean and Vietnam wars and is the most decorated living American veteran.

As you read, consider the following questions:

1. What examples of inappropriate behavior by homosexuals does Hackworth provide?
2. What aspects of military life does the author argue most people do not fully comprehend?
3. Who opposes lifting the ban on gays and lesbians in the military, according to Hackworth?

David Hackworth, "A Voice from the Trenches Says Keep Gays Out of the Military," *The Washington Post National Weekly Edition*, July 6-12, 1992. Reprinted with permission.

Democratic Rep. Pat Schroeder of Colorado wanted to give women "equality and opportunity" by making them rucksack-toting grunts. Now she aims at putting homosexuals in the foxholes to "end the final bastion of discrimination."

I cannot think of a better way to destroy fighting spirit and gut U.S. combat effectiveness. My credentials for saying this are more than four decades' experience as a soldier or military reporter.

Inappropriate Behavior

Despite the ban on service by homosexuals, gays have long served in the armed forces, some with distinction. Many perhaps felt no sexual inclination toward their heterosexual fellow soldiers. If they did, they had their buddies' attitudes and the Uniform Code of Military Justice hanging over their heads. Still, I have seen countless examples of inappropriate and morale-busting behavior.

In Italy, for example, in the postwar occupation, a gay soldier could not keep his hands off other soldiers in my squad. He disrupted discipline, mangled trust among squad members and zeroed out morale. In the same unit, the personnel major was gay. He had affairs with ambitious teenage soldiers in exchange for kicking up their test scores. This corrupted the command's promotion system and led to the commissioning of William Calley-like lieutenants not fit to lead combat soldiers.

During my second tour in the Korean War, a gay commanding officer gave combat awards to his lovers who had never been on the line. In Vietnam, a young captain in my unit was asked by the commander to go to bed with him. This almost destroyed the esprit of a fine parachute unit.

These are not isolated incidents: During my Army career I saw countless officers and NCOs who couldn't stop themselves from hitting on soldiers. The absoluteness of their authority, the lack of privacy, enforced intimacy and a 24-hour duty day made sexual urges difficult to control. The objects of their affection were impressionable lads who, searching for a caring role model, sometimes ended up in a gay relationship they might not have sought.

A majority of American citizens, according to polls, support Schroeder's bill. Many people look at the armed forces as they do the post office, the Bank of America or General Motors—an 8-to-5 institution where discrimination on the basis of sexual orientation is against basic freedom, human rights and the American way of life. If these polls are true, a lot of people don't understand what war is about.

Sure, banning gays from defending their country is discriminatory. But discrimination is necessary when a larger public purpose is served. Civilian standards of fairness and equality don't apply down where the body bags are filled.

On the battlefield, what allows men to survive is combat units made up of disciplined team players, who are realistically trained and led by caring skippers who set the example and know their trade. When all of these factors are in sync, a unit has the right stuff. It becomes tight, a family, and clicks like a professional football team. Spirited men who place their lives in their buddies' hands are the most essential element in warfare. The members of such combat teams trust one another totally.

NEWS ITEM: HOUSE BILL WOULD LIFT BAN OF HOMOSEXUALS IN THE MILITARY.

Ramirez/Copley News Service. Reprinted with permission.

One doesn't need to be a field marshal to understand that sex between service members undermines those critical factors that produce discipline, military orders, spirit and combat effectiveness. Mix boys and girls, gays and straights in close quarters such as the barracks or the battlefield, and both sexual contact and the consequent breakdown of morale are inevitable

Many bright people are pushing for the ban to be lifted. I suspect that few if any have been down in the trenches, but I have no doubt their psychological/sociological/political clout will have considerable influence even if they don't have a clue what combat is about.

Unfortunately, most of the top brass won't sound off. They duck and weave and offer hollow and spurious Pentagonese double-talk reasons for continuing the ban—reasons that only fuel the pro-gay argument. But they have told me in the "G" ring of the Pentagon that they're "against it, but sounding off would be the kiss of death, like opposing women in combat—a career killer, you know."

Gays Not Wanted

I hope that our lawmakers will visit Quantico and Fort Benning before they vote, and ask Marine gunnery sergeants and army platoon sergeants what a few gays would do to the fighting spirit of units. These pros told me: Gays are not wanted by straight men or women in their showers, toilets, foxholes or fighting units. They say that in combat young men face death constantly, and what allows them to make it through the hell of it all is a feeling of toughness, invincibility and total trust in their buddies.

My experience with warriors in more than eight years of roaming the killing fields in seven wars confirms what these old salts are saying.

A serving lieutenant general recently wrote to me, "Ask Pat Schroeder if she'd like her kids under a gay first sergeant who might use his rank and authority to demand sexual favors from his subordinate 18-year-old kids. We just had that occur in my command."

No doubt advocates of gays in combat units will argue that they don't approve of demanding sexual favors and that the first sergeant deserved what he got—a court-martial. The problem is, all the court-martials and regulations in the world can't prevent the kind of morale problems that a change in the law is bound to create. Sure, the first sergeant is serving hard time at Fort Leavenworth, but Pat Schroeder and the two dozen lawmakers who support her bill must also ask themselves what happened to the morale and fighting spirit of his unit.

> *"Problems gay and lesbian teens have are not a result of their sexuality, but come from the homophobia that permeates the society around them."*

School Programs Should Stress Acceptance of Homosexuality

Bruce Mirken

Bruce Mirken is a free-lance writer who has written for the *L.A. Reader* and *GENRE*, a magazine for gay men. In the following viewpoint, he writes of the anguish and social isolation faced by many gay teens, and describes school programs that have been developed to help them. Such programs, including Project 10 in Los Angeles and the Harvey Milk School in New York City, provide essential social and emotional support for gay and lesbian adolescents, Mirken maintains, and should be emulated throughout the United States.

As you read, consider the following questions:

1. Why are gay and lesbian teens at high risk for suicide, according to Mirken?
2. What problems do gay and lesbian teens face, according to the author?
3. How do programs such as Project 10 help teens, according to Mirken?

Bruce Mirken, "Gay Teens," *Genre*, August/September 1992. Reprinted with permission.

Matt Marco, who turns 19 this June, came out two and a half years ago. He almost didn't live through it. Growing up in the St. Louis suburb of Edwardsville, Illinois—"a cow town," he calls it—Marco didn't know anyone who was gay or lesbian. When he came to terms with his sexuality at 16 he had no one he could confide in. "I was not by any means out of the closet," he recalls. "I was really, really depressed."

He finally decided to tell his younger brother, Mike, with whom he had always been close. When Mike heard the news, Marco remembers, "he ran out of the room. He ran five miles into town to his best friend's house, hysterical all the way." Mike told their mother, who at first wouldn't speak to the older boy at all and then started calling psychiatrists in hopes of finding one who would "cure" him. Worst of all, he says, she pulled him out of a study-abroad program for which he had already qualified and considered an important step in his plans for college and beyond.

When relations with his mother hit bottom, Marco went to live with his father, which had the advantage of putting him in close proximity to his boyfriend, Tim. But things quickly went from bad to worse: At the end of the first week, father and son got into an argument which turned violent. "It ended up outside in the snow, with my head between his legs and he was squeezing," he recalls. "He told me to take back what I had said. He was squeezing me so hard I couldn't talk." Remembering the moment, Marco suddenly becomes quiet, choked up with emotion: "I thought I was going to die."

He apparently passed out and doesn't know exactly what happened. The next thing he remembers is being inside the house with his father gone and Tim and his grandmother taking care of him. He moved out on his own, and hasn't spoken to either of his parents in well over a year.

It was difficult, but Marco made it, working 60-hour weeks to support himself while graduating from high school two years early with a 3.6 grade point average. Now a sophomore at Southern Illinois University at Edwardsville, he is president of the school's Gay and Lesbian Association of Students, a group he founded. He serves on the National Steering Committee for the 1993 March on Washington for Lesbian, Gay and Bi Equal Rights and Liberation. "I finally started to get complete control over my life," he says with a smile. "It's been wonderful."

Peer Support

Marco credits his survival almost entirely to a gay and lesbian youth group in St. Louis called Growing American Youth. That group, he says, gave him his first sense of acceptance and belonging, not to mention his first gay friends. "I celebrate a coming-out day every year on the anniversary of my coming to the youth group," he says.

Too much of what Marco went through is typical for gay, lesbian, and bisexual teens. "The thing that they all have in common is isolation," notes Joyce Hunter, a co-founder of New York's Hetrick-Martin Institute and current President of the National Lesbian and Gay Health Foundation. "Until this young person develops a social support network, he's going to have a rough time."

Bobby Griffith never found such a support network. On August 27, 1983, just two months after his twentieth birthday, he jumped off a freeway overpass in front of an oncoming truck which killed him instantly. Growing up in a Christian fundamentalist family where he often heard talk of how homosexuals were sinful and would go to hell, Bobby believed what he heard. Earlier in the year he had written in his diary:

"Why did you do this to me, God? Am I going to hell? That's the gnawing question that's always drilling little holes in the back of my mind. Please don't send me to hell. I'm not bad, am I? I want to be good. I want to amount to something. I need your seal of approval. If I had that I would be happy. Life is so cruel and unfair."

Healthy Sexual Development

I propose that healthy sexual development for homosexually oriented persons is the evolution of sexual attitudes, feelings, and behaviors which, *overall*, enhance adaptation in the various subcultures to which they belong. At the very least, healthy sexual development demands a positive homosexual core identity and the skills to adapt to other subgroups as well. Both conditions are essential to a healthy sexuality. Assimilation within the majority culture, without positive homosexual identity, can lead to self-hatred or disastrous consequences, as in the case of the lesbian adolescent who becomes pregnant to hide her homosexual feelings. Conversely, inability to "fit" within nongay subcultures can lead to extreme vulnerability. Witness the relentless maltreatment of gay-identified boys in most American schools.

Gary Remafedi, *SIECUS Report*, May/July 1989.

"Gay and lesbian kids," says Hunter, "are at extremely high risk for suicide." A 1989 report commissioned by the federal Department of Health and Human Services—and squelched under right-wing pressure—found gay and lesbian teens two to three times more likely to kill themselves than their heterosexual peers. No one knows for sure how many respond to the rejection and isolation they feel by dropping out of school, running away from home or turning to drugs or alcohol.

Bobby Griffith's mother, Mary, reacted to her family's tragedy by setting out to make sure that other kids wouldn't have to go through what her son did. She became a strong advocate of Project 10, the Los Angeles Unified School District's pioneering counseling program for gay, lesbian and bisexual teens. At a 1988 hearing she testified: "Correct education about homosexuality would have prevented this tragedy. Bobby's hopes and dreams should not have been taken from him, but they were. We can't have Bobby back. Please don't let this happen again."

Project 10

Project 10 is the brainchild of Fairfax High science teacher Virginia Uribe, a plain-spoken, middle-aged lesbian whose direct manner seems to connect well with the kids. Now reaching 50 schools in the district, it began in November, 1984, after an incident in which a seventeen-year-old was verbally and physically harassed out of a series of schools, including Fairfax. "He had been thrown out of his home for telling his parents he was gay," Uribe remembers. "He came to L.A., lived on the streets. Wherever he went he was harassed. He was a young man who everybody said was a really nice guy and he basically got systematically harassed out of school." Uribe began meeting at lunch with self-identified gay and lesbian students and began seeing firsthand the loneliness, the sense of rejection and isolation among kids who literally had no one they could talk to. "Everything I'd read in the literature about stigmatized gay kids was coming true in front of me," Uribe recalls. The lunchtime discussions quickly grew. Now the district pays Uribe to work on Project 10 half her time—running rap groups, doing one-on-one counseling, training teachers at Fairfax as well as other schools, and working with the school district administration.

But Uribe has had to fight to keep the program alive in the face of relentless right-wing attacks. In 1989, Traditional Values Coalition Chairman, Rev. Lou Sheldon, who scorns Project 10 as a "homosexual recruitment program," set up what he called SHAPE: Stop Homosexual Advocacy in Public Education. SHAPE worked with conservative state legislators in a nearly successful effort to cut off state funding for any school district with a program like Project 10.

But for the kids, Project 10 is a lifeline, a place where they can socialize, make friends, talk about things they don't feel safe discussing anywhere else, and finally relax. Laurence Perry, 15, has had to face harassment at school. "Our school's very macho," he says, recalling one rather effeminate boy who dropped out because he couldn't take the harassment. Perry has the advantage of being big for his age, gregarious and resilient. "I play around with it," he says. "They say, 'Hey baby!' and I say, 'Hey baby!' back." But Project 10 has provided his first contact with other gay kids. Before, he muses, "I was isolated and I felt it."

Perry is out to his parents, who have handled it reasonably well, but many of the young people in Project 10 are not. Judith (not her real name), 17, is one of them. "If my mom found out she'd wig," she says. "She can't accept that I'm not like her." Judith stopped going to Project 10 meetings for a while "out of paranoia"—fear that her friends would see her and know where she was going. "Now it's after school so it's okay," she comments. The times and locations of Project 10 meetings are generally not publicized so that the kids will feel safe.

The Hetrick-Martin Institute

In New York City, the Hetrick-Martin Institute is a major source of support and services for lesbian and gay youth. Founded in 1979, after a 15-year-old boy who had been gang-raped at a city shelter was thrown out because he had supposedly invited the attack simply by being gay, Hetrick-Martin now provides a range of programs, including counseling services, HIV/AIDS education, an after-school drop-in center which provides a safe place for kids to socialize, and Project First Step, which assists homeless teenagers on the streets of the city.

Like Project 10, one of Hetrick-Martin's most vital functions is to provide a safe place where gay, lesbian and bisexual adolescents can meet other kids like themselves. Hunter, who until recently headed HMI's department of Social Work Services, remarks, "The thing that most are looking for is: 'How do I meet other people my own age? I don't know anybody that's gay.' What they lack are role models, both adult and peer."

The feeling most often expressed by the youths who find their way to a program like HMI or Project 10 is relief that the loneliness is finally over. When a panel of HMI youth spoke in July, 1990, at the Lesbian and Gay Health Conference in Washington, D.C., Clive, 19, described coming out at age 16. A school social worker had suggested he contact HMI. Clive recalled that "it was exciting to find out that there were other gay teenagers like myself. I started to go five times a week to the drop-in center. I remember keeping it a secret, telling my mother and brother that I was going to a new type of boys' club. I truthfully and honestly found my first friend at HMI." Hunter stresses that problems gay and lesbian teens have are not a result of their sexuality, but come from the homophobia that permeates the society around them. "If we provide a safe and happy environment for these kids," she declares, "they're just as noisy, just as ornery, just as loving as other kids."

Harvey Milk High School, perhaps Hetrick-Martin's most famous program, is just such a safe and happy environment, designed for gay and lesbian kids who couldn't function in traditional schools. A fully accredited high school, the institute runs under the auspices of the school board's Alternative High Schools and programs division, Harvey Milk is small, with just two teachers, two classrooms and a few dozen students. With an open-classroom policy, a *New York Times Magazine* article described the atmosphere as "often noisy and confusing"—but also, in the words of one student, "fabulous." Harvey Milk, long the only school of its type, is about to have a west coast counterpart: An as yet unnamed school to be operated by Los Angeles' Gay and Lesbian Adolescent Social Services under an arrangement similar to the one in New York.

No Other Place to Go

For most American adolescents, high school is a time of social growth, sexual awakening and intellectual blossoming. But it can be a traumatic experience for gays and lesbians, some of whom are harassed by students and teachers and drop out of mainstream schools.

The Harvey Milk School, named after the gay San Francisco supervisor who was assassinated in 1978, is a refuge for such teenagers. A survey of the student body showed that more than 58% of them had been beaten up by their peers and feared that they would never be able to complete their education.

"We're talking about kids who have been humiliated and ostracized, and for whom there is no other place to go," says Joyce Hunter, a licensed social worker with the Hetrick-Martin Institute for Lesbian and Gay Youth, which set up the school with the cooperation of New York City officials.

Michael Quintanilla, *Los Angeles Times*, December 7, 1989.

But there are some who have criticized the very concept of gay schools, saying that gay kids need to integrate into the rest of society rather than be segregated, and that such specialized programs take boards of education off the hook for meeting the needs of gay and lesbian students in all school settings. But GLASS Executive Director Teresa DeCrescenzo feels the special schools are important. "I don't believe in ghettoizing," she declares. "I believe in mainstreaming. This is intended to fill an identified educational need for kids whose educational problems stem from the inability to function in a mainstream school."

Many of the gay teenagers who end up in places like L.A., New York or San Francisco started off somewhere else. Hunter says she's seen "lots" of kids fleeing small towns and rural states—"Iowa, Tennessee . . . I've seen kids from all over the U.S." They come from places where there is literally no place for young gays and lesbians to turn, hoping to find acceptance in urban gay communities. For these kids it can be incredibly rough.

Lost in Los Angeles

Isaac Reddick III knows all about how rough it can be. Now 21, the wholesome-looking youth with an easy grin and a quirky sense of humor arrived in Los Angeles at age 19 with $80 in his pocket and nowhere to stay, having fled a small town in upstate New York where, he says, "I couldn't be gay." He'd even participated in gay-bashing with high school friends.

He remembers the day he arrived in L.A. as "the worst day of my life. I was lost and alone and in the world, for the first time on my own." With no idea of where to go or what to do, he looked up "gay" in the phone book and found the number of the Gay and Lesbian Community Services Center. Soon he was living in Citrus House, GLCSC's youth shelter, "with a lot of kids like myself—throwaways and runaways. Eight out of ten of them were street kids," youths with no home other than the streets of Hollywood, many of whom had supported themselves through prostitution.

Although his first months in Los Angeles were tumultuous, including several days of homelessness, he got a job—he now does data entry for a local courier service—and began putting his skill at cartooning to use. His comic strip, "The Lazarus Heart"—sort of a gay "Doonesbury" with a lead character strikingly similar to Reddick—is now a regular feature of the local gay newspaper *Vanguard*, and he hopes someday to make his living as a cartoonist.

Reddick also regularly volunteers on GLCSC's Youth Talkline, lending an ear and a comforting word to kids feeling the same sort of isolation that he felt a couple of years ago. That such resources exist in more and more places is surely progress, but even a large agency like Hetrick-Martin reaches what Hunter admits is "the tip of the iceberg. A lot of these kids don't have access or are afraid to call." Only when the larger problem of society's homophobia is dealt with, Hunter feels, will the needs of gay and lesbian youth really be addressed. Virginia Uribe puts it this way: "We're supposed to be teaching our kids how to live in a diverse society. The education must begin with the adults."

112

"Project 10 recruits vulnerable young teens into homosexuality."

School Programs Should Not Stress Acceptance of Homosexuality

Patricia Smith

Patricia Smith, author and teacher, currently serves as research director for the Oregon Citizens Alliance, a group opposed to minority status "special rights" based on homosexuality. In the following viewpoint, she criticizes Project 10, a program developed in Los Angeles schools for gay and lesbian youth. Smith argues that Project 10 and similar programs promote homosexuality as normal, positive, and healthy to teens. Smith objects to this viewpoint, maintaining that homosexual behaviors are unhealthy and abnormal.

As you read, consider the following questions:

1. What false assumptions is Project 10 based upon, according to Smith?
2. How are the rights of parents violated by Project 10, according to the author?
3. What does Smith advocate should be done for gay and lesbian teens?

From Patricia Smith, "Project 10: Not What It Seems," *The Family*, November 1992. The original article is documented with thirty-seven footnotes that have not been included in this reprint. Reprinted by permission.

Virginia Uribe, a science teacher at Los Angeles' Fairfax High School, noticed that a daily-abused gay male student had dropped out of school. Disturbed by this incident, she began writing a counseling program for homosexual youth, labeling it: "Project 10."

Ms. Uribe, a lesbian herself, aimed the program to help gay and lesbian students raise their self-esteem, stay in school, avoid drug abuse, and practice "responsible sex." Uribe explains: "We don't know the statistics, but it does appear that students who are dealing with issues of sexual orientation have a much higher risk of suicide. . . . Substance abuse is a real problem in the gay and lesbian community." Homosexual youth also experience greater risks of internal conflict, exposure to disease (AIDS & S.T.D. [sexually transmitted disease]), and difficulty with intimate relationships.

Reasons for Opposition

Project 10, designed to meet the unique needs of homosexual youth, seems to be launched from caring, compassionate motives. Why, then, are thousands of parents and educators nationwide voicing committed opposition to the spread of Uribe's counseling program throughout America's junior highs and high schools?

Seven reasons deserve analysis.

1. Project 10 is built upon false assumptions.

The title, "Project 10," refers to the 1948 Kinsey study which asserted that "10% of the population is born homosexual." However, the Kinsey study, which relied on voluntary subjects (many of whom lived in prison), proved to be unscientific.

Current scientific surveys place the figure at 2% to 4%. The 1 in 10 figure, though a myth, is useful for the homosexual agenda because it suggests normalcy and creates a bandwagon "me too" effect. A "10% student population" figure also helps justify tax funding $31,000/year for Project 10 in San Francisco.

Ms. Uribe's program does not take into account the fact that homosexuality is a complex psychological, physical, and spiritual phenomenon. There are a variety of scientific theories about the origins of homosexuality—childhood experiences, hormonal and genetic influences, etc. The majority of researchers on the origins of homosexuality favor the theory that psychogenetic factors predominate in the development of this orientation. It is beyond doubt that cultural factors, such as pro-homosexual authority figures and societal acceptance of the gay scene, will strongly influence youth toward homosexuality. Project 10 includes both.

The most fundamental fallacy supposes that the way to lower the high rate of alcohol/drug abuse, exposure to AIDS, suicide and dropouts among homosexual students is to reinforce the student's gay identity. This reinforcement then intensifies the student's involvement in the sub-culture pervaded with the very risks for which Project 10 supposedly seeks reduction.

Advocating Homosexuality

2. Project 10 advocates homosexuality as an "alternate lifestyle."

"Alternate" suggests no healthy-unhealthy, normal-abnormal, right-wrong value judgments—merely a choice among many choices of equal value. No society in human history, including modern America, has accepted sodomy as morally neutral.

A U.S. Department of Health and Human Services [DHHS] Task Force Report of August 1989 states: "Public and private schools need to take responsibility for providing all students at junior high and high school level with positive information about homosexuality. . . . Family life classes should present homosexuality as a natural and healthy form of sexual expression." This sugar-coated approach conceals truth. If students are to make a rational choice from available "alternatives," they need to know the negative facts about homosexual behavior— e.g., sex play with human feces and urine; exploitive sex acts in public bathrooms, porno shops and bars; the offensive sex acts which spread venereal disease and AIDS; crime and abuse.

Inappropriate Counselors

Turning sensitive, impressionable teens and preteens over to practicing gay and lesbian counselors, as is done by "Project 10," is like inviting drunken, unrecovered alcoholics to take teens to bars and teach them how to drink liquor, or like inviting practicing cocaine addicts to show teens how to use cocaine while lecturing on drug addiction.

Lou Sheldon in *New Dimensions*, January 1990.

Project 10 refers to the "stable, long-lasting relationship" of gay living but fails to tell students that promiscuity, infidelity, and anonymous sexual contacts compose the major reality of male homosexual behavior.

Sex education which sterilizes homosexuality misrepresents the truth, leading vulnerable children and teens, who do not know the facts, into a deadly and disease-ridden lifestyle.

3. Project 10 increases risk of disease by encouraging homosexual contacts and behavior.

Male homosexuals experience higher rates of disease than the general population: fourteen times more apt to experience syphilis, three times greater risk for genital warts, eight times more vulnerable to hepatitis, and 5,000 times greater chance of contracting AIDS. Of the homosexuals going to S.T.D. clinics in San Francisco, 80% test HIV positive.

So-called "safe sex" or "condomania" is a myth in homosexual circles due to a lifestyle built upon instant sexual gratification, unsanitary behaviors and impersonal contacts with many partners. Homosexuals also own a 414% greater incidence of deliberate infection of others than do heterosexuals.

When adolescents are many more times likely to contact a sexually transmitted disease from homosexual contact than from heterosexual contact, why would caring adults want to fund programs in schools that teach sodomy as "normal" or "healthy"?

4. Project 10 uses sexually explicit materials, offensive to most students and parents.

One Los Angeles school discontinued use of the Project 10 book *One Teenager in 10: Testimony of Gay and Lesbian Youth* when the public protested its graphic descriptions of unnatural sexual behavior. A pornographic chapter describes how a twelve-year-old girl is seduced by her teacher into a three-year relationship. Another chapter tells how young people were "brought out" of their oppressive heterosexuality into the "blissful" gay lifestyle.

Violating Privacy

5. Project 10 violates parent-child privacy.

On February 24, 1988, Virginia Uribe spoke to a group of 150 students during regular classtime at San Fernando High School. She explained how she practices "safe sex," told them it was okay for them to have sexual feelings for those of the same sex, and that "10% of them were probably gay." Elizabeth R., like most of the students, had no interest in homosexuality, but was forced to attend. Contrary to California law (Ed. code Sec. 51240), parents were not notified prior to Uribe's class presentation. Parents protested: "We don't feel that the school should be a forum for homosexuality. These are family issues that involve family values."

But Project 10 carries no respect for parental values. The Project 10 book *How to Come Out to Your Parents* advises students not to discuss it with their parents until they are securely settled into the lifestyle: "Parents . . . are part of a guilty society, a homophobic society." Indeed, parents could be an overwhelming obstacle to recruitment of teens into the homosexual subculture.

6. Project 10 recruits vulnerable young teens into homosexuality.

In the aggressive search for the so-called 10%, Project 10 adults impose the program on all students. Virginia Uribe sent the following memo regarding *Reach* magazine to counselors in all Los Angeles junior and senior high schools: "Please make *Reach*, a publication of Temenos, the Youth Department program at the Gay and Lesbian Community Services Center, available to your counselors and to the students. Perhaps you could ask your librarian to put some copies in the library." The magazine was recommended not just to students with sexual identity conflict, but to *all* students.

The magazine issue Uribe recommended explained how a teen girl made a lesbian contact after her teacher invited lesbians to speak in class. "After the discussion, literature was available and that's where I found various names, addresses, and phone numbers of different organizations within the community." When curious teenagers call these numbers, the phone counselor may then say things such as: "You feel this way because you've been born a homosexual or lesbian and you need to face the fact and accept it as your lifestyle." Blatant recruiting!

Project 10 material contains a series of general questions designed to lead students into phone contact with homosexual individuals and organizations. Some of the questions include: Have you ever had sexual feelings that were confusing or upsetting to you?; Are you worried about AIDS and the other sexually transmitted diseases that you keep hearing about in school and on TV?; Do you think that someone you know might be using drugs and sharing dirty needles? Obviously, most people could answer "yes" to several of these questions, regardless of gender identity. Vulnerable young teens, not yet mature enough to see through this manipulation, call the numbers, where exploitive persuasion can continue.

Educators and parents might assume that counselors using Project 10 materials are value-neutral. But Project 10 specifies that counselors are to be "gay identified," meaning "counselors should be gay." The 1989 U.S. DHHS report states: "It is important for schools to hire openly gay male and lesbian teachers to serve as role models and resource people for gay youth."

Concern over "gay-identified" counselors intensifies with the fact that over 60% of homosexuals claim their first partner was older. One quarter of gays admit to having had sex with children and underage teens. In one study, 4% of the gays reported their first homosexual experience was with a teacher. One study revealed that two-thirds of the males whose first experience was homosexual practiced homosexuality as adults.

A Larger Agenda

7. Project 10 exists as part of a larger gay agenda.

A gay magazine article summarizes the strategy for imposing this radical agenda upon American citizens: "Talk about gays as loudly and as often as possible. . . . Portray gays as victims, not as aggressive challengers. . . . Make gays look good. . . . Make the victimizers (e.g., heterosexuals) look bad. . . . Solicit funds."

The 1972 Gay Rights Platform called for: "Federal encouragement and support for sex education courses, prepared and taught by gay women and men, presenting homosexuality as a valid, healthy preference and lifestyle, as a viable alternative to heterosexuality."

The ultimate goal of the "gay liberation" movement is to achieve sexual freedom for all, which means not just "equal rights" for homosexuals, but free sexual expression for youth and children. The National Gay Task Force, a strong influence on AIDS curricula, states the priority goal of removing age of consent laws to permit "voluntary" sex with children:

Radical feminists say: "Compulsory heterosexuality is basic to women's oppression. . . . Lesbianism threatens male supremacy at its core. . . ." "The first condition for escaping from forced motherhood and sexual slavery is escape from the patriarchal institution of marriage."

In California, the ACLU [American Civil Liberties Union] opposed "Abstinence Education" legislation, saying: "It is our position that teaching monogamous, heterosexual sexual intercourse within marriage . . . is an unconstitutional establishment of a religious doctrine in public school." But, of course, the ACLU defends the teaching of homosexuality in public schools.

Opposition to Project 10

Conservative Christians and others have fought a running battle against Project 10 and its director, Virginia Uribe, for about three years. The Rev. Louis Sheldon, president of the Traditional Values Coalition in Anaheim, says referring students to gay groups and gay literature isn't balanced counseling. He wants Project 10 to tell students that choosing heterosexuality is a possible solution. . . .

Project 10 has faced other vocal critics. Talks to students around Los Angeles have been scaled back after parental complaints and heated reactions at some schools. "God created Adam and Eve," one combative student at a largely Hispanic school told Mrs. Uribe, "not Adam and Steve."

Gary Putka, *The Wall Street Journal*, June 12, 1990.

The National Education Association has joined these leftist political agendas. The 1990 annual NEA convention endorsed homosexuals teaching in the classroom even if they have AIDS, and counseling of students by homosexuals. "Managing Heterosexism and Homophobia," from the Gay and Lesbian Caucus of the NEA, calls for use of gay and lesbian speakers in classes, support for openly gay school staff members, inclusion of homosexual issues in lesson plans, information regarding local gay and lesbian resources; this document *requires* comprehensive sex education which teaches diversity of sexual orientation and encourages the inclusion of gay-sensitive literature in school libraries.

Yes, all students deserve freedom from name-calling, whether the name be "queer" or "homophobe." All students deserve the opportunity to attend school without discrimination or abuse. But it is cruelty, rather than compassion, which encourages people to take pride in behavior that is destroying them. This program of the political gay agenda deserves no time, space or funding in our nation's schools because it shows compassion neither to the troubled homosexual, nor to society at large.

a critical thinking activity

Distinguishing Between Fact and Opinion

This activity is designed to help develop the basic reading and thinking skill of distinguishing between fact and opinion. Consider the following statement: "Homosexuals are officially barred from serving in the U.S. military." This statement is a fact which can be verified by looking up Defense Department rules or by reading newspaper or magazine articles on the subject. But the statement "Changing the rules to allow homosexuals to serve in the military would destroy morale" is clearly an opinion. Experts within and outside the military disagree as to whether allowing homosexuals to openly serve in the military would have such an effect.

When investigating controversial issues it is important that one be able to distinguish between statements of fact and statements of opinion. It is also important to recognize that not all statements of fact are true. They may be based on inaccurate, false, or dated information (for instance, the factual statement that homosexuals are officially barred from the military, while true in 1992, may become false in subsequent years). For this activity, however, we are concerned with understanding the difference between those statements that appear to be factual and those that appear to be based primarily on opinion.

Most of the following statements are taken from the viewpoints in this chapter. Consider each statement carefully. *Mark O for any statement you believe is an opinion or interpretation of facts. Mark F for any statement you believe is a fact. Mark I for any statement you believe is impossible to judge.*

If you are doing this activity as a member of a class or group, compare your answers with those of other class or group members. Be able to defend your answers. You may discover that others come to different conclusions than you do. Listening to the reasons others present for their answers may give you valuable insights into distinguishing between fact and opinion.

> O = *opinion*
> F = *fact*
> I = *impossible to judge*

1. More than seven thousand hate-motivated incidents have been reported to the National Gay and Lesbian Task Force.

2. The vast majority of antigay episodes in U.S. towns and cities are never reported.

3. We have an epidemic of antigay violence in this country.

4. People do not routinely discriminate against homosexuals.

5. On radio stations across America, lesbians and gay men are the subject of ugly jokes.

6. The 1990 Federal Hate Crimes Statistics Act includes sexual orientation among the hate crimes for which data must be collected.

7. Male homosexuals experience higher rates of sexually transmitted disease than the general population.

8. The teen suicide rate is three times higher for lesbians and gays than for their heterosexual peers.

9. Many homosexuals live in well-furnished homes in nice neighborhoods.

10. The homosexual lobby speaks of itself as struggling for civil rights, but is really after special privileges for homosexuals.

11. Members of the group Queer Nation have held demonstrations in many U.S. cities featuring public kissing and embracing.

12. Gay people are immoral and thus unfit to work.

13. Discrimination against lesbians and gay men runs throughout American society.

14. The countries of Holland, Denmark, and Israel have already integrated gays into their armed forces.

15. Other countries have demonstrated that a military with gays can work.

16. Letting gays in the U.S. military would destroy combat morale and effectiveness.

17. About 10 percent of Americans are homosexual.

18. Homosexuals have all the same civil rights heterosexuals do.

19. School programs for gay teens such as Project 10 carry no respect for parental values.

20. No society in human history, including modern America, has accepted sodomy as morally neutral.

21. The Supreme Court held in 1986 that "To hold that the act of homosexual sodomy is somehow protected as a fundamental right would be to cast aside a millennia of moral teaching."

Periodical Bibliography

The following articles have been selected to supplement the diverse views presented in this chapter.

Jonathan Alter   "Degrees of Discomfort," *Newsweek*, March 12, 1990.

Martha Barron Barrett   "Double Lives: What It's Like to Be a Lesbian Today," *Glamour*, September 1989.

Michael Cunningham   "Queer/Straight," *Mother Jones*, May/June 1992.

Don Feder   "Media Distortion of the Gay Rights Debate," *New Dimensions*, November 1990.

Peter Freiberg   "Gay on the Job," *Genre*, April/May 1992. Available from Genre Publishing, 8033 Sunset Blvd. #261, Los Angeles, CA 90046.

Nancy Gibbs   "Marching Out of the Closet," *Time*, August 19, 1991.

William Norman Grigg   "Oregon's Morality Measure," *The New American*, October 19, 1992.

David Hackworth   "The Key Issue Is Trust," *Newsweek*, November 23, 1992.

Pete Hamill   "Confessions of a Heterosexual," *Esquire*, August 1990.

John Leo   "The Politics of Intimidation," *U.S. News & World Report*, April 16, 1992.

Arthur S. Leonard   "Report from the Legal Front," *The Nation*, July 2, 1990.

Donna Minkowitz   "Why Heterosexuals Need to Support Gay Rights," *Utne Reader*, March/April 1991.

E.L. Pattullo   "Straight Talk About Gays," *Commentary*, December 1992.

Charles E. Rice   "A Crime Against Nature," *The New American*, September 21, 1992.

Darrell Yates Rist   "Homosexuals and Human Rights," *The Nation*, April 9, 1990.

Eloise Salholz et al.   "The Future of Gay America," *Newsweek*,
                               March 12, 1990.

Jeffrey Schmalz   "Gay Politics Goes Mainstream," *The New
                               York Times Magazine*, October 11, 1992.

Joseph P. Shapiro   "The True State of Gay America," *U.S. News
                               & World Report*, October 19, 1992.

Thomas Short   "Gay Rights or Closet Virtues?" *National
                               Review*, September 17, 1990.

Thomas A. Stewart   "Gay in Corporate America," *Fortune*,
                               December 16, 1991.

Robert E. Sullivan Jr.   "Bashers," *The New Republic*, September 21,
                               1992.

Andrew Tobias   "Three-Dollar Bills," *Time*, March 23, 1992.

Bill Turque et al.   "Gays Under Fire," *Newsweek*, September
                               14, 1992.

Ernest van den Haag   "Sodom and Begorrah," *National Review*,
                               April 29, 1991.

Jacob Weisberg   "Gays in Arms," *The New Republic*, February
                               19, 1990.

Can Homosexuals Change Their Sexual Orientation?

Chapter Preface

In the late nineteenth and early twentieth centuries, the medical profession almost universally regarded homosexuality as an illness that required a cure. Among the methods attempted to make homosexuals heterosexual were castration, hysterectomy, lobotomy, and electroshock therapy. By the mid-twentieth century psychotherapy had become the most common method of "curing" homosexuality. Many homosexuals spent years in analysis attempting to change their sexual orientation.

In the 1950s and 1960s a growing number of psychiatrists began to question whether such efforts were misguided. What mental and emotional problems homosexuals faced, they reasoned, stemmed from coping with society's anti-gay prejudices rather than from homosexuality itself. In 1973 Ronald Gold became the first openly gay psychiatrist to address the American Psychiatric Association. "Your profession of psychiatry, dedicated to making people well," he stated in a panel discussion on gays and psychiatry, "is the cornerstone of a system of oppression that makes people sick." Later in 1973 the APA removed homosexuality from its official list of mental disorders. Other medical institutions soon followed the APA's example, and health practitioners began to focus on helping gays and lesbians accept and affirm their homosexuality rather than change it.

In spite of the APA's official change of status of homosexuality, some psychiatrists still debate whether homosexuals can learn to change their sexual orientation. As psychiatrist Joseph Nicolosi wrote in the February 1989 issue of *California Psychiatrist*, "Many members of our profession still privately express the opinion that homosexual development is not normal. The 1973 APA ruling did not resolve the issue—it simply silenced eighty years of psychoanalytic observation." Nicolosi and a few other psychotherapists maintain that homosexuality is a changeable condition and offer therapy designed to effect that change. In addition, numerous religious organizations have sprung up to aid gays who want to change their sexual orientation.

Some experts have strongly criticized these programs and treatments as doing more harm than good for gays and lesbians. Author Roger E. Biery writes that "homosexuality simply has and needs no cure."

The following chapter examines the questions of whether sexual orientation can be changed and whether such attempts are desirable.

"As a result of treatment, many men have been supported in their desired commitment to celibacy, while others have been able to progress to the goal of heterosexual marriage."

Psychotherapy Can Change Sexual Orientation

Joseph Nicolosi

Joseph Nicolosi is the director of the Thomas Aquinas Psychology Clinic in Encino, California. Much of his practice is with men seeking to change their homosexuality. In the following viewpoint, taken from Nicolosi's book *Reparative Therapy of Male Homosexuality*, Nicolosi calls such people "non-gay homosexuals," and argues that they have been unfairly neglected by the mental health profession, which instead seeks to make homosexuals accept their condition. He asserts that homosexuality is caused by a weak sense of masculinity that can be traced to childhood and family problems, and that psychotherapy can enable homosexuals to change by bolstering their sense of male identity and wholeness. Nicolosi examines the treatment of several of his clients and their progress toward changing their homosexuality.

As you read, consider the following questions:

1. What distinction does Nicolosi make between homosexuals and gays?
2. What are the author's views of masculinity, femininity, and androgyny?
3. What basic steps does Nicolosi prescribe for men wishing to change their homosexuality?

From Joseph Nicolosi, *Reparative Therapy of Male Homosexuality*, pages xv-xviii, 162-68. Northvale, NJ: Jason Aronson Inc. Copyright © 1991 by Jason Aronson Inc. Reprinted with permission of the publisher.

There are homosexual men who reject the label of "gay" along with all of the implications that label would bestow upon them. Although "homosexual" may name an undeniable aspect of their psychology, "gay" describes a life-style and values they do not claim. These men experience conflict between their values and their sexual orientation. Experiencing their personal development to be encumbered by homoerotic desires, they seek not to surrender to but to surmount their homosexual attractions.

In recent years, the psychiatric profession has reversed its opinion that homosexuality is unhealthy. This has resulted in the abandonment of these men, whom I call *non-gay homosexuals*. Although psychology claims to work from a value-free philosophy, in fact it chooses to devalue their struggles and to counsel them instead for what it invariably interprets to be self-hatred due to internalized homophobia.

A Developmental Problem

In reality, the homosexual condition is a developmental problem—and one that often results from early problems between father and son. Heterosexual development necessitates the support and cooperation of both parents as the boy disidentifies from mother and identifies with father. Failure in relationship with father may result in failure to internalize male gender-identity. A large proportion of the men seen in psychotherapy for treatment of homosexuality fit this developmental syndrome.

Failure to fully gender-identify results in an alienation not only from father, but from male peers in childhood. The twin phenomena of nonmasculine behavior in boyhood and problems with male peers are widely acknowledged in the literature as forerunners of homosexuality. This disenfranchisement from males—and from the empowerment of one's gender—leads to an eroticization of maleness. There is often an alienation from the body characterized by either excessive inhibition or exhibitionism. There is also a deficit in sense of personal power. The resultant homosexuality is understood to represent the drive to repair the original gender-identity injury.

A review of the physiological literature demonstrates that genetic and hormonal factors do not seem to play a predetermining role in homosexual development. However some predisposing factors may make some boys more vulnerable to gender-identity injury.

Problems associated with homosexuality include assertion difficulties, the sexualization of dependency and aggression, and defensive detachment from other males. Male homosexuals typically have difficulty with nonerotic male friendships.

Taking a look at gay relationships, we see there are many inherent limitations in same-sex love. Gay couplings are known for their volatility and instability. Research consistently reveals great promiscuity and a strong emphasis on sexuality in gay relationships. Without the stabilizing element of the feminine influence, male couples have a great deal of difficulty maintaining monogamy.

In spite of the gay man's stated valuing of androgyny, there is a contradictory search in the gay world for the masculine archetype, with nonmasculine men perceived to be lower in the status hierarchy. Gay relationships are also inherently troubled by the limitations of sexual sameness, making the sex act characteristically isolated and narcissistic through the necessity of "my turn-your turn" sexual techniques. There is not only an inherent anatomical unsuitability, but a psychological insufficiency that prevents a man from taking in another in the full and open way of heterosexual couples. . . .

Reparative Therapy

Reparative therapy for homosexuality is based upon object relations theory and empirical studies in gender identity. One of the first goals in therapy is to clarify the family dynamics that may have led to a man's homosexual condition. Making peace with father is one early issue. Preliminary treatment goals include growth in self-acceptance and an alleviation of excessive guilt. There is considerable discussion of gender difference, and an acknowledgment of the empowering effects of growing fully into one's gender. Growing out of the false self of the compliant "good little boy" is a goal for many clients. There are many initiatory challenges for ego-strengthening and self-assertion. In group therapy the client is challenged to develop self-assertion through effective verbalization. Male bonding is an especially important goal through the development of mutuality in nonerotic same-sex friendships. For the homosexual, defensive detachment usually creates a resistance to making friends with ordinary, "nonmysterious" males. . . .

Reparative therapy is not a "cure" in the sense of erasing all homosexual feelings. However it can do much to improve a man's way of relating to other men and to strengthen masculine identification. As a result of treatment, many men have been supported in their desired commitment to celibacy, while others have been able to progress to the goal of heterosexual marriage. . . .

Factors Affecting Prognosis

Motivation to change has repeatedly been found to be a primary predictor of success in treatment. Motivation means the client is unambivalent in rejecting a homosexual identity and is striving toward heterosexuality. Other indicators of favorable prognosis are lack of indulgence in self-pity, a positive sense of self, and the ego-strength to tolerate stress and frustration. Heterosexual fantasies and dreams are also strongly favorable. Also the stronger family relationships the client has, the better his prognosis.

Traditional values and the sense of oneself as a member of heterosexual society are also strongly supportive in providing a framework from which to reflect on the homosexual experience. Clients who enter reparative therapy are strong in the conviction that psychological development does not come from a surrendering of identity into the gay subculture. Other factors in treatment success are the ability to resist impulsive behaviors and to postpone gratification, the ability to set goals, and the capacity to reflect upon, verbalize, and learn from past experiences. Clients who believe they have power in shaping their own destinies have a far greater likelihood of overcoming their homosexuality than do those who submit to a fatalistic attitude or who see life as happening *to* them. The ability to be honest with oneself and others is significant to treatment success, as is the ability to identify what one is feeling. An appreciation for the value of gender differences also does much to support the treatment plan.

Can Homosexuals Be Changed To Heterosexuals?

| | | Years in Practice | | | | Size of Community | | |
	Total	Less than 5	5 to 15	16 to 25	More than 25	Under 200,000	200,000 to 1,000,000	Over 1,000,000
(Base)	(207)	(3)	(72)	(69)	(63)	(52)	(78)	(77)
Yes	53%	33%	46%	54%	60%	48%	53%	56%
No	22	33	22	22	21	15	19	29
Not sure	24	33	30	24	14	35	26	14
No response	1	0	1	0	5	2	2	1

A survey conducted by Opinion Research Corporation, a research organization in Princeton, New Jersey, asked practicing psychiatrists for their opinions on various aspects of sexuality. 207 of 1072 psychiatrists who received questionnaires responded.

Source: Opinion Research Corporation.

Those men who have been less sexually active have better prognoses. Considering the habit-forming nature of sexual behavior, the more homosexually active the client is, the more difficult the course of treatment. . . .

Two final qualities that are of the utmost value—second only to motivation to change—are *patience* with oneself and an *acceptance* of the ongoing nature of the struggle. . . .

Cure

Growth through reparative therapy is in one way like the gay model of coming out of the closet. That is, it is an ongoing process. Usually some homosexual desires will persist or recur during certain times in the life cycle.

Therefore, rather than "cure," we refer to the goal of "change," a meaning shift beginning with a change in identification of self. As one married ex-gay man described it: "For many years I thought I was gay. I finally realized I was not a homosexual, but really a heterosexual man with a homosexual problem."

Within that essential change in view of self are new ways of understanding the nature of homosexual behavior and its motivational basis in unmet early love needs. One client who had been in reparative therapy for about a year described his feelings as follows:

> What my homosexual feelings used to be, they aren't now. They're still around, they're still there, but they're not as upsetting. The improvement is in how they affect me emotionally, how much they shake me up, affect my self-esteem—how compulsive they are, how much I am preoccupied by them.

Another man, a former female impersonator, now married with three teenage sons, commented, "Now those homosexual fantasies are more like a gnat buzzing around my ear." Another man explained: "A problem that used to have a capital 'H' now has a small 'h.'"

While some therapies focus directly on heterosexual conversion, reparative therapy takes a wider view of the homosexual condition as it affects issues of personal power, gender identity, and self-image. Reparative therapy views change as a long-term process, and one that is in fact most probably lifelong. One 25-year-old client explained his process of change in the following letter:

> I've been in group therapy now for 13 months, and I can say this time has been the most revealing, growthful, and important period in my life.
>
> My love for my Catholic faith originally led me to seek help for my homosexuality, as I felt guilty and unhappy. However, today I continue to come to therapy because I am motivated by my own progress and the progress of the other men in the group.
>
> The therapy has helped me understand a lot about myself, my past, and the things that have contributed to my situation. For example, my father left my mother when I was 3 years old, and I grew up never having a close male figure to identify or bond with. Consequently I never felt a true sense of maleness about myself, and as I grew up, I never really felt like one of

the guys. This eventually led to an exclusive attraction to males, which I remember started around age six.

Therapy has broken down most of the fantasy world I had built up around other males. My self-esteem and sense of masculinity have improved, and this is reflected in my success at work and my newly established male friendships. I have even started dating, and now I definitely see marriage and children in my future. While my relationship.with my father is still not so good, I have made him aware of my situation and he has shown compassion.

The attraction to other men has still not gone away completely, but it has certainly diminished. Other men who used to both intimidate and attract me are much less threatening today. While I do not think that my same-sex attraction will disappear 100 percent, I do think I will reach a point where my attraction to the opposite sex prevails, and I will be able to move on with my life. All of this growth comes about, I have found, through the wholesome male friendships which I have learned how to develop through therapy, a prayer life, and the sacraments of my church.

Change Is Possible

A textbook I began using says unequivocally that psychotherapy for homosexuality "has been ineffective." This is an erroneous conclusion. Change is possible for some. Every study of conversion (from homosexual to heterosexual) reports some successes, ranging from 33 percent to 60 percent. In a curious non sequitur, however, opponents of such therapies use the modest cure rates to argue that no cure is possible.

Stanton L. Jones, *Christianity Today*, August 18, 1989.

If our use of the word *change* rather than *cure* sounds pessimistic, one should consider the use of the word *cure* as it applies to other psychiatric conditions. Indeed, except for the most elementary behavior-modification programs such as smoking-cessation and treatment of certain phobias, no psychological treatment can be conceptualized in terms of absolute cure. The alcoholic is never fully cured of his desire to drink, but successful treatment does offer him an effective way of dealing with his lifelong condition. The client with low self-esteem is never fully freed of his doubts and insecurities, but he grows in self-assurance. And are the issues of Adult Children of Alcoholics (ACAs) ever no longer their issues? So rather than "cure" of homosexuality, we should think in terms of growth, by laying the right foundation of healthy nonerotic male relationships. Then for some, celibacy will be the solution; for others, heterosexual marriage is the hoped-for goal.

The validity of any therapy—no matter what the treatment method or goal—is found in its overall effect on the life of the client. Good therapy must do more than alleviate a specific symptom. If the treatment is right for the person, then the freedom and well-being it brings will radiate throughout all aspects of the personality. Most important, the move to health will bring a growing awareness of personal power.

"The effort to change the sexual orientation of a gay man is harmful to him."

Psychotherapy Should Help Gay Men Accept Their Homosexuality

Richard A. Isay

Richard A. Isay is a psychoanalyst at Cornell University in Ithaca, New York, and chairperson of the American Psychoanalytic Association's Committee on Gay, Lesbian and Bisexual Issues. The following viewpoint is taken from his book *Being Homosexual: Gay Men and Their Development*. Isay argues that homosexuality is not something that can be "cured" by psychotherapy, and that many men have been psychologically harmed by efforts to change their sexual orientation. The overriding goal of the therapy of gay men should be to improve their total well-being, Isay writes, which should include the acceptance of their homosexuality.

As you read, consider the following questions:

1. How do efforts to change sexual orientation harm gay men, according to Isay?
2. What examples of homophobia demonstrated by psychiatrists does the author describe?
3. According to Isay, what stance should psychotherapists have toward sexual orientation?

My perspective on the therapy of gay men is based on two convictions. First, gay men can live, as homosexuals, well-adjusted and productive lives with gratifying and stable love relationships. This is an observation based on my clinical experience and on extensive personal observation.

Many readers will believe this to be a self-evident proposition. Most dynamically oriented therapists and psychoanalysts, however, contend that the same conflicts in the early lives of homosexual men that have caused their homosexuality have produced such severe personality problems that it is impossible for a gay man to establish stable relationships and live a reasonably happy life. These therapists believe that it is in the best interest of the homosexual patient to change his sexual orientation from homosexuality to heterosexuality. A homosexual man will then presumably be happier, not only because he will be in less conflict with society but because warring intrapsychic structures will have been brought into greater harmony through his understanding and resolution of his early conflicts. After successful treatment his homosexual impulses will theoretically have become successfully sublimated by a strengthened ego.

Attempts at Change Harmful

My second conviction is one established by clinical experience: the effort to change the sexual orientation of a gay man is harmful to him. The psychoanalytic literature is replete with recommendations for modifications of analytic technique that are deemed to be appropriate to the treatment of homosexual men in order to change their sexual object choice. For example, Lawrence Kolb and Adelaide Johnson state that analytic neutrality should at times be abandoned so that the homosexual patient not misconstrue neutrality as permission for him to act out homosexual behavior. They indicate that under some circumstances therapists should terminate treatment if homosexual behavior persists. Lionel Ovesey suggests that a patient should be given an ultimatum if he is making insufficient effort to perform heterosexually. "There is only one way that the homosexual can overcome this phobia and learn to have heterosexual intercourse, and that way is in bed with a woman." He and others maintain that only those therapists who are convinced that a homosexual can be changed to heterosexual should undertake the treatment of a homosexual patient. Charles Socarides suggests that the gratification of a homosexual be spoiled by interpretation of the meaning of his "perverse acts," and that he be counseled how to engage in heterosexual sex. . . .

Through certain therapies, homosexual behavior can be curtailed for varying periods of time and heterosexual behavior can be manifest for varying periods of time in some gay men motivated to attempt heterosexuality. Claims of achieving behavioral change in a highly motivated population of male and female homosexual patients have in fact varied from about 20 percent to 50 percent, with a variety of therapeutic techniques. Such techniques, however, rely on behavioral modification with positive and/or negative reinforcement or, in a supposedly "neutral" analytic therapy, on the exploitation of transference. All these treatments depend for their efficacy on making homosexuality appear less desirable than heterosexuality, or on "spoiling the gratification." Such treatment has the ultimate effect of undermining the self-esteem of the patient by making him feel that his sexual orientation is unacceptable to the therapist as long as he remains homosexual.

Alfred Kinsey and his co-workers for many years attempted to find patients who had been converted from homosexuality to heterosexuality during therapy, and were surprised that they could not find one whose sexual orientation had been changed. When they interviewed persons who claimed they had been homosexuals but were now functioning heterosexually, they found that all these men were simply suppressing homosexual behavior, that they still had an active homosexual fantasy life, and that they used homosexual fantasies to maintain potency when they attempted intercourse. One man proclaimed that, although he had once been actively homosexual, he had now "cut out all of that and don't even think of men except when I masturbate."

In a study of 106 gay men, Irving Bieber and his associates claimed that 19 percent of those who had been exclusively homosexual switched to heterosexuality as a result of psychoanalytic treatment. Wardell Pomeroy, a co-author of the Kinsey Report, has maintained a standing offer to administer the Kinsey research questionnaires to any of the patients who were reportedly cured. Bieber acknowledged to Pomeroy that he had only one case that would qualify, but he was on such bad terms with the patient that he could not call on him.

Harmful Consequences

My clinical follow-up of many gay men treated by another therapist has demonstrated to me that there may be severe emotional and social consequences in the attempt to change from homosexuality to heterosexuality. I will illustrate this conclusion with [two] patients whom I saw in long-term psychoanalytically oriented psychotherapy ten to fifteen years after the completion of a prior analysis in which such a change was attempted. In the prior treatment, sexual behavior was temporarily modified. Each patient remained homosexual in his sexual orientation, however, as evidenced by the continuing predominance of homoerotic fantasy, which remained unchanged by the treatment.

Each of these men now had the additional difficult social and personal complication of a family.

When Milton consulted me, he was forty-seven and the father of two adolescent girls. He had married in his late twenties, shortly after the completion of a five-year analysis. Before starting the analysis he had had an active homosexual life, including a relationship with a young man who, he told me, had been the only passion of his life. He had never enjoyed sex with women before his analysis and during the analysis "learned" to enjoy sex with them. Although sex with men was not specifically prohibited, the love affair was proscribed by the analyst and sex with women was prescribed. There had been no homosexual sex since the marriage. Milton sought therapeutic help from me because of persistent depression, no zest for living, low self-esteem, apathy in his work, and no sexual interest in his wife, with whom he had not had sexual relations since the birth of his last child fifteen years ago. His masturbatory and other sexual fantasies were exclusively homosexual. He longed for the love of his lost youth.

Ethics and Conversion Therapy

Psychological ethics mandate that mental health professionals subscribe to methods that support human dignity and are effective in their stated purpose. Conversion therapy qualifies as neither. It reinforces the social stigma associated with homosexuality, and there is no evidence from any of the studies to suggest that sexual orientation can be changed. Perhaps conversion therapy seemed viable when homosexuality was still thought to be an illness; at this point, it is an idea whose time has come and gone.

Douglas C. Haldeman in *Homosexuality*, 1991.

Milton was a devoted father and husband. His wife knew nothing of his past homosexual life. He had no regrets over the change in his sexual behavior, except that he felt something was missing in his life—he called it a "passion." Even though he was not actively homosexual, I considered him homosexual because he still had an active homosexual fantasy life and continued to long for the love of other men.

This man expressed a great deal of anger toward his prior analyst for "manipulating" him. He grieved at having given up the passion that he spoke of so often. During his three years of therapy with me, his depression gradually decreased as he became more tolerant of his homosexual impulses and was able to think of himself as gay. He never resumed his homosexual life, because he felt it would disrupt his marriage, and he sublimated many of his homosexual impulses into successful creative endeavors and into his love for his children and male friends.

Milton always believed that his previous analysis had been a success. He had a wife and children, from whom he gained enormous pleasure. He liked the conventionality, the relative lack of stress in his life, and his professional success. It became clear in our work, however, that the denial, repression, and unanalyzed acquiescence that had been necessary for him to achieve the renunciation of his homosexual behavior had affected his zest for life and interfered with professional accomplishment, and that his analyst's failure to analyze these transference manifestations and defenses in his first treatment was in part responsible for the depression that motivated him to seek further help.

Low Self-Esteem

The question of whether or not he would have been happier living an active homosexual life is unanswerable. But it would appear that the first analyst's "health" values made it impossible for either the patient or the analyst to explore this other option. It was clear to me from my work with this man that much of the depression that followed the termination of his previous analysis was caused by the exacerbation of his low self-esteem and poor self-image, which were reinforced by the negative way the therapist perceived and interpreted this patient's homosexuality. These symptoms were greatly alleviated in the subsequent therapy as he became more tolerant of his sexual feelings, encouraged by an accepting, neutral therapeutic stance.

Another patient, Larry, had previously been in analysis for five years, during which time he had married and then separated. According to his recollection, he had felt homosexual since early adolescence and had engaged in homosexual sex since that time. He entered treatment in his twenties because of several unhappy relationships with other men and because of depression and ambivalence about being gay. He met his wife during this analysis; she was the first woman he had ever had sex with. Although his sexual relationship was not "great," he perceived it as adequate and for a time he gave up all homosexual activity. Subsequently, however, his work seemed increasingly tedious and he became depressed, argumentative, and apathetic. He resumed having occasional surreptitious homosexual sex, and the relationship with his wife continued to deteriorate, until they eventually separated. He stopped his analysis at the time of his separation, ostensibly because he felt his analyst was unempathic and rigid. He sought consultation several years later, when he was thirty, because of continuing depression connected with his low self-esteem.

When I first saw Larry, he had no interest in women and not much interest in having sex with other men, although he readily acknowledged that he was gay. He wanted a stable relationship, which his previous analyst encouraged him to believe would be possible only in a conventional marriage. This analyst had made the same technical modifications as had Milton's: he had questioned homosexual behavior without actually prohibiting it, and encouraged dating and any heterosexual involvement. During three years of therapy with me, Larry mourned the loss of his wife and the probability that he would never have children, and he began to have an active sex life with other men and in fact entered into a relationship.

Sexual Preference Cannot Be Changed

Homosexuality is almost impossible to change. The reason we say almost is that there are people who claim they have changed from gay to straight, thanks to therapy or a religious conversion, or for no reason at all. But there is no way to know whether these people have really changed for good, are denying their homosexuality, or were never really gay in the first place.

The evidence is overwhelming that the vast majority of gay people can't change their sexual preference no matter what they do and no matter what is done to them. Over the years gays have been tortured and imprisoned, been given electroshock treatments, psychoanalysis, and hormone injections, and been prayed for. Nothing worked. They remained gay. You can make someone miserable but you can't make them straight.

Susan and Daniel Cohen, *When Someone You Know Is Gay*, 1989.

In both these cases the man's homoerotic behavior was inhibited by the previous analyst's reinforcing what he believed was the more acceptable heterosexual behavior and by his use of a probably unconscious, disapproving attitude that served negatively to reinforce the man's homosexual behavior. For instance, the previous analysts had stated that homosexual relations would probably be of short duration, reinforcing the notion that heterosexual relationships were intrinsically better and more stable. Furthermore, both analysts used whatever ambivalence their patients felt about their socially discordant sexuality and the pain caused by social rejection to reinforce the idea that homosexuality was a result of childhood conflict and to encourage their patients to change. Neither analyst appeared to recognize that his patient's willingness to acquiesce to attempting to change his sexuality was a manifestation, in the transference, of a childhood desire to please and be loved by the father. Instead, the need to be loved was used by the analysts to help these men suppress their homosexuality. . . .

Gay Positive Therapy

Positive regard and affirmation must be provided by the therapist if there is to be an atmosphere in which the patient may safely project, witness, understand, and untangle the negative self-images he has acquired from childhood experiences and relationships. A therapist who does not accept his patient as gay will reinforce earlier images that are reflected in the patient's self-deprecatory, paranoid, masochistic, or sadistic attitudes which are now interfering with his capacity for more positive relationships and experiences. . . .

It is my suggestion to gay men currently seeking psychotherapy that if they are to unravel and untangle the internalized homophobia and other aspects of childhood development that may contribute to their low self-esteem, they must have a therapist who regards them as capable of gratifying and loving relationships as homosexual men. Guiding a therapeutic endeavor with any gay man must be the therapist's conviction that his patient's homosexuality is for him normal and natural. Such an attitude, it seems to me, can be convincingly sustained only by a therapist who holds the theoretical perspective that homosexuality is a normal developmental end point for some men.

"I was once homosexual and now experience heterosexuality. Every turn of the path I walked is filled with signs of the gracious persistence of God."

Christianity Can Help Gays Change Their Sexual Orientation

Colin Cook

Many homosexuals who wish to change their sexual orientation do so because of their religious beliefs. In the following viewpoint, Colin Cook writes that Christianity can help lesbians and gays cope with and even change their sexual orientation. Colin Cook, a counseling minister, has founded and worked in ministries for gay and lesbian Christians. He writes that change from homosexuality to heterosexuality is possible with the help of God but that such changes often do not come easily or overnight. Instead, they are often part of a slow and difficult process.

As you read, consider the following questions:

1. What two reasons does Cook give for recounting his past?
2. What important turning points marked the author's struggle with homosexuality?
3. Why should Christians be hopeful about changing homosexuality, according to Cook?

From Colin Cook, "I Found Freedom," *Christianity Today*, August 18, 1989, © 1989 by Christianity Today. Reprinted with permission.

I am writing this story because I was once homosexual and now experience heterosexuality. Every turn of the path I walked is filled with signs of the gracious persistence of God.

Yet it is not easy to retrace my labyrinthine ways. To the embarrassment of my family and friends, I suffered the loss of a pastoral ministry in 1974 when my homosexuality was first exposed. Then, in 1986, because my recovery from the blinding deception and obsessiveness of homosexuality was not yet complete, I lost the homosexual healing ministry I had built over the years. I have gotten back up again, in possession of a deeper level of healing than I have ever known, and with new inner boundaries. I am back to counseling now with the sound checks and balances of supervision, church accountability, and an innovative counselor-evaluation system. So you can easily imagine that a large part of me would simply like to put the past behind me and forget it.

But I cannot, for two reasons. First, I would be selfish and disobedient to God if I kept silent for the sake of my own comfort and peace. Unless I—and others like me—confirm from personal experience that recovery and change can happen, thousands of Christians will yield to the despairing persuasion that homosexuality is an irreversible fate.

Second, I cannot recount what has happened without God's grace becoming gloriously evident. To tell my story is to say more about God than about me. God's manner of dealing with sinners is a constant astonishment. Every ounce of his being repudiates sin, yet, in order to save me, his stubborn love overcame his repugnance toward my sinfulness. My story is therefore a recounting of *his* victory—not mine—in the midst of struggle. If my story can lead many staid and "circumcised believers" to be "astonished that the gift of the Holy Spirit has been poured out even on" homosexual "Gentiles" (cf. Acts 10:45, NIV), then the glory coming to God will make the shame coming to me worth the effort of putting this painful story into ink.

First Glimmers of Freedom

I was found by Christ when I was a 15-year-old boy. I say *he* found me, because I was not even aware that I was lost or that it was him I was looking for. My boyhood fascination with flying saucers led me to what I thought was a public lecture on the subject in my home town in England. In fact, it was an evangelistic meeting on the Second Coming. From the mysterious, silent universe, whose dark skies I had gazed upon night after night and whose stillness seemed to echo the vacancy in my own soul, was to come the living, loving God. At the thought that Jesus was coming for me, I was filled with immense joy that remained in me, uninterrupted, for six months. I accepted

Jesus as my Savior, gave my life over to him, and became a member of the church.

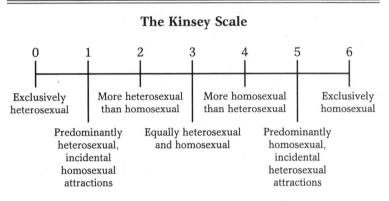

The Kinsey Scale

0	1	2	3	4	5	6

Exclusively heterosexual	More heterosexual than homosexual	More homosexual than heterosexual	Exclusively homosexual

Predominantly heterosexual, incidental homosexual attractions	Equally heterosexual and homosexual	Predominantly homosexual, incidental heterosexual attractions

In 1948 sex researcher Alfred Kinsey concluded that classifying people into two distinct categories of heterosexual and homosexual was inadequate. He devised the Kinsey Scale to measure sexual orientation in the U.S. population.

Before the first year of my conversion had come full circle, however, the conflict I felt over my sexual feelings was becoming marked. I went to the half-dozen school friends with whom I had mutually masturbated and asked them to forgive me. I was a Christian now, I told them. I remember the embarrassed shrugs and nods, and that was it. The bridges were burned. I was not to have another homosexual act for ten years.

But that was not it. Like any healthy youth, I was sexually in my prime. But every arousal, every longing, every fantasy was for men. Far from conversion solving the homosexual problem, it seemed to worsen it. For conversion created a necessary war that was to rage unabated in my soul for the next 15 years, until faith found a deeper source.

The Agony of Holiness

It was at Newbold College, nestled in the "green belt," that great circle of countryside known as the "lungs of London," that my struggle with homosexuality took a desperate turn. I had gone there to study for the ministry. My studies brought me face to face with my deep need for holiness. Bob and Will and I were spiritual brothers at different periods in my college days. We often prayed and read our Bibles together, but I never told them of the struggle deep in my troubled, aching soul.

We wanted to be holy for our God. We wanted to be like

Jesus. Will and I examined as many angles as we knew to the holy life—Andrew Murray's absolute surrender, John Wesley's "second blessing," Brother Lawrence's "practice of the presence of God." For long periods I would spend half a night in prayer every week. Each day I would spend an hour in prayer in the morning and a half-hour in the evening. I developed the habit of fasting one day a week for about a year. Yet homosexuality still seemed like an impenetrable wall. Many times I wept before the Lord for my sins. "How long," my journal records, "will it be till I am made clean?"

Never more vivid to me was the struggle with homosexuality than in the attempt to develop friendships. I could not feel inwardly relaxed with men or women. To most people, I suppose I appeared to be outgoing, spiritual, and assertive. I was voted student chaplain in my senior year. But emotionally, I was insulated. How could I reveal the terrifyingly real me?

Loneliness and Loathing

It was the days of ministry, ten years after my conversion, that were to see the collapse of my moral world. The motivation for wanting to be free from homosexuality was gradually, subtly shifting to a basic longing for love, a home, a family. Yet the stronger the longing, the more it appeared unreachable. I was stunned by the loneliness of the ministry as a single man, struggling to be a friend even to myself. In a new city, without the comfort of college friends and the reassuring order of dormitory life, I closed down to everything I knew to be right and good and went out one night into the darkness and, in a momentary attempt at comfort, gave my body to a stranger.

I loathed what I had done. I came back to my apartment almost nauseated. In enormous distress I poured out my soul to God in repentance. The only hope I could find in the rubble of my wickedness was that perhaps the shock of my sin might keep me from it forever.

But the repugnance faded in the memory of its brief pleasure. I sought more. Now I was to know guilt and the constant fear of exposure in a deeper way than ever before. I guarded my terrible secret during four years of ministry in England and another three in New York City, where nearly all restraints were lost. What a moral schizophrenia! Loving and serving God, then proceeding to defy all he stands for as I cruised gay streets, furtively exited X-rated movie houses, or took to the illusory cocoon of the gay bathhouse, only to return to my apartment, pounding with anxiety or overcome with depression.

The crisis of identity, of my "place" in the world and in God's kingdom, was becoming gargantuan. Who was I? A lecherous wolf in sheep's clothing, fleecing the flock, "beguiling unstable souls?" Or a child of God, with a besetting sin, trapped in the struggle described by Paul in Romans 7, hating what I did?

A Switch Is Flipped

I had left England in 1971 to complete an M.A. degree at Andrews University in Michigan, after which I was to return to ministry in New York City. New to the campus, I felt uncertain and lonely and far removed from the familiar climes of England. I soon heard about a class that had seminarians buzzing: Prof. Hans LaRondelle's systematic theology course on righteousness by faith. LaRondelle, who had received his doctorate under the Reformed theologian G.C. Berkouwer in Holland, is a short, stocky man with a thick, Dutch accent and a subdued, mischievous joy.

The Christian Response

Q. What is the responsibility of the person who wants to be a Christian but struggles with a deeply ingrained attraction to members of his or her own sex?

A. If I interpret Scripture properly, that person is obligated to subject his sexual desires to the same measure of self-control the heterosexual single adults must exercise. In other words, he must refrain from the expression of his lusts. . . .

Second, I would recommend that the homosexual enter into a therapeutic relationship with a Christian psychologist or psychiatrist who is equally committed to Christian virtues. This condition can be treated successfully when the individual wants to be helped and when a knowledgeable professional is dedicated to the same goal.

James C. Dobson, *Focus on the Family*, March 1991.

The classroom was packed. Expectations were high. LaRondelle's lectures were proclamations, fit for any hour of devotion with God. From the first moment, I knew I was listening to something enormously significant to me.

There can be no renovation of man's sinful nature. . . . Christ is the Substitute for the human race, the Propitiation. . . . In Christ we are treated as righteous. . . . We expand with joy because Christ, our Peace, makes us certain of glorification. . . .

Condemned in the first Adam, we are justified in the Second Adam. . . . We therefore give our bodies to his obedient service, treating them as if they were resurrected in his resurrection. . . . We struggle and thrash against sin . . . but we are freed from its power by the justifying atonement of Jesus. . . . Christ has triumphed over the evil powers by the Cross. . . . We now live in the Spirit who puts to death our carnality.

As I walked back from class each day and sat at my desk in my little bachelor bedroom no bigger than a one-man prison cell, my mind began to expand far beyond the poky confines of my quarters. Thoughts sped through my brain at enormous velocity. Segments of truth heretofore disconnected, in a flash made linkages that formed a unified whole. A switch seemed to flip on in my mind from a negative to a positive mindset. Never since my conversion had I so greatly sensed the magnificence of Jesus. Little did I realize then that I was at the beginnings of a personality reconstruction.

Christ, I could now see, had broken the powers of homosexuality at the Cross. My Jesus had been too small. It was not merely a matter of my keeping Christ in my heart. I was by the throne in him. In Jesus I was identified as whole, a heterosexual man. I had been judging myself by how I felt, not by who I was in him. God created all humankind heterosexual in Adam. Homosexuality is an illusory, false state, primarily due to the Fall and the brokenness of human relationships that ensue. It is accounted dead with Christ. My sexual lust was being stimulated by fear of abandonment and condemnation (Rom. 7:5). I had been reinforcing homosexuality for years by neurotic, whining, faithless prayer that pleads for a deliverance that is already provided.

In that little room, reality that would take years to unfold through experience was telescoped into weeks of time. The prison door was open. No matter how long it took, I knew now that I could ultimately walk free.

What God showed me about the gospel of Jesus at seminary, he was to weave into my life in astonishing ways over the next 17 years. The battle was now joined, but now I saw it as a faith war, rather than a sin war. Homosexual behavior gradually decreased in frequency and intensity as the reality of grace filled my mind and began to remake and remold my identity. The Lord began to awaken heterosexual desires in me, and in 1978 he led me to Sharon, who became my wife. If God had not given me first the assurance of being reckoned with Christ, I believe my spirit would have been knocked out by the events and trials about to happen that instead became instruments of healing.

A Hurricane Passes By

Both the loss of my pastoral ministry three years after seminary and the loss in 1986 of Quest Learning Center, the homosexual healing ministry I founded, came about because of homosexual behavior. In the last instance, the behavior involved some of my counselees.

Though I had discovered the experience of heterosexual love, I was still blinded to its greater component, that of loyalty to my bride. I had rationalized certain behaviors for years, like an alcoholic trying to swap beer for the hard stuff. Some behavior, I told myself, like prolonged holding and hugging and massages without clothes was not sexual because it was not genital, *even though it was arousing*. I told myself it helped me and others to desensitize sexual feelings or fulfill child-parent needs long neglected. I look back in amazement today, that I actually believed this and fooled myself into denying that an erotic, nongenital massage was disloyal to my wife.

Exposure burst my secrecy wide open and showed me my dishonesty. God shook me awake through Christian friends and brought me to face him, myself, and others. I came to see that while there is a legitimate desensitizing and reparenting in the healing of homosexuality, mine was mixed with seduction. I was shocked at the level of denial. I was shocked at the hurt I had brought upon trusting friends and vulnerable counselees. I was almost overwhelmed by the pain this meant to my wife.

A Long-Term Process

Thousands of men and women have come out of homosexuality. However, for most of them, healing has been a long-term process.

Most former homosexuals report that victory is a process of day-to-day discipleship. Temptations may sometimes occur, similar to a Christian previously addicted to alcohol or gambling.

One former homosexual, now married, remembers his early struggles. "Even two years into my Christian walk, I fell back into homosexual activity. I'd secretly been holding onto homosexual desires and had isolated myself from other Christians."

Afterward, he repented of his actions, confessed to a Christian friend and kept pushing forward. In the 11 years since, he's learned more about the grace and mercy of God and has not fallen back into homosexual behavior.

Bob Davies, *Focus on the Family*, March 1991.

Nevertheless, the pain of these trials led us to Christ and to the healing of our marriage. It was Mother Teresa, I believe, who said, "You will never know that Jesus is all you need until Jesus is all you've got." My reputation, mind games, and lewd distractions, were seen for the pathetic little heap they were when Jehovah the Hurricane passed by.

As my faith grabbed the truth I had learned and imposed it

upon all my homosexual feeling, I came to experience viscerally that the "I" that is crucified with Christ and now lives by faith in the Son of God is not the "I" of homosexuality. Personhood and homosexuality are not the same. They are like two circles, the one (homosexuality) superimposed on the other (personhood) so that they are confused as one.

Slowly those two circles pulled apart, the homosexual circle diminishing in size over the years, its steely bonds gradually disintegrating into powder, drifting away before the gentle, invincible wind of God's Spirit.

A Power Finally Broken

The Lord taught me never to ask for homosexual healing again, but to begin to praise him that Jesus had broken the power of homosexuality at the Cross. Often he would encourage me not to turn my eyes away from an attractive man (my principal way of counterfeiting Christ's victory), but to reframe the significance of what I saw before me through affirming what I am in Jesus and who this man is I see before me in the great love of God. I had to learn to experience something of being a man among men before I could be a man among women. Before and throughout my marriage, God has brought several heterosexual men into my life who have loved me and shown me affection with not a whiff of homosexuality.

Gradually this focused faith in all that Christ can do led to the breakup of all the guilt, shame, and fear that had stimulated so much sexual sin. My sexual compulsions—and a crippling homosexual romanticism—finally disappeared as I learned to see my worth in Jesus. The fantasies shifted first from being a compulsion, to becoming a pleasant diversion, to becoming, finally, something I did not want, because the false need for them had gone, and I could say good-bye to them.

Sometimes the fight of faith seemed near to tearing me apart as the only "self" I had ever known was pushed aside and my true self was allowed to emerge. But a bruised reed Jesus will not break. I have come to know that God can do what he promises.

Despite my stumbling, God did not let go of me. By his grace and the love and courage of my wife, I now stand free: blissfully, gratefully free.

"Accepting my homosexuality within the context of my Christian faith led me to a reconciliation with God, with myself, with my family and friends, and with my church."

Gay Christians Should Accept Their Homosexuality

Chris Glaser

Chris Glaser, a pastor and author, served on the Presbyterian Task Force to Study Homosexuality and was director of the Lazarus Project, a ministry of reconciliation between the church and the lesbian and gay community. His books include *Uncommon Calling: A Gay Man's Struggle to Serve the Church*, and *Come Home!*, from which this viewpoint is excerpted. Glaser criticizes Christian ministries and groups which purport to cure or change homosexuality, arguing that these programs actually cause homosexual desires to simply be suppressed or redirected in unhealthy ways. A true Christian healing, Glaser asserts, involves the acceptance of homosexuality, whether in oneself or in other Christians.

As you read, consider the following questions:

1. How are homosexuals "healed" by many Christian groups, according to Glaser?
2. What alternatives to changing one's homosexuality does the author present?
3. How are gay Christians affecting the church, according to Glaser?

Planners of a churchwide educational event in Texas invited me to co-lead a workshop on homosexuality and the church. The other workshop leader was to be a person who had begun a "healing ministry" for homosexual persons. He was bringing a "healed" homosexual man to participate in the workshop, so I taped an interview with a black church member who had experienced another so-called healing ministry, and I used portions of the tape in the class. The workshop participants heard of the sexual exploitation and spiritual domination this individual endured at the hands of such ministry. It was only when he began worshiping with our congregation and attending the Lazarus Project Bible study group that he enjoyed true healing.

Truly Healed?

But those attending the workshop could have learned the bogus nature of ministries which claim to change homosexuals by listening carefully to the prime example of the healing ministry showcased by my co-leader. The supposedly "healed" homosexual revealed that the ministry's counseling worked by having the clients develop a deep emotional attachment to their same-gender counselors. This satisfied their need for such a relationship while denying them an opportunity for sexual expression. In response to a question, the healed homosexual surprised many when he confessed that he still had homosexual fantasies. He described as an example passing a jogger in his car and mentally undressing him. Then he gave a detailed description of what he would enjoy doing with the runner's genitals, a description I would blush to record here! I thought to myself, "Here I am the professing gay person, and though I may admire a male jogger, I don't get into such an elaborate fantasy!"

His fantasy life was apparently compensating for his loss of real-life experience. Jesus condemned those who judge sins of the body when the judges themselves indulged in sins of the mind: "every one who looks at a woman lustfully has already committed adultery with her in his heart" (Matt. 5:28). And to think that the relationship that the healed homosexual had with his counselor was intended to serve as a substitute for a truly loving relationship—such "counseling" violates good ethics and good sense! It would make the client dependent on the therapist, when good psychotherapy seeks to help the client realize his or her independence.

In the workshop, I presented another alternative. I reclaimed the words "healed" and "healing" by offering myself as an example of a healed homosexual leading a ministry that was healing to other homosexual persons as well as healing for the church. In my own healing process, accepting my homosexuality within the context of my Christian faith led me to a reconciliation with

God, with myself, with my family and friends, and with my church. The Spirit enabled me to integrate my spirituality and my sexuality, to give thanks to God for both, and to praise God for God's wonderful deeds in liberating me from my own homophobia and the homophobia of others. My worship became more holistic, my gratitude more authentic, and my ministry an outgrowth of what God had done for me. I then sought to reconcile externally what the Holy Spirit had reconciled internally: homosexuality and Christianity.

The Healing of Jesus

When Jesus healed, he removed obstacles that prevented the worship of God. The cleansed lepers could return to their worshiping community by showing the priests that they were no longer infectious outcasts. The woman healed of a hemorrhage by touching his garment would no longer be considered "unclean" by the strict religious code. The demoniac could worship Jesus when the demons which crazed him were sent into a herd of pigs. The hungry multitudes could better listen to Jesus' words after he healed their hunger by feeding them.

Jesus healed more than met the eye. When he healed the beloved servant of a Roman centurion, Jesus acknowledged the faith of a Gentile, and someone who represented the oppressor. "Not even in all of Israel," Jesus exclaimed, "have I found such faith." When he allowed the woman of ill-repute to wash his feet, over the objection of the Pharisee with whom he was dining, he welcomed her into intimate communion with himself and healed her of her estrangement from the community of faith. Healing was not the arbitrary restoration of a person's abilities or health, it was the removal of that which interfered with an individual's worship of God. In these latter two stories, the healing overcame questions of condition and morality, and welcomed the Roman and the woman into spiritual community and communion.

Lesbian and gay Christians have experienced this kind of healing within our own lives. Our affirmation of this healing is often perceived as an affront to the church, I believe, because of its own failure to adequately reconcile sexuality and spirituality. Regardless of their viewpoint on whether or not homosexual persons are "broken" and in need of "healing," many Christians hold the view that homosexuality is an issue wounding the church, causing brokenness. What they fail to see is that homophobia and heterosexism are what is truly wounding the church, and that the church, in turn, is wounding its gay family members and neighbors and encouraging society at large to do so.

A recent General Assembly of the Presbyterian Church, meeting in St. Louis, approved guidelines for its own exhibit hall, an area set aside for church agencies and organizations to display their programs and ministries. In a list of things which would not be tolerated in exhibits, a list which included things like racism and sexism, this national governing body voted not to include homophobia, though previous assemblies have declared it to be a sin. Just after the vote, a gay seminarian sat down near me. Hurt by the assembly's action, he said, "I just can't believe they wouldn't include homophobia in that list. I guess it's okay to hurl abuse at gay people.."

That very night, as I walked a gay Pentecostal to his car after a two-hour counseling and prayer session, a car of drunken young men careened toward us, hurling abusive language attached to the word *faggots*. Our goodbye hug must have seemed suspicious to them. On their third pass, they drove as if they intended to run us down. My friend, nervously trying to catch his breath, urged me to get into his car. He drove me the short block back to my hotel.

Therapy Ineffective

Recently, founders of yet another prominent "ex-gay" ministry, Exodus International, denounced their conversion therapy procedures as ineffective. Michael Busse and Gary Cooper, cofounders of Exodus and lovers for 13 years, were involved with the organization from 1976 to 1979. The program was described by these men as "ineffective . . . not one person was healed." They stated that the program often exacerbated already prominent feelings of guilt and personal failure among the counselees; many were driven to suicidal thoughts as a result of the failed "reparative therapy."

Douglas C. Haldeman in *Homosexuality*, 1991.

Ironically, one of the arguments that our opponents use is that church opinions should not be "dictated" by society, as if our society embraces gays and lesbians! That night, in the General Assembly vote and in these abusive men, I personally witnessed how the church and society become conspirators in their dysfunctional relationship with homosexual persons.

The incident with the gay-bashers reminded me of a similar experience one Sunday as members of my congregation enjoyed coffee hour after worship. Another group of young men drove past those of us standing outside the sanctuary and, instead of hurling the usual anti-gay epithets, simply shouted one word: "AIDS!"

The same evening that the General Assembly refused to in-

151

clude homophobia in its guidelines, it debated a fairly enlightened policy statement on AIDS. But the assembly removed an affirmation that AIDS should not be viewed "as punishment for behavior deemed immoral." In effect, they declined to take issue with the judgment that AIDS is God's judgment on homosexuality. From a gay perspective, it was difficult for me to discern a difference between the church's position and that of those who drove past our church shouting, "AIDS!"

Gay Christians

Gay Christians are seeking to bring healing to the church, to restore its "peace, unity, and purity" by restoring gays and lesbians to the church and by restoring the church to gays and lesbians. The healing of our sexuality and spirituality may lead to the healing of the sexuality and spirituality of our heterosexual counterparts in the church. Our healing presence may lead the church to a more inclusive prayer life, a more inclusive ministry, and a more inclusive community. We are evangelicals in the radical sense of the term. We are bearers of good news.

I believe lesbian and gay Christians are living reminders of the healing that Jesus offered persons of faith. The goal of this healing is integrity rather than uniformity. "Your faith has made you whole," Jesus told the woman healed of the hemorrhage, not "Your faith has made you like everybody else." The healings effected, the demons cast out, enabled those who benefited to return to their homes, neighborhoods, and synagogues. Families, communities, and congregations were made more whole by the reintegration of those who had been exiled. Both individuals and groups enjoyed greater integrity, greater wholeness.

I define integrity as an integration within the self of what one believes, thinks, says, is, feels, and does, accompanied by an integration of that self with community, creation, and Creator. Created in God's image, human beings reflect God's ability at integration, though not God's capacity. Lacking trust in God, we reach for God's capacity in the prideful belief that we may do so and play God's role. This is illustrated by Adam and Eve's eating the forbidden fruit of the tree of the knowledge of good and evil to "become like gods." Another biblical example is the building of the tower of Babel, a human attempt to reach into the heavens. In trespassing on God's turf, we "dis-integrate" ourselves from harmony with God, with creation, and with our community. Biblically, such harmony is represented in the past by Eden, and in the future by the kingdom, or commonwealth, of God.

The Law of Moses became a means of reintegration, harmonizing the self with the community, and the community with God. The Law was the people's side of the Covenant between God and the people of Israel, indicating the mutuality of the brokenness. When the Law became perceived as a new Tower of Babel, that is, a human attempt to reach into God's heaven, Jesus Christ was called to reintegrate us with God and the cosmos. The Church was charged with this ministry of reconciliation: to reintegrate the self, and the self with God, creation, and community, by putting us within the healing touch of Jesus Christ.

I define brokenness as denying our interior wholeness and denying our integrity with the Creator, creation, and community. The story of creation tells us that we are made in the image of God. Jesus' healing touch proclaims "the kingdom of heaven is within you" and "your faith has made you whole." The Fall was not a fall from perfection, but a fall from integrity—a "dis-integration." Adam and Eve did not trust their integrity with God, with one another, with all of creation. They believed that the knowledge of good and evil would lead to their perfection, to their becoming "as the gods."

Homosexuality Part of God's Creation

Some argue that since homosexual behavior is "unnatural," it is contrary to the order of creation. Behind this pronouncement are stereotypic definitions of masculinity and femininity that reflect the rigid gender categories of patriarchal society. There is nothing unnatural about any shared love, even between two of the same gender, if that experience calls both partners into a fuller state of being. Contemporary research is uncovering new facts that are producing a rising conviction that homosexuality, far from being a sickness, sin, perversion or unnatural act, is a healthy, natural, and affirming form of human sexuality for some people. Findings indicate that homosexuality is a given fact in the nature of a significant portion of people, and that it is unchangeable.

Our prejudice rejects people or things outside our understanding. But the God of creation speaks and declares, "I have looked out on *everything* I have made and 'behold it (is) very good.'" (Gen. 1:31) The word of God in Christ says that we are loved, valued, redeemed, and counted as precious no matter how we might be valued by a prejudiced world.

John S. Spong in *Is Homosexuality a Sin?*, 1992.

People of faith throughout the centuries have supposed that knowing and doing good would lead to their perfection, to their becoming godly. The perfectionist ideal unprovidentially led to debilitating anxiety ("If I can't become a saint like Mother Teresa, I won't pray regularly!") or undue pride ("I'm on the road to perfection while these slobs are whiling away their lives!"). In present-time America, I believe this has led to the opposite experiences of low self-esteem and the unquestioned self. I believe that most Americans suffer from low self-esteem, unable to affirm their integrity as people made in the image of God. Christian admonitions against pride are rendered meaningless and even destructive in the face of this sense of worthlessness. Those who need to hear it the most cannot: the unquestioned selves, those who are too sure of themselves, their answers, and their god.

I define healing as affirming our wholeness and affirming our integrity. Healing implies "returning to its original state." Our original state is wholeness and integrity, having been made in God's image. *Therapy*, derived from the New Testament Greek term for healing, is the process of returning to our original state of wholeness. Healing means change, and change may be painful or discomforting. But healing is engineered into the process of life: a cut hand heals, certain blood cells fight foreign bodies to prevent infection. So, our brokenness may be healed, whether of flesh from flesh or flesh from spirit. God's Spirit leads us to affirm our wholeness and integrity, heals disintegration, even (as our faith affirms) the ultimate disintegration of death.

Unity and Uniformity

Many Christians mistakenly believe that the healing of our integrity leads to uniformity. I believe that the healing of our integrity leads to unity. Unity respects the integrity of an individual or group, while harmonizing such within a broader scheme. Uniformity disregards the integrity of the individual or group in favor of normality as defined by selective biblical criteria or majority practice. Unity enables broader levels of harmonizing, so that, for example, religion and science are not viewed as opposing forces, but complementary endeavors. Uniformity disables such harmonizing, setting religion against science. Christians who view uniformity as the goal of healing want sexual minorities to conform to heterosexual lifestyles. These Christians cannot accept the findings of science regarding homosexuality and bisexuality, because science is also perceived as the opposition. Christians who view unity as the goal of healing may be more tolerant of sexual diversity, believing that unity may lead to shared experience and insights. These Christians more readily accept scientific information related to sexuality.

The liability of Christians seeking uniformity is that they are readily seduced into believing that sexual orientation may be changed, or that directing homosexually oriented persons into celibacy or heterosexual expression will not carry severe psychological, emotional, and spiritual penalties. The liability of Christians seeking unity is that they are readily seduced into seeking unity at all costs, even if it means ignoring or suppressing diversity within the church.

These two kinds of Christians—those seeking uniformity and those seeking unity—are not always separate groups: the boundaries between them are sometimes quite fluid. A Christian may seek uniformity on one issue, while seeking unity on another. Gay and lesbian Christians, in the process of integrating our sexuality and spirituality, most likely find ourselves seeking unity, but that does not necessarily mean that we do not experience or express uniformity of belief and practice.

I believe that Jesus Christ himself opted for unity over uniformity. Class, condition, morality, or theology did not determine to whom he brought the gospel, or whom he chose to heal, or whom he called to serve. He looked for a person's faith in God as healer when he restored people to their integrity, to their community, to their God. In his final prayer for his disciples and all "those who believe in me through their word," Jesus did not pray for uniformity of belief, but for unity, "that they may be one even as we are one, I in them and thou in me, that they may become perfectly one, so that the world may know that thou has sent me and hast loved them even as thou hast loved me" (John 17:22-23).

The Goal of Integrity

The goal of becoming "perfectly one," as either church or individual, is not perfection, but integrity. Our healing as a church or as a community is found in our unity more than our uniformity. Our healing as individuals is found in our faith in Jesus Christ, not the Babel tower of a heterosexual law.

Evaluating Sources of Information

When historians study and interpret past events, they use two kinds of sources: primary and secondary. Primary sources are eyewitness accounts. For example, a magazine article written by a gay man describing his experiences with psychoanalysis would be a primary source. A book giving a general history of the psychiatric profession's views toward homosexuality would be a secondary source. Primary and secondary sources may be decades or even hundreds of years old, and often historians find that the sources offer conflicting and contradictory information. To fully evaluate documents and assess their accuracy, historians analyze the credibility of the documents' authors and, in the case of secondary sources, analyze the credibility of the information the authors used.

Historians are not the only people who encounter conflicting information, however. Anyone who reads a daily newspaper, watches television, or just talks to different people will encounter many different views. Writers and speakers use sources of information to support their own statements. Thus, critical thinkers, just like historians, must question the writer's or speaker's sources of information as well as the writer or speaker.

While there are many criteria that can be applied to assess the accuracy of a primary or secondary source, for this activity you will be asked to apply three. For each source listed on the following page, ask yourself the following questions: First, did the person actually see or participate in the event he or she is reporting? This will help you determine the credibility of the information—an eyewitness to an event is an extremely valuable source. Second, does the person have a vested interest in the report? Assessing the person's social status, professional affiliations, nationality, and religious or political beliefs will be helpful in considering this question. By evaluating this you will be able to determine how objective the person's report may be. Third, how qualified is the author to be making the statements he or she is making? Consider what the person's profession is and how he or she might know about the event. Someone who has spent years being involved with or studying the issue may be able to offer more information than someone who simply is offering an uneducated opinion; for example, a politician or layperson.

Keeping the above criteria in mind, imagine you are are writing a paper on whether homosexuality can be changed. You decide to cite an equal number of primary and secondary sources. Listed below are several sources that may be useful for your research. *Place a P next to those descriptions you believe are primary sources. Place an S next to those descriptions you believe are secondary sources.* Next, based on the above criteria, *rank the primary sources, assigning the number (1) to what appears to be the most valuable, (2) to the source likely to be the second-most valuable, and so on, until all the primary sources are ranked. Then rank the secondary sources, again using the above criteria.*

		Rank in Importance
P or S		
_____	1. A television report on psychiatrists who work to change the sexual orientation of unhappy gay patients.	_____
_____	2. A pamphlet by the Metropolitan Community Church titled *Not a Sin, Not a Sickness*.	_____
_____	3. Historian Martin Duberman's book *Cures: A Gay Man's Odyssey*, in which he describes his own years in psychotherapy before accepting his homosexuality.	_____
_____	4. Historian Martin Duberman's book *Hidden from History: Reclaiming the Gay and Lesbian Past*, a historical study of gay and lesbian people.	_____
_____	5. A 1962 book titled *Homosexuality: Disease or Way of Life?* in which case histories of homosexual psychiatric patients are described.	_____
_____	6. A journal by a woman who left a lesbian relationship to become married and have children.	_____
_____	7. A research survey of psychiatrists asking how they treated homosexuals and whether they attempted to change their clients' sexual orientation.	_____
_____	8. A position statement by the American Psychiatric Association saying homosexuality is not an illness.	_____
_____	9. An article in the *Advocate*, a gay-oriented magazine, about religious programs for changing homosexuality.	_____
_____	10. An interview in a Christian magazine with a founder of an ex-gay ministry.	_____

Periodical Bibliography

The following articles have been selected to supplement the diverse views presented in this chapter.

Tom Bethell	"Exodus," *The American Spectator*, October 1991.
Elizabeth Carl	"Gays and the Churches: Wading Back?" *Christianity and Crisis*, November 18, 1991. Available from PO Box 6415, Syracuse, NY 13217.
Bob Davies	"What Homosexuals Need Most," *Focus on the Family*, March 1991. Available from PO Box 35500, Colorado Springs, CO 80935-3550.
Randy Frame	"The Evangelical Closet," *Christianity Today*, November 5, 1990.
William Main	"Gay but Unhappy: A New Approach May Offer Hope for Homosexuals," *Crisis*, March 1990. Available from the Brownson Institute, Inc., PO Box 1006, Notre Dame, IN 46556.
Laura M. Markowitz	"Homosexuality: Are We Still in the Dark?" *The Family Therapy Networker*, January/February 1991. Available from 7705 13th St. NW, Washington, DC 20012.
Douglas Martin	"They Are Gay, and Beseeching God to Make Them Not So," *The New York Times*, July 12, 1990.
Roy Masters	"Sex and Power: Inside the Secret World of Homosexuality and Trauma Conditioning," *New Dimensions*, January 1990.
Robert Pela	"The Ex-Ex-Gay," *The Advocate*, June 30, 1992. Available from Liberation Publications, Inc., 6922 Hollywood Blvd., Tenth Fl., Los Angeles, CA 90028.
Scott Schrader	"Get Thee Behind Me, Homosexuality," *The Advocate*, January 17, 1989.
Tim Stafford	"Coming Out," *Christianity Today*, August 18, 1989.

Should Society Legally Sanction Gay Relationships?

Chapter Preface

Should the definition of *family* include gay and lesbian partnerships? Many segments of society hotly argue this question. Currently, gay and lesbian couples cannot legally marry. They are thus denied many of the benefits society grants married couples. These advantages include health insurance provided for spouses by employers, inheritance and community property rights, hospital visitation rights, and other privileges. Gays have demanded and in a few cases received some of these privileges. For instance, some employers include partners of gays in health insurance plans. However, many gay activists assert that despite these small gains, society still refuses to accept gay and lesbian relationships. Brooklyn Law School professor Nan D. Hunter writes:

> The fundamental inequity is that . . . virtually any straight couple has the option to marry and thus establish a next-of-kin relationship that the state will enforce. No lesbian or gay couple can. Under the law, two women or two men are forever strangers, regardless of the relationship.

Some people believe that society *should* discriminate in favor of heterosexuality when it comes to granting marriage licenses. One reason, these people say, is that gay marriage is especially harmful to children. Bradley P. Hayton, a family counselor and former research analyst with the conservative Family Research Council, writes:

> Homosexuals cannot meet the psychological, emotional, spiritual, social, and educational needs of children. Homosexuals have very unstable relationships. . . . The average couple only stays together nine to sixty months. . . . These unstable relationships are not conducive to the stable social and emotional development of children. By nature homosexuality is physically and emotionally abnormal, and thus trains children in behaviors and virtues that are destructive to the social fabric.

Hayton and others believe the trend toward acceptance of openly gay couples is destructive of the traditional family.

While some studies have suggested that children are not unduly harmed by being raised by gay parents, many Americans share Hayton's misgivings. An August 27, 1992, *Newsweek* poll revealed that while a majority of Americans were willing to support such rights as health insurance and inheritance rights for gay partners, 58 percent were against legally sanctioned gay marriages, and 61 percent were against adoption rights for homosexuals. The viewpoints in this chapter evaluate whether gay relationships enrich or weaken family values in the United States.

VIEWPOINT

"Depriving millions of gay American adults the marriages of their choice . . . denies equal protection of the law."

Society Should Sanction Gay Partnerships

Thomas B. Stoddard and Patricia Horn

The following two-part viewpoint argues for greater societal recognition of homosexuals who live in long-term, monogamous relationships. In Part I, Thomas B. Stoddard describes the plight of Karen Thompson, who was denied contact with her lesbian lover, Sharon Kowalski, following Kowalski's disabling auto accident (Thompson was eventually granted custody of Kowalski in 1991) and concludes that marriage should be a basic civil right for homosexuals. Stoddard, a lawyer, is a former executive director of the Lambda Legal Defense and Education Fund, a gay rights organization. In Part II, Patricia Horn, a staff editor of *Dollars & Sense* magazine, describes the concept of domestic partnerships. Gay couples, she writes, can in some municipalities and corporations register their commitment to each other and be eligible for spousal benefits. She argues that such arrangements, in lieu of marriage, can greatly help homosexuals.

As you read, consider the following questions:

1. How has the lack of legal same-sex marriage harmed homosexuals, according to the authors?
2. How does Stoddard reply to the argument that homosexual marriages would be anti-family?

Thomas B. Stoddard, "Gay Marriages: Make Them Legal," *The New York Times*, March 4, 1989. Copyright © 1989 by The New York Times Company. Reprinted by permission. Patricia Horn, "To Love and to Cherish," *Dollars & Sense*, June 1990. Reprinted with permission. *Dollars & Sense* is a progressive economics magazine published ten times a year. First-year subscriptions cost $16.95 and may be ordered by writing *Dollars & Sense*, One Summer St., Somerville, MA 02143 or calling 617-628-2025.

I

"In sickness and in health, 'til death do us part." With those familiar words, millions of people each year are married, a public affirmation of a private bond that both society and the newlyweds hope will endure. Yet for nearly four years, Karen Thompson was denied the company of the one person to whom she had pledged lifelong devotion. Her partner is a woman, Sharon Kowalski, and their home state of Minnesota, like every other jurisdiction in the United States, refuses to permit two individuals of the same sex to marry.

Tragic Separation

Karen Thompson and Sharon Kowalski are spouses in every respect except the legal. They exchanged vows and rings; they lived together until Nov. 13, 1983—when Ms. Kowalski was severely injured when her car was struck by a drunk driver. She lost the capacity to walk or to speak more than several words at a time, and needed constant care.

Ms. Thompson sought a court ruling granting her guardianship over her partner, but Ms. Kowalski's parents opposed the petition and obtained sole guardianship. They moved Ms. Kowalski to a nursing home 300 miles away from Ms. Thompson and forbade all visits between the two women. In 1989, as part of a reevaluation of Ms. Kowalski's mental competency, Ms. Thompson was permitted to visit her partner again. But the prolonged injustice and anguish inflicted on both women hold a moral for everyone.

Marriage, the Supreme Court declared in 1967, is "one of the basic civil rights of man" (and, presumably, of woman as well). The freedom to marry, said the Court, is "essential to the orderly pursuit of happiness."

Marriage is not just a symbolic state. It can be the key to survival, emotional and financial. Marriage triggers a universe of rights, privileges and presumptions. A married person can share in a spouse's estate even when there is no will. She is typically entitled to the group insurance and pension programs offered by the spouse's employer, and she enjoys tax advantages. She cannot be compelled to testify against her spouse in legal proceedings.

Individual Decision

The decision whether or not to marry belongs properly to individuals—not the Government. Yet at present, all 50 states deny that choice to millions of gay and lesbian Americans. While marriage has historically required a male partner and a female partner, history alone cannot sanctify injustice. If tradition were the only measure, most states would still limit matrimony to partners of the same race.

As recently as 1967, before the Supreme Court declared mis-cegenation statutes unconstitutional, 16 states still prohibited marriages between a white person and a black person. When all the excuses were stripped away, it was clear that the only purpose of those laws was, in the words of the Supreme Court, "to maintain white supremacy."

Those who argue against reforming the marriage statutes because they believe that same sex marriage would be "anti-family" overlook the obvious: marriage creates families and promotes social stability. In an increasingly loveless world, those who wish to commit themselves to a relationship founded upon devotion should be encouraged, not scorned. Government has no legitimate interest in how that love is expressed.

And it can no longer be argued—if it ever could—that marriage is fundamentally a procreative unit. Otherwise, states would forbid marriage between those who, by reason of age or infertility, cannot have children, as well as those who elect not to.

As the case of Sharon Kowalski and Karen Thompson demonstrates, sanctimonious illusions lead directly to the suffering of others. Denied the right to marry, these two women are left subject to the whims and prejudices of others, and of the law.

End the Injustice

Depriving millions of gay American adults the marriages of their choice, and the rights that flow from marriage, denies equal protection of the law. They, their families and friends, together with fair-minded people everywhere, should demand an end to this monstrous injustice.

II

Tom Brougham and Barry Warren share a home in Berkeley, California. They consider themselves life partners—a family. When the city of Berkeley passed a law allowing unmarried partners to register as domestic partners, they were one of the first couples to register.

A Sweet Moment

For the two men, registering was a sweet moment. Ten years ago, Brougham and Warren were pioneers in the domestic partners movement. Like many other committed couples who lived together, they could not receive family health benefits at their jobs. Each worked beside married employees whose partners were automatically covered, even if their relationships had not endured as long as Brougham and Warren's had. Fed up with what they considered discrimination, each asked his employer to extend the benefits enjoyed by married employees and their families to domestic partner families.

Warren's employer, the University of California, refused, citing the difficulty of verifying these relationships and the high cost of extending health benefits to unmarried couples. Brougham's employer, the city of Berkeley, asked for time to study the proposal.

The two men continued to develop their ideas on the rights of domestic partners and shared them with others. One person they spoke with was gay San Francisco Supervisor Harry Britt, whom they urged to push for the rights of gay families in San Francisco. In 1982, with the support of many gay rights organizations, Britt introduced a city ordinance that would allow unmarried city employees to include their partners on the city's health-care plan.

Britt's initiative created controversy in San Francisco and throughout the country. The media labeled it the "live-in lover law." Politicians, gay rights groups, and some churches focused on the law as a gay and lesbian issue only, inflaming the nation's fear of homosexuals. Though the legislation passed the Board of Supervisors by a vote of six to two, Mayor Diane Feinstein vetoed it.

Brougham, Warren, and Britt's initiatives inspired a national movement that is questioning conventional definitions of family. The domestic partner movement encompasses issues relevant not only to gays and lesbians but also to unmarried heterosexual couples and persons in other non-traditional families. Marriage should not be the only factor that qualifies people for the legal rights and economic benefits that families enjoy, assert organizers. That criterion discriminates against many of the nation's self-declared families. . . .

Discrimination Against Gay and Lesbian Families

At the vanguard of the domestic partner movement are gay and lesbian organizations. While straight unmarried couples face the same legal and economic discrimination as gays, they can choose to marry if they need the benefits. Gay and lesbian couples, however, do not have the option of marrying. They are legally cut off from ever receiving those benefits and rights.

In the last 10 years two developments have made the economic and legal discrimination against gay and lesbian families hit home, mobilizing the community to political and legal action. The first is AIDS. In the last decade tens of thousands of gay men have died of AIDS. As their partners and friends died, homosexuals grew more aware of their lack of family rights. They could not get their partners included on their companies' health plans, and without a will they had no claims on their lovers' property, nor even the right to go to the funeral.

At the same time, an increasing number of gay and lesbian

couples had children or adopted them. In the San Francisco area alone, at least 1,000 children have been born to or adopted by gay or lesbian couples since 1985. In addition, an estimated three million to five million lesbian and gay parents have children from former heterosexual relationships. As more gays and lesbians formed families with children, they wanted to protect them in the same ways straight parents did—with good health care, child care, and a secure household.

As gays and lesbians became more politically organized around these issues, they took the domestic partner movement into courts, legislatures, unions, and work places. Eight cities now provide health benefits, sick leave, and/or bereavement leave for domestic partners: Berkeley, West Hollywood, Santa Cruz, and Los Angeles, California; Madison, Wisconsin; Takoma Park, Maryland; Seattle, Washington; and New York City. Domestic partner legislation is being discussed in other cities, including Washington, D.C., and Philadelphia, and in the states of Illinois and New York. . . .

Domestic Partner Recognitions in the U.S.

Prepared by the National Gay and Lesbian Task Force Policy Institute

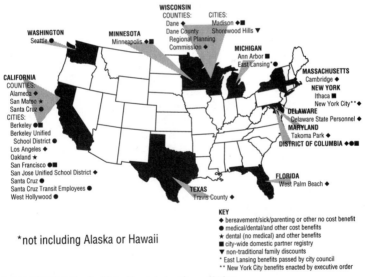

WISCONSIN
COUNTIES:
Dane ◆
Dane County ◆
Regional Planning Commission ◆

CITIES:
Madison ◆■
Shorewood Hills ▼

WASHINGTON
Seattle ●

MINNESOTA
Minneapolis ◆■

MICHIGAN
Ann Arbor ■
East Lansing * ●

CALIFORNIA
COUNTIES:
Alameda ◆
San Mateo ★
Santa Cruz ●
CITIES:
Berkeley ●■
Berkeley Unified
School District ●
Los Angeles ◆
Oakland ★
San Francisco ●■
San Jose Unified School District ◆
Santa Cruz ●
Santa Cruz Transit Employees ●
West Hollywood ●

MASSACHUSETTS
Cambridge ◆
NEW YORK
Ithaca ■
New York City ** ◆
DELAWARE
Delaware State Personnel ◆
MARYLAND
Takoma Park ◆
DISTRICT OF COLUMBIA ◆●■

FLORIDA
West Palm Beach ◆

TEXAS
Travis County ◆

*not including Alaska or Hawaii

KEY
◆ bereavement/sick/parenting or other no cost benefit
● medical/dental/and other cost benefits
★ dental (no medical) and other benefits
■ city-wide domestic partner registry
▼ non-traditional family discounts
* East Lansing benefits passed by city council
** New York City benefits enacted by executive order

© 1992 NGLTF Policy Institute. Reprinted with permission.

In the courtrooms, legal-rights organizations are pursuing and winning more sexual orientation and marital status discrimination cases as well. In 1989, the American Civil Liberties Union, with the support of the national gay and lesbian legal rights organization Lambda Legal Defense and Education Fund, won a precedent-setting case in the Court of Appeals in New York state. The court granted a gay man whose partner had died the right to stay in a rent-controlled apartment that was leased in his partner's name.

The fiercest foes of efforts to win domestic partner rights and stop marital status discrimination are Christian fundamentalists, orthodox Jewish organizations, and the Roman Catholic Church hierarchy. These organizations have crowned themselves the protectors of the traditional institution of marriage. Church groups were the principal opponents of the first domestic partner law in San Francisco. In Madison, they helped thwart the city's attempt to extend health benefits to domestic partners.

Traditional values rule in the courts as well. For this reason, many activists anticipate that most progress will be made not in the courtroom but in work places, unions, businesses, and legislatures. "In many ways society has moved ahead of the government," explains Evan Wolfson, staff attorney at Lambda. "The judiciary is especially a problem. It will be dominated by anti-gay, anti-equality, and anti-minority appointments for years to come."

Savvy Politicking

Because gay and lesbian organizations have led the fight for domestic partner rights, the issue has become a gay issue rather than one embraced by a broader range of non-traditional families. Homophobia has prevented straight unmarried people from joining the movement and inhibited cities, courts, and businesses from changing rulings and policies.

"When I give presentations about domestic partner rights, I downplay the gay issue and talk more about straight folk," says Ginny Cutting, the convener of the Gay and Lesbian Concerns Committee for Local 509 of the Service Employees International Union in Massachusetts. "At times this is difficult, but I'm savvy enough to know if I don't sell it this way I am sinking myself before I even get started.". . .

Cutting, who is fighting for domestic partner provisions in her union's labor contract, says her present task is to educate people. "Education is what it is all about right now," she comments. "We are bringing the issue to the forefront." The issue may fall by the wayside, but "in a few years we'll do it all over again. This isn't a one shot deal."

2 VIEWPOINT

"Authorizing the marriage of homosexuals, like sanctioning polygamy, would be unenlightened social policy."

Society Should Not Sanction Gay Partnerships

Bruce Fein and Dinesh D'Souza

In the following two-part viewpoint, Bruce Fein and Dinesh D'Souza question whether society should give greater official sanction to gay relationships. Fein, an assistant attorney general in the Reagan administration and a noted columnist on constitutional law, argues in Part I that society has legitimate reasons for limiting marriage to heterosexual couples. In Part II, D'Souza, a research fellow at the American Enterprise Institute in Washington, D.C., and author of *Illiberal Education*, questions the merit of domestic partnership arrangements, arguing that they harm society by weakening its concept of family.

As you read, consider the following questions:

1. What wrong message would society convey in sanctioning gay marriages or partnerships, according to the authors?
2. What stake does society have in marriage, according to the authors?
3. What is the homosexual community demanding from society, in D'Souza's opinion?

Bruce Fein, "No: Reserve Marriage for Heterosexuals," *ABA Journal*, January 1990, © 1990 by the American Bar Association. Reprinted by permission of the *ABA Journal*. Dinesh D'Souza, "From Tolerance to Subsidy," *Crisis*, September 1989. Reprinted by permission of *Crisis* magazine, PO Box 1006, Notre Dame, IN 46556.

I

Authorizing the marriage of homosexuals, like sanctioning polygamy, would be unenlightened social policy. The law should reserve the celebration of marriage vows for monogamous male-female attachments to further the goal of psychologically, emotionally and educationally balanced offspring.

Experience

As Justice Oliver Wendell Holmes noted, the life of the law has not been logic; it has been experience. Experience confirms that child development is skewed, scarred or retarded when either a father or mother is absent in the household.

In the area of adoption, married couples are favored over singles. The recent preferences for joint child-custody decrees in divorce proceedings tacitly acknowledge the desirability of child intimacies with both a mother and father.

As Supreme Court Justice Byron White recognized in *Taylor v. Louisiana* (1975): "[T]he two sexes are not fungible; a community made up exclusively of one is different from a community of both; the subtle interplay of influence one on the other is among the imponderables" (quoting from *Ballard v. United States*).

A child receives incalculable benefits in the maturing process by the joint instruction, consolation, oversight and love of a father and mother—benefits that are unavailable in homosexual households. The child enjoys the opportunity to understand and respect both sexes in a uniquely intimate climate. The likelihood of gender prejudice is thus reduced, an exceptionally worthy social objective.

Protect Children

The law should encourage male-female marriage vows over homosexual attachments in the interests of physically, mentally, and psychologically healthy children, the nation's most valuable asset.

Crowning homosexual relationships with the solemnity of legal marriage would wrongly send social cues that male-female marriages are not preferable. And there is no constitutional right to homosexual marriage since homosexual sodomy can be criminalized. See *Bowers v. Hardwick* (1986).

The fact that some traditional marriages end in fractious divorce, yield no offspring, or result in families with mistreated children does not discredit limiting marriage to monogamous female-male-male relationships. Anti-polygamy laws are instructive. They seek to discourage female docility, male autocracy, and intra-family rancor and jealousies that are promoted by polygamous marriages. That some might not exhibit such deplorable characteristics is no reason for their repeal or a finding of constitutional infirmity.

To deny the right of homosexual marriage is not an argument for limiting other rights to gays, because of community animosity or vengeance. These are unacceptable policy motivations if law is to be civilized.

Several states and localities protect homosexuals against discrimination in employment or housing. In New York, a state law confers on a homosexual the rent-control benefits of a deceased partner. Other jurisdictions have eschewed special legal rights for homosexuals, and the military excludes them. Experience will adjudge which of the varied legal approaches to homosexual rights has been the most enlightened.

Asay, by permission of the *Colorado Springs Gazette Telegraph*.

Sober debate over homosexual rights is in short supply. The subject challenges deep-rooted and passionately held images of manhood, womanhood and parenthood, and evokes sublimated fears of community ostracism or degradation.

Each legal issue regarding homosexuality should be examined discretely with the recognition that time has upset many fighting faiths and with the goal of balancing individual liberty against community interests. With regard to homosexual marriage, that balance is negative.

II

The city of San Francisco has legalized "domestic partnerships" for homosexual couples and unmarried heterosexuals who live together. The law entitles "domestic partners" to be treated no differently from married partners. It allows hospital visitation rights that family members currently enjoy; city employees get bereavement leave if a partner dies; couples may sign up for joint health insurance policies. . . . Sponsors of the legislation are hoping it will be a model for cities across the country, and New York State has now enacted a similar law regarding the inheritance of rent-controlled apartments.

At first glance, the ordinance seems unobjectionable; what could be wrong with treating enduring non-marital relationships, both homosexual and heterosexual, with the same social regard as marriage? The law says that San Francisco "shall not discriminate against domestic partners or domestic partnerships in any way," and isn't it about time we outlawed all forms of discrimination? Further, nonmarital living arrangements have proliferated to the point where we are all accustomed to dealing with them in our daily existence; the rule appears merely to codify that which we take for granted.

Reason for Alarm

A close analysis of the rule, however, gives reason for pause and indeed alarm. First, the even-handedness of the ordinance, its dual applicability to heterosexuals and homosexuals alike, is confusing and deceptive. Think about why heterosexual couples live together: is it not precisely to escape those legal tangles and obligations that accrue to married couples? Heterosexual non-marital arrangements are mechanisms for avoiding the binding commitment of the law. We may safely predict that heterosexuals will not line up in large numbers for "domestic partnerships."

This is a homosexual rights ordinance, then, whose provisions such as hospital visitation and bereavement leave are specifically aimed at the AIDS epidemic. No doubt AIDS has devastated the homosexual community in San Francisco. But precisely because AIDS is so bad—individually lethal and socially lacerating—isn't it important that society stop promoting behavior that increases the likelihood of AIDS transmission? It is a strange way to fight an epidemic by encouraging the agents of its proliferation.

With the current ordinance, the homosexual community has gone from demanding social tolerance to social recognition and subsidy. Now it is one thing to argue that homosexuals, like all Americans, have a basic right to be left alone, a right not to be harassed or persecuted, a right against government interference. This is quite different from extending to homosexuals—or unmarried heterosexuals for that matter—the same special privileges that society, for very good reasons, extends to marriage.

Interest in Marriage

Society's interest in marriage is not limited to self-preservation or self-perpetuation. Society makes very heavy demands on parents: they must devote large segments of their lives to raising children, caring for their illness, ensuring their moral and vocational education. When married couples don't do this, when the family unit disintegrates, society must then contend with the debris: single mothers who are dependent on the state, children who are uprooted. Government policy should encourage marriage and intact families because they are the basic units of social order, stability, and growth.

Society has no comparable interest in promoting non-marital relationships. This does not mean it should outlaw them. It can simply leave them alone. Individuals who choose those relationships will lose some of the societal privileges of marriage, but that is hardly an outrage since they have not assumed the enormous responsibilities of marriage. It is significant that the San Francisco law gives "domestic partnerships" claims against the government but outlines no accompanying obligations. If one wishes to inherit the life insurance benefits of one's homosexual partner, isn't it only fair that one should bear joint responsibility for paying for his medical expenses if he suffers from AIDS?

With the San Francisco ordinance, we are watching a familiar pattern unfold. First a group says, "Don't persecute me." Next it says, "I deserve recognition by society." Finally it announces, "I am now ready to receive handouts." Soon the same advocates of legal recognition for "domestic partnerships" will demand homosexual adoption rights, tax breaks for homosexual couples, perhaps even preferential treatment to counter historic discrimination.

"Same-sex marriage would most likely increase desegregation and acceptance of the gay and lesbian community."

Legalizing Gay Marriage Would Help Homosexuals

Craig R. Dean

An increasing number of gay and lesbian couples have been fighting for the right to legally marry. While some churches and other organizations perform ceremonies of same-sex marriages, none of the fifty states grant marriage licenses and status for gays and lesbians. In the following viewpoint, Craig R. Dean, an attorney and founder of the Equal Marriage Rights Fund, argues that granting marriage rights to gays and lesbians would restore fundamental justice to homosexuals and increase their acceptance in U.S. society. Dean and his partner, Patrick Gill, filed a lawsuit against the District of Columbia after it refused to grant them a marriage license. They argued that the district had violated its Human Rights Act prohibiting discrimination on the basis of sexual orientation.

As you read, consider the following questions:

1. What does Dean say is the main reason for fighting for the right to marry?
2. How does the author describe his treatment by the mainstream media?
3. How does Dean respond to the argument that gays and lesbians should not mimic heterosexual marriages and life-styles?

From Craig R. Dean, "Gay Marriage: Lead, Follow, or Get Out of the Way," *New York Native*, August 26, 1991. Reprinted with permission.

My lover, Patrick Gill, and I filed for a marriage license with the District of Columbia. We did so because the Mayor of Washington, Sharon Pratt Dixon, said during her campaign that she favored legalizing same-sex marriage and that "society is a changing place and it [gay and lesbian marriage] is something we should accept." So, based upon her campaign promise, Patrick and I filed for a marriage license after Dixon was elected Mayor. Yet, the District government denied us the right to marry because we are a gay male couple.

So we filed a lawsuit alleging a two-fold discrimination: 1) violation of the District's gender-neutral marriage law, and 2) violation of the District's Human Rights Act, which explicitly prohibits discrimination based on sexual orientation. The Human Rights Act mandates that "every individual shall have an equal opportunity to participate fully in the economic, cultural, and intellectual life of the District and to have an equal opportunity to participate in all aspects of life." The Act further states that the intent behind this legislation is to "end . . . discrimination [in the District of Columbia] for any reason . . . [including] sexual orientation."

What good are such gay-rights laws in D.C., New York, or anywhere else, if they are not used?

Taking the Lead

The main reason that Patrick and I are demanding equality for gay and lesbian relationships is because it is the right thing to do. Otherwise, if we didn't demand our rights, we would be agreeing with the homophobes who posit that homosexual relationships do not have the same quality and value as heterosexual relationships. Homophobes live in terror of the day when states will legally recognize homosexual relationships. Unless we assert ourselves and fight for our right to marry, we would be giving in to homophobia—perhaps even our own homophobia.

It's been tough. But our love for each other gives us the strength to carry on this battle for what we know is just. We do not believe our love is of any less magnitude or importance than that of any other couple in a long-term committed relationship. For that reason, we want legal recognition of our upcoming holy union ceremony, which would be offered without question if one of us were female. We demand the same rights and benefits that are automatically bestowed upon heterosexual couples. These rights and benefits protect and reinforce relationships. Yet these rights are denied to us for only one reason—because we're gay!

Married couples have many significant rights that unmarried couples—even "domestic partners" cannot have. For instance, married couples have the automatic right to be on each other's health, disability, and life insurance policies, as well as to be on each other's pension plans. Married couples get special tax preferences for exemptions, deductions, and refunds. As a matter of right, married couples are also able to own real estate and personal property jointly, and to protect that property from each other's creditors. Spouses automatically inherit property and have rights of survivorship. While for same-sex couples the family is the next of kin, for married couples, a spouse is the next of kin in case of death or medical emergencies, and spouses may therefore make important decisions for their partners. Last, and certainly not least in light of the epidemic, a spouse can make financial decisions in the case of a partner's incapacity. Need we be reminded of the plight of Karen Thompson and Sharon Kowalski?

In the District of Columbia alone there are more than 100 automatic marriage-based rights. In D.C., heterosexuals can meet each other tonight in a bar, and have more rights through marriage within five days than Patrick and I are able to obtain after five years of being together. This is an incredible act of multiple-discrimination against lesbians and gays. It is outrageous, and we are doing something about it.

Following

No one can take the lead on every issue. It's gratifying that many have chosen to help us on the issue of same-sex marriage. We have received letters and expressions of support from thousands of lesbians and gays all over the world. We were honored to be the Grand Marshalls of Gay Pride parades from Baltimore to Hawaii. National groups such as the National Organization for Women, the National Gay and Lesbian Task Force, Parents and Friends of Lesbians and Gays and many Washington, D.C., groups have expressed support for our case. The Human Rights Campaign Fund has written D.C.'s Mayor on our behalf, saying:

> The discrimination that thousands of lesbian and gay residents of the District experience is reinforced when the government of the District treats these lesbian and gay men differently from non-Gay residents and denies them benefits, licenses and privileges based solely on their sex and sexual orientation. There is no legal barrier; in fact, current District law requires no discrimination. Neither is there a policy barrier; the same policies that support civil marriage between men and women apply with the same force to same-sex couples. If two individuals desire to establish a union, which by law imposes certain responsibilities and creates certain benefits, the government and the society that it serves have the same interest in validating that union regardless of . . . sexual orientation.

We are fortunate that the mainstream media is following this issue, too. In fact, the media has shown an intense fascination with the gay marriage issue. There was a time—not so long ago—when the news media completely ignored gay issues. But in the wake of the massive AIDS coverage during the past few years, the media seems ready to cover other, more positive gay issues.

Enter the gay marriage proposal. As far as Pat and I can tell, coverage of our fight represents the first time the media has been willing to consistently portray a gay issue in a positive manner for such a broad audience. It is difficult to know how many millions we have reached, but by adding the estimated viewership of our television appearances alone, the number of people we've reached could be as high as 50 million. We have appeared on the *Oprah Winfrey Show*, twice on *Donahue*, *CBS Morning News*, *CBS Nightwatch*, *Fox Morning News*, *CNN*, and various local TV and radio news and talk shows around the country. In addition, because AP [Associated Press] is following our story, hundreds of newspaper articles have been written on same-sex marriage.

People of color got a good deal of momentum for their civil rights struggles when television brought their plight into American homes. Our movement will also gain momentum from the coverage in mainstream media. Furthermore, because marriage is such a familiar institution to which nearly everyone can relate, gay marriage could potentially build a broader coalition for the gay civil rights movement.

Indeed, the response of straight America has been overwhelming I believe that we are seeing a tremendous shift in the public's perception of lesbians and gays. We have even made inroads into Hollywood—sitcoms such as *Golden Girls* have run strongly supportive shows on the issue of same-sex marriage. And to a large extent, as the *Golden Girls* go, so goes America! . . .

Marriage and Homosexuals

As for whether gays and lesbians should seek marriage at all, some critics say that homosexuals should not mimic heterosexual lifestyles. This argument is dangerous because it tends to buy into homophobic fears that gays and lesbians should not be married lest it make a farce of the marital institution. The issue is not whether all gays and lesbians should get married; the issue is whether homosexuals should have the same choices as heterosexuals available to them, and the right to define our own family structures. Whether gays and lesbians should serve in the military is considered a legitimate point of debate, and no one in the gay community seriously argues that gays should be denied the option of joining. It is the *option*, the *choice*, that counts. Marriage has traditionally been an attractive option for people because it can provide stability and the respect of society in general. Same-sex marriage would most likely increase desegregation and acceptance of the gay and lesbian community.

We demand full and immediate equality now. Anything less is unacceptable. If you agree with us, help take the lead or try to follow. If you disagree, please do not stand in the way. Some have said that gay marriage is merely a shortcut to equal rights. For us, the real shortcut is to give into homophobia and give up without a fight.

"Marriage runs contrary to . . . the affirmation of gay identity and culture and the validation of many forms of relationships. "

Marriage Is Not a Path to Liberation

Paula L. Ettelbrick

Paula L. Ettelbrick is the legal director of the Lambda Legal Defense and Education Fund, a gay rights organization in New York City. In the following viewpoint, she questions whether the legalizing of same-sex marriage will have a positive effect on the gay and lesbian community. Ettelbrick contends that legalizing and encouraging marriage among homosexuals would undercut efforts to establish a distinctive gay identity and culture, and argues that gays and lesbians should work to make society accept their differences, rather than conform to the heterosexual model of marriage.

As you read, consider the following questions:

1. What are the two major reasons why Ettelbrick is disturbed by the movement to legalize same-sex marriage?
2. What is necessary to achieve justice for gays and lesbians, according to the author?
3. What family-related goals for the gay and lesbian movement does Ettelbrick advocate?

Paula L. Ettelbrick, "Since When Is Marriage a Path to Liberation?" *Out/Look*, Fall 1989. Reprinted with permission.

"Marriage is a great institution . . . if you like living in institutions," according to a bit of T-shirt philosophy I saw recently. Certainly, marriage is an institution. It is one of the most venerable, impenetrable institutions in modern society. Marriage provides the ultimate form of acceptance for personal intimate relationships in our society, and gives those who marry an insider status of the most powerful kind.

Steeped in a patriarchal system that looks to ownership, property, and dominance of men over women as its basis, the institution of marriage long has been the focus of radical feminist revulsion. Marriage defines certain relationships as more valid than all others. Lesbian and gay relationships, being neither legally sanctioned or commingled by blood, are always at the bottom of the heap of social acceptance and importance.

Given the imprimatur of social and personal approval which marriage provides, it is not surprising that some lesbians and gay men among us would look to legal marriage for self-affirmation. After all, those who marry can be instantaneously transformed from "outsiders" to "insiders," and we have a desperate need to become insiders.

It could make us feel OK about ourselves, perhaps even relieve some of the internalized homophobia that we all know so well. Society will then celebrate the birth of our children and mourn the death of our spouses. It would be easier to get health insurance for our spouses, family memberships to the local museum, and a right to inherit our spouse's cherished collection of lesbian mystery novels even if she failed to draft a will. Never again would we have to go to a family reunion and debate about the correct term for introducing our lover/partner/significant other to Aunt Flora. Everything would be quite easy and very nice.

Marriage Is No Liberation

So why does this unlikely event so deeply disturb me? For two major reasons. First, marriage will not liberate us as lesbians and gay men. In fact, it will constrain us, make us more invisible, force our assimilation into the mainstream, and undermine the goals of gay liberation. Second, attaining the right to marry will not transform our society from one that makes narrow, but dramatic, distinctions between those who are married and those who are not married to one that respects and encourages choice of relationships and family diversity. Marriage runs contrary to two of the primary goals of the lesbian and gay movement: the affirmation of gay identity and culture; and the validation of many forms of relationships.

When analyzed from the standpoint of civil rights, certainly lesbians and gay men should have a right to marry. But obtaining a right does not always result in justice. White male firefighters in Birmingham, Alabama, have been fighting for their "rights" to retain their jobs by overturning the city's affirmative action guidelines. If their "rights" prevail, the courts will have failed in rendering justice. The "right" fought for by the white male firefighters as well as those who advocate strongly for the "rights" to legal marriage for gay people, will result, at best, in limited or narrowed "justice" for those closest to power at the expense of those who have been historically marginalized.

The fight for justice has as its goal the realignment of power imbalances among individuals and classes of people in society. A pure "rights" analysis often fails to incorporate a broader understanding of the underlying inequities that operate to deny justice to a fuller range of people and groups. In setting our priorities as a community we just combine the concept of both rights and justice. At this point in time, making legal marriage for lesbian and gay couples a priority would set an agenda of gaining rights for a few, but would do nothing to correct the power imbalances between those who are married (whether gay or straight) and those who are not. Thus, justice would not be gained.

Accepted with Our Differences

Justice for gay men and lesbians will be achieved only when we are accepted and supported in this society *despite* our differences from the dominant culture and the choices we make regarding our relationships. Being queer is more than setting up house, sleeping with a person of the same gender, and seeking state approval for doing so. It is an identity, a culture with many variations. It is a way of dealing with the world by diminishing the constraints of gender roles which have for so long kept women and gay people oppressed and invisible. Being queer means pushing the parameters of sex, sexuality, and family, and in the process transforming the very fabric of society. Gay liberation is inexorably linked to women's liberation. Each is essential to the other.

The moment we argue, as some among us insist on doing, that we should be treated as equals because we are really just like married couples and hold the same values to be true, we undermine the very purpose of our movement and begin the dangerous process of silencing our different voices. As a lesbian, I am fundamentally different from non-lesbian women. That's the point. Marriage, as it exists today, is antithetical to my liberation as a lesbian and as a woman because it mainstreams my life and voice. I do not want to be known as "Mrs. Attached-To-Somebody Else." Nor do I want to give the state the power to regulate my primary relationship.

Yet, the concept of equality in our legal system does not support differences, it only supports sameness. The very standard for equal protection is that people who are similarly situated must be treated equally. To make an argument for equal protection, we will be required to claim that gay and lesbian relationships are the same as straight relationships. To gain the right, we must compare ourselves to married couples. The law looks to the insiders as the norm, regardless of how flawed or unjust their institutions, and requires that those seeking the law's equal protection situate themselves in a similar posture to those who are already protected. In arguing for the right to legal marriage, lesbians and gay men would be forced to claim that we are just like heterosexual couples, have the same goals and purposes, and vow to structure our lives similarly. The law provides no room to argue that we are different, but are nonetheless entitled to equal protection.

"I never feel lonely when I've just spoken to some of my married friends."

PUNCH

© Punch/Rothco. Reprinted with permission.

The thought of emphasizing our sameness to married heterosexuals in order to obtain this "right" terrifies me. It rips away the very heart and soul of what I believe it is to be a lesbian in this world. It robs me of the opportunity to make a difference. We end up mimicking all that is bad about the institution of marriage in our effort to appear to be the same as straight couples.

By looking to our sameness and deemphasizing our differences, we don't even place ourselves in a position of power that would allow us to transform marriage from an institution that emphasizes property and state regulation of relationships to an institution which recognizes one of many types of valid and respected relationships. Until the Constitution is interpreted to respect and encourage differences, pursuing the legalization of same-sex marriage would be leading our movement into a trap; we would be demanding access to the very institution which, in its current form, would undermine *our* movement to recognize many different kinds of relationships. We would be perpetuating the elevation of married relationships and of "couples" in general, and further eclipsing other relationships of choice.

Outlawing Gay Sex

Ironically, gay marriage, instead of liberating gay sex and sexuality, would further outlaw all gay and lesbian sex which is not performed in a marital context. Just as sexually active non-married women face stigma and double standards around sex and sexual activity, so too would non-married gay people. The only legitimate gay sex would be that which is cloaked in and regulated by marriage. Its legitimacy would stem not from an acceptance of gay sexuality, but because the Supreme Court and society in general fiercely protect the privacy of marital relationships. Lesbians and gay men who do not seek the state's stamp of approval would clearly face increased sexual oppression.

Undoubtedly, whether we admit it or not, we all need to be accepted by the broader society. That motivation fuels our work to eliminate discrimination in the workplace and elsewhere, fight for custody of our children, create our own families and so on. The growing discussion about the right to marry may be explained in part by this need for acceptance. Those closer to the norm or to power in this country are more likely to see marriage as a principle of freedom and equality. Those who are more acceptable to the mainstream because of race, gender, and economic status are more likely to want the right to marry. It is the final acceptance, the ultimate affirmation of identity.

On the other hand, more marginal members of the lesbian and gay community (women, people of color, working class and poor) are less likely to see marriage as having relevance to our struggles for survival. After all, what good is the affirmation of our relationships (that is, marital relationships) if we are rejected as women, black, or working class?

The path to acceptance is much more complicated for many of us. For instance, if we choose legal marriage, we may enjoy the right to add our spouse to our health insurance policy at work, since most employment policies are defined by one's marital status, not family relationship. However, that choice assumes that we have a job *and* that our employer provides us with health benefits. For women, particularly women of color who tend to occupy the low-paying jobs that do not provide health care benefits at all, it will not matter one bit if they are able to marry their woman partners. The opportunity to marry will neither get them health benefits nor transform them from outsider to insider.

Of course, a white man who marries another white man who has a full-time job with benefits will certainly be able to share in those benefits and overcome the only obstacle left to full societal assimilation—the goal of many in his class. In other words, gay marriage will not topple the system that allows only the privileged few to obtain decent health care. Nor will it close the privilege gap between those who are married and those who are not.

Marriage creates a two-tier system that allows the state to regulate relationships. It has become a facile mechanism for employers to dole out benefits, for businesses to provide special deals and incentives and for the law to make distinctions in distributing meager public funds. None of these entities bothers to consider the relationship among people; the love, respect, and need to protect that exists among all kinds of family members. Rather, a simple certificate of the state, regardless of whether the spouses love, respect, or even see each other on a regular basis, dominates and is supported. None of this dynamic will change if gay men and lesbians are given the option of marriage. . . .

Redefining the Family

If the laws change tomorrow and lesbians and gay men were allowed to marry, where would we find the incentive to continue the progressive movement we have started that is pushing for societal and legal recognition of all kinds of family relationships? To create other options and alternatives? To find a place in the law for the elderly couple who, for companionship and economic reasons, live together but do not marry? To recognize the right of a long-time, but unmarried, gay partner to stay in his rent-controlled apartment after the death of his lover, the only named tenant on the lease? To recognize the family relationship of the lesbian couple and the two gay men who are jointly sharing child-raising responsibilities? To get the law to acknowledge that we may have more than one relationship worthy of legal protection?

Marriage for lesbians and gay men still will not provide a real choice unless we continue the work our community has begun to spread the privilege around to other relationships. We must first break the tradition of piling benefits and privileges onto those who are married, while ignoring the real life needs of those who are not. Only when we de-institutionalize marriage and bridge the economic and privilege gap between the married and the unmarried will each of us have a true choice. Otherwise, our choice not to marry will continue to lack legal protection and societal respect.

The lesbian and gay community has laid the groundwork for revolutionizing society's views of family. The domestic partnership movement has been an important part of this progress insofar as it validates non-marital relationships. Because it is not limited to sexual or romantic relationships, domestic partnership provides an important opportunity for many who are not related by blood or marriage to claim certain minimal protections.

It is crucial, though, that we avoid the pitfall of framing the push for legal recognition of domestic partners (those who share a primary residence and financial responsibility for each other) as a stepping stone to marriage. We must keep our eyes on the goals of providing true alternatives to marriage and of radically reordering society's view of family.

The goals of lesbian and gay liberation must simply be broader than the right to marry. Gay and lesbian marriages may minimally transform the institution of marriage by diluting its traditional patriarchal dynamic, but they will not transform society. They will not demolish the two-tier system of the "haves" and the "have nots." We must not fool ourselves into believing that marriage will make it acceptable to be gay or lesbian. We will be liberated only when we are respected and accepted for our differences and the diversity we provide to this society. Marriage is not a path to that liberation.

"We cannot find, by the current measures available, that any evidence of homosexuality in a parent has a specific detrimental effect."

Homosexuals Should Have Greater Parental Rights

Scott Harris

An estimated 6 to 14 million gay and lesbian Americans are parents. While most of the parents had children within heterosexual marriages, an increasing number of gay and lesbian couples are raising children acquired via adoption, artificial insemination, or other means. In the following viewpoint, Scott Harris, a staff writer for the *Los Angeles Times*, examines the growing phenomenon of gay and lesbian parents. He writes that the growing number of such families has enabled many gays and lesbians to gain greater acceptance within their local communities, and cites studies demonstrating that the sexual orientation of the parents has no special negative effects on children.

As you read, consider the following questions:

1. What stereotypes have gay and lesbian parents rejected, according to Harris?
2. Why is the number of children raised by gay parents difficult to quantify, according to the author?
3. How do children react to news of their parents' sexual orientation, according to Harris?

Scott Harris, "2 Moms or 2 Dads—and a Baby," *Los Angeles Times*, October 20, 1991. Copyright, 1991, Los Angeles Times. Reprinted with permission.

To look at her, Alanna Gabrielle Handler seems an altogether conventional baby. Just 14 weeks old, she scrunches her tiny face and inspires the usual oohs and ahhs. The nursery in her family's Van Nuys apartment is pastel and girlish and graced with a banner proclaiming, "Welcome Alanna—Grandma and Grandpa."

But Alanna is not a typical infant. She was not conceived the traditional way and her parents are not a conventional couple—or should we say trio? No, Alanna is different. She is a tribute to lesbian romance and a product of artificial insemination, a baby whose very existence challenges traditional views of nature and family.

And for the gay rights movement, she is a tiny bundle of hope.

Little Alanna was born into the brave new world of "gay families." The notion of gays bringing up children may seem contradictory to those who assume that homosexuals are not inclined to propagate; it may alarm and disturb people who disapprove of gays as role models. But thousands of gays and lesbians are doing just that.

The Gayby Boom

Children are added to gay households in a variety of ways: by winning custody of offspring in the dissolution of heterosexual marriages, by adoption, by alternative means of conception. Experts suggest that Alanna is one of hundreds of babies, probably thousands, born to lesbians nationwide in recent years via artificial insemination—in some cases with sperm donated by gay men. A small number of gay men, meanwhile, have enlisted surrogates to help them fulfill paternal desires. The "gayby boom," some activists call it.

These parents have, in effect, rejected stereotypes held both outside and inside the gay community about what it means to be homosexual. At a time when the gay rights movement has been radicalized by the AIDS epidemic and such controversies as California Gov. Pete Wilson's veto of gay rights legislation, some activists believe such families may do more to alter society's attitudes about homosexuals than any protest march, lawsuit or legislation.

Such change, activists predict, would be evolutionary and incremental—but could ultimately lead to legal recognition of gay marriage. Gay rights proponents, still battling for such fundamental civil rights as job and housing protection, predict that redefining laws governing an institution as sacred as the family will prove their most difficult challenge.

Surveys suggest that a large majority of the American public, although generally favoring anti-discrimination laws, is uncomfortable with gays as parents. A 1989 Time Magazine-CNN poll, for example, showed that 17% say that gay couples should be legally permitted to adopt children, with 75% opposing and 8% uncertain.

Such attitudes are distressing to gay parents. "I would like the day to come when there's nothing to talk about, period," said Jeff Carron of Hollywood, the adoptive father of 5-year-old Jenny. "Whether I'm married to Susan or Steve, big deal. Am I nice? Am I good? Am I a loving parent? That's the important thing."

Courts have increasingly agreed with Carron's view. Judges, persuaded by growing research data that gays are as able as heterosexuals to be worthy parents, have increasingly granted gays custody of children and approved adoptions by gays. Meanwhile, alternative means of conception have brought more babies—and more gay parents—into the world.

Unknown Numbers

The number of gays bringing up children is difficult to quantify because many people remain closeted, fearful that they will lose their children, said Don Harrelson of the Gay and Lesbian Parents of Los Angeles. This is especially true outside cosmopolitan gay centers such as San Francisco, New York and Los Angeles, suggests Harrelson, the adoptive father of two sons.

In the San Francisco Bay Area alone, there are 5,000 gay households with children, according to the "educated guess" of Cynthia Underhill, director of the lesbian and gay parenting program at Lyon-Martin Women's Health Services in San Francisco. The program's mailing list numbers 2,000.

Medical professionals, meanwhile, can easily document hundreds of cases in the last decade in which lesbians have conceived via artificial insemination. Records at the Oakland-based Sperm Bank of California show that of the 405 women who conceived there from 1982 to June 1991, 208 identified themselves as lesbian, said executive director Barbara Raboy. Suzanne Gage, director of the artificial insemination program at Wholistic Health Care in West Hollywood, says more than 100 women who identified themselves as lesbian have conceived there over the last five years.

These two programs "are probably the tip of the iceberg," Raboy said, noting that substantial numbers of lesbians have conceived through artificial insemination programs at women's clinics in New York, Boston and Washington and in smaller numbers in clinics elsewhere. Raboy and other experts suggest that these numbers are equaled, if not surpassed, by those who do artificial insemination with assistance from a private physician or who do it themselves.

Alanna Handler was a do-it-yourselfer. Helene Handler was inseminated by her companion, Celia Noriega, in their bedroom using a syringe with a tube attached. The semen was donated by a friend.

Another homemade artificial insemination baby is year-old Lennon Marley Gunter, the pride and joy of biological mother Nadja Judin and "co-parent" Renee Gunter, as well as Jim Olarte, Lennon's biological father, and his longtime companion, Larry Craig.

The infant is named for musical artists John Lennon and Bob Marley—not just for their music, Judin explained, but "because they were social revolutionaries." Lennon lives with Judin and Gunter in their Studio City home. Olarte and Craig, who live in Laguna Beach, visit frequently.

Judin—now in the process of changing her name to Judin-Gunter—said it was important to find a donor who wanted to play an active role in their child's life.

"When he's older, he'll spend some weekends with his daddy. He'll know that Jim is his daddy. But he has two mamas too," Judin said.

False Concerns

There is concern among the general population that a child who grows up with a homosexual parent will develop same-sex orientation. This concern is grounded in the false assumption that children develop their sexual orientation by emulating their parents. It is important to note that the vast majority of homosexuals were raised by heterosexual parents. Current scientific research on the causes of homosexuality has dispelled the myth that any correlation exists between the parent's sexual orientation and the child's sexual orientation. Further, every study on the subject reveals that the incidence of same-sex orientation among children of homosexuals occurs as frequently and in the same proportion as in the general population.

National Center for Lesbian Rights, *Lesbian and Gay Parenting: A Psychological and Legal Perspective*, 1987.

Olarte said he envisions himself taking Lennon to the beach and the mountains, teaching him to surf and ski.

Many lesbians seeking to become pregnant are wary of gay donors because of the prevalence of the AIDS virus among gay men. A wrong decision could infect both mother and baby with potentially lethal results. Judin placed her trust in a battery of tests that showed that Olarte was free of the virus, as well as assurances that he and Craig have been in a monogamous relationship for 11 years.

Now the couples are discussing the possibility of a second

child—only this time Gunter and Craig would be the biological parents.

Many gays see the "gayby boom" as part of the maturation process for a community that used to jokingly refer to heterosexuals as "breeders."

"I think maybe 20 years ago, gays and lesbians were in many ways fighting their own homophobia, and their own feelings of where self-worth was coming from," said Roberta Bennett, a 48-year-old lesbian mother and an attorney who specializes in adoptions. "Times have certainly changed. I think politically and emotionally, the gay and lesbian community as a whole feels they're just like everybody else—and that they can raise a child just as well, if not better, than anybody else."

Bennett and her companion of 18 years have brought up five children—two each from prior heterosexual unions, and now a grandchild. She sees a spiritual link between AIDS and the gay-family phenomenon. Amid so much tragedy, Bennett asks, what is more emotionally enriching and life-affirming than bringing up children?

Many gay parents say having children simply represents a personal quest.

"Being gay has nothing to do with your desire or need to raise children," said a would-be father who is a member of Gay and Lesbian Parents of Los Angeles. "Heterosexuals have such an easy time having children they sometimes don't appreciate what a gift it is."

This man, who asked to be identified only as "Ralph," is among a handful of gay men seeking to father children with the aid of a surrogate. He plans to have two; the process costs about $35,000 for each child.

"Many gays don't understand it," he added. "They think you want to have children because you're trying to pass as a heterosexual. That's not what it is. You want to be a parent because you want to know what it's like. You want to change diapers. You want all of that experience."

Having children, Ralph says, is "the ultimate liberation of a gay person."

Political Implications

Gay parents see political implications in small and large ways. On personal levels, many speak of how children have brought greater acceptance from relatives, neighbors and people they meet at the PTA and Little League.

Parents, regardless of their sexual orientation, are able to relate to each other, said Diane Goodman, a lesbian attorney and adoptive mother of a toddler son. "It's waking up five times a night; it's 'I'm thirsty, I need to go to the bathroom'—it's all the same stuff," she said. "It's like the lesbian title is gone—because I'm a mother."

Alanna Handler's arrival, her mother Helene says, has softened her own family's attitude. Her parents and grandparents stood opposite her and Noriega during a recent Jewish naming ritual—"and the rabbi very much included Celia."

Winning Society's Trust

Winning society's trust is something else. To change family laws, gays would have to do much more than overcome opposition from people who see them as sinners. Many others grow squeamish at the notion of gays and children in close company.

"Any time you're dealing with children, it brings out the most primitive kind of reaction to lesbians and gay men," said Jon W. Davidson, a gay lawyer with the American Civil Liberties Union. "People raise concerns about molestation and role modeling. And will children turn out to be lesbian and gay?"

Gay parents and lawyers who represent them say such fears reflect erroneous stereotypes. Their contentions are supported by psychiatric research, said Dr. Martha J. Kirkpatrick, a professor at the UCLA School of Medicine.

"Whatever goes on in a family has an effect on the child. But we cannot find, by the current measures available, that any evidence of homosexuality in a parent has a specific detrimental effect," said Kirkpatrick, who has studied children brought up by lesbians.

Moreover, researchers have not found any more or less of a tendency in children brought up by gays and lesbians to be homosexual themselves, Kirkpatrick said. . . .

Some gays wryly point out that, as far as they know, their own parents were heterosexual. But they, too, wonder if homosexuality is a matter of nature, nurture or both. Many gay mothers and fathers—no doubt like their parents before them—worry whether their own children might be homosexual.

"I was born this way," asserted Bruce Zisterer of Altadena, recently granted joint custody of his 10-year-old son, Joel, after the dissolution of a 15-year marriage. "I believe it's an innate thing you're born with.

"Now, if I had my say, I would hope my son grows up straight. . . . He would not have to go through the emotional pain I have gone through."

Although more openly gay people are bringing up more children than ever before, gays say it is absurd to think of homosexuals having children as some apocalyptic turn of events. "As long as there have been lesbians and gays, there have been lesbian mothers and gay fathers," said Roberta Achtenburg, the former executive director of the National Center for Lesbian

Rights and now a member of the San Francisco County Board of Supervisors.

Parental rights have been a key issue since the gay liberation movement started in the late 1960s. California law since 1967 has held that a parent cannot be denied custody of a child solely on the grounds of homosexuality. But as more gays and lesbians came out of the closet, their lawyers discovered that such disclosures greatly jeopardized their standing in custody battles.

The courts gradually became more tolerant. A key reason, some suggest, was the American Psychiatric Assn.'s decision in 1973 removing homosexuality from its diagnostic manual of disease categories. When San Francisco's Lesbian Rights Project was founded in 1977, "the primary emphasis of the legal work was in the defense of mothers, because the kids were being taken away from them for no good reason," Achtenburg said.

Data Supports Homosexual Parents

The psychological and sociological data indicate that the sexual orientation of a parent is not a predictor of whether or not children parented by them will develop either major psychological problems, or same-sex sexual orientation. There is no competent social science data developed in the last twenty years which indicates anything other than that homosexuals are as qualified as heterosexuals to parent children. It is crucial that this be understood if we are not to end up relying on prejudice, misunderstanding and stereotype, to the detriment of not only the homosexual seeking to parent but, more important, to the child in need of that parent's love and home.

National Center for Lesbian Rights, *Lesbian and Gay Parenting: A Psychological and Legal Perspective*, 1987.

In more recent years, studies such as Kirkpatrick's have made the homosexuality of a parent less of an issue in custody disputes. But Kirkpatrick says that more long-term studies are needed to better understand the dynamics of "gay families" and their influence on children.

Domestic scenes in gay households rattle classic notions of the nuclear family.

Zisterer, who lives with companion Nick Paul, decided that he had to "come out" to his son more than a year ago during a contentious custody battle. His former wife, Zisterer said, "tried to make an issue of homosexuality. . . . It didn't work."

He gave Joel a reading lesson with a primer called "Daddy's Roommate," trying to explain his relationship with his live-in companion, Nick Paul.

Joel showed the book to a visitor, matter-of-factly reading how the two men "live together, work together, eat together, sleep together, shave together." Being gay, the book explains, "is just one more kind of love. And love is the best kind of happiness."

Younger children, gay parents say, tend to take news of a parent's homosexuality in stride. But the arrival of adolescence makes a parent's sexual orientation more of an issue.

Thirteen-year-old Alice—not her real name—said she has confided in only a few friends that her father is gay. One, she said, responded by revealing that her aunt is a lesbian.

But Alice said she still hasn't told "my very, very best friend in the whole world."

One day, Alice explained, her friend asked her if she was prejudiced against any group. "I said, 'Not really. Just ignorant people, I guess.' Then she said she was just prejudiced against gay people. . . . I didn't say anything."

Zisterer and other gay parents say it is important to convey to their children that homosexuality is nothing to be ashamed of. Zisterer said his unorthodox household has encountered largely accepting attitudes at church, the PTA and among neighbors whose children play with Joel.

"Nick," he added, "is an excellent co-parent."

"Co-parent" is the term many gay fathers and lesbian mothers use to describe their domestic partners. But the term is meaningless in the eyes of the law.

Attorneys who have tried to explain the new realities of gay families to the courts say laws need to be revised to offer protection for children and adults. . . .

Consider the case of Alanna Handler. If Helene Handler had been artificially inseminated under a doctor's supervision, the sperm donor would have no legal rights or responsibilities under existing California law.

But because Celia inseminated Helene at home, the friend who donated the sperm is legally the child's father—regardless of whether he wants such responsibility. . . .

In some instances, "co-parents" may attain parental status by legally adopting the child. But Alanna's biological father would complicate any attempt by Noriega to adopt Alanna. Helene Handler said that, to protect both her companion and her daughter, she intends to draw up a will naming Noriega as Alanna's guardian if she dies.

But what if Handler and Noriega split up? In two groundbreaking custody battles between lesbians, the court sided with the biological mother. Activists view the decisions as setbacks for the gay rights movement.

Both the child and society would benefit, Goodman argues, if "co-parents" are granted greater rights.

"Most Americans would hasten to reject governmental authorization of homosexual parenting, seeing such family arrangements as perverse."

Homosexuals Should Not Have Greater Parental Rights

Human Events

The growing number of gay and lesbian couples raising children has alarmed many. The following viewpoint, an editorial taken from the conservative newspaper *Human Events*, summarizes many of the fears and concerns of those who oppose homosexuals raising children. The editorial questions studies that purport to show that children are not harmed by their parents' homosexuality, and argues that such children run greater risks of child abuse and psychological trauma.

As you read, consider the following questions:

1. Why do most Americans reject the notion of homosexual parenting, according to *Human Events*?
2. What is a favorite tactic of homosexual activists, according to the author?
3. What are some of the possible detrimental effects on children being raised by gays and lesbians, according to *Human Events*?

"Homosexuals Push for Parental Rights," *Human Events*, December 7, 1991. Reprinted with permission.

America's homosexual activists have as their eventual goal the complete legitimization of homosexuality in every sphere of life. While many Americans have noted their efforts to place homosexual behavior under the protection of the civil rights laws, probably not many are aware that these same activists have turned their eyes on the family itself—specifically, the rearing of children—as an area to press for equal legal status with heterosexuals.

Thus, added to the usual demands for the legalization of homosexual marriage, we are now seeing a push towards legalized homosexual adoption of children.

In addition, some state courts have ordered placement of children with homosexual parents who are involved in custody disputes with their estranged heterosexual spouses. Judges have also ordered children into homosexual foster homes and, even more bizarre, lesbians have taken to having themselves artificially inseminated so as to have their own children—sometimes as part of an agreement with a homosexual male friend to use his semen in exchange for handing over to him a second child.

Most Americans Reject Homosexual Parenting

Whatever state courts and homosexual activists may be quietly doing, however, most Americans would hasten to reject governmental authorization of homosexual parenting, seeing such family arrangements as perverse and, in an age of AIDS and pedophilia, more dangerous than ever before. At the least, most would harbor fears for the psychic health of children reared in such an environment.

Indeed, most would probably echo the words of former Supreme Court Chief Justice Warren Burger, who wrote in upholding the constitutionality of Georgia's anti-sodomy statute in 1986, "Condemnation of homosexuality is firmly rooted in Judeo-Christian moral and ethical standards."

Notwithstanding such High Court judgments, however, the battle still rages across the country.

In trying to further their cause, a favorite tactic of homosexual activists is to invoke allegedly "scientific" studies that purport to demonstrate that homosexuals make fine parents and that they have been unfairly treated by courts and adoption agencies for years.

Not surprisingly, California is the state where such arguments have been most widely accepted, though judges and governmental authorities in other states have begun to show signs of subscribing to the same "enlightened" doctrines.

A *Los Angeles Times* article by Scott Harris on the topic of homosexual parenting is the latest salvo directed at those Americans whose common sense and moral beliefs lead them to reject such legal innovations out of hand.

Harris' lengthy apologia for homosexual parenting drew heavily on the work of UCLA's Dr. Martha Kirkpatrick. Indeed, Harris himself told *Human Events* that Kirkpatrick's studies of children reared by lesbians provided the foundation for his article.

Homosexuality and Child Abuse

Homosexuals often say that they are no more likely to be child molesters than heterosexuals, and that most molestation cases involve heterosexuals. But these assertions are misleading. Most molestations are committed by heterosexuals, but only because the vast majority of people are heterosexual. Even though homosexuals represent less than three percent of the U.S. population, at least one-third of all child molestations involve homosexual activity. Thus, the propensity for pedophilia is far higher among homosexuals.

Robert Knight, *Family Policy*, June 1992.

He quotes Kirkpatrick's conclusion: "Whatever goes on in a family has an effect on the child. But we cannot find, by the current measures available, that any evidence of homosexuality in a parent has a specific detrimental effect on a child."

Kirkpatrick also says that children reared by homosexuals do not show any increased tendency to become homosexuals themselves.

Elsewhere Harris notes, "Judges, persuaded by growing research data that gays are as able as heterosexuals to be worthy parents, have increasingly granted gays custody of children and approved adoption by gays."

Faulty Data

But how reliable are such research data? A careful reading of Kirkpatrick's monograph, "Homosexuality and Parenting," reveals that, far from having clinched the case in favor of such families, scientific studies of the phenomenon are in their infancy and are conducted with the crudest of research methods. One such method is the Toy Preference Test in which inferences are drawn about a mother's influence on a child's acquisition of a sex role based on what toys his mother would choose for him.

Even more disquieting for anyone hoping to rely on the research of Kirkpatrick and others in the field is her own admission that absolutely no long-term studies (termed "longitudinal studies" in the jargon of researchers) have been conducted to determine if children reared in homosexual homes grow up to be well adjusted.

Studies of children reared in homosexual homes from birth are only just now getting under way; such studies as have been done have focused on children reared by divorced lesbians, etc.

No follow-up studies have been done even of the mothers and children who have been subjected to some testing by researchers. Kirkpatrick herself lamented to us on the phone that the frequent moving around of her subjects made such follow-up studies virtually impossible.

Furthermore, according to Kirkpatrick, the research done on homosexual males as parents is *even more sparse* than that done on lesbians as child rearers.

Kirkpatrick, whose study group numbered only 20, told us that she once served on the board of directors of National Gay Rights Advocates, but she stressed that she had gotten involved with the advocacy group only after she had begun doing research in the field and had decided homosexual parenting posed no risks for children.

"I don't think we know the best way to raise healthy children," Kirkpatrick told us, "but I don't think it depends as much on the structure of the family as on the function of the family. I don't think it depends on the sexual orientation of the parents or kinship relationship between those caring for the children, the amount of money they have, or whether a father is present.

"In my mind all these things are less important than whether the family as a unit feels comfortable with each other, is supportive and respectful, and deals openly about disagreements."

Children Shocked by Homosexuality

Nevertheless, even Kirkpatrick concedes that her research showed that many children, when informed of their mother's homosexuality, were "shocked, confused, hurt and embarrassed. Young children need to deny the meaning of the information: older children may be burdened by the secret or have concerns for their own sexual development, with an increased pressure to act out their heterosexuality for reassurance."

Despite her repeated claims to *Times* reporter Harris and to us that the sexual orientation of parents was relatively unimportant, her "Homosexuality and Parenting" ends by cautioning, "We cannot assume that a parent's homosexuality has no effect on a child, only that the effects are variable in direction and extent, and there is specific or inevitable effect."

This is well short of a clear scientific statement that a judge could rely on in deciding, for example, a custody case.

Not surprisingly, there are some researchers who downplay the significance of the work of Kirkpatrick and other students of homosexual parenting. Dr. Judith Reisman, author of *Kinsey, Sex* and Fraud and "Softporn" Plays Hardball, reaffirmed to *Human Events* that there was insufficient data to come to any conclusions on the topic, and termed the *Los Angeles Times* article "a puff piece."

"You have a broad spectrum of detrimental effects," said Reisman about children brought up by homosexuals. She said that those detrimental effects were widely recognized in the medical community until it became "politically incorrect" to mention them.

Society Should Not Sanction Homosexual Families

It must be concluded that when compared to the traditional heterosexual marriage form of the family, homosexual partnerships greatly lack social benefit. Homosexuals highly sexualize human relationships which are usually very temporary. They cannot reproduce children, except through extraordinary technology and influence children in unhealthy ways, not unlike other forms of single parenthood or stepfamily relationships. Homosexual parents also model what society has traditionally called immoral sexual behavior. Today, in face of an epidemic of STDs [sexually transmitted diseases], AIDS, and teenage pregnancy, we must not teach our children that sexual promiscuity is merely an alternative lifestyle. Rather, children should be encouraged to live in mutual monogamy with one sexual partner in marriage. This is not the behavior that is either desired nor lived by the homosexual community.

Bradley P. Hayton, *To Marry or Not: The Legalization and Adoption of Homosexual Couples*, February 1992.

"To state only the most obvious and easily checked problems," she added, "homosexual men have the highest rates of *all* communicable diseases—hepatitis, tuberculosis, etc."

She said, "We do know what makes for healthy children: a mom and a dad with an extended family to provide backup if parents get sick, or have financial problems, etc. It is simply true to say that we take better care of our kin than of others."

Child Abuse

Reisman pointed with horror to a study in the *Journal of Sex Research* indicating that "31 per cent of lesbians and 12 per cent of homosexual males reported being victims of forced sex by their current or most recent partner," with battery being part of the coercion involved.

"You've got a lot of angry people in these groups," Reisman said, "and it's frightening to think of this violence being visited on children, particularly in a sexual context."

The potential for abuse by pedophiles was a major concern of Reisman. "Children are not guinea pigs to be experimented with," she said, and advised interested readers to look at the advertisements in the back of homosexual magazines for evidence of how widespread a desire for "young people" is among homosexuals.

She said that she feared that male pedophiles would increase their desire for children as the AIDS epidemic worsened because they are thought to be safe and warned that a Duke University Department of Pediatrics report states that 14 per cent of children with AIDS were identified as victims of sexual abuse.

"You won't learn about that from the L.A. *Times* article," she added ruefully.

Another source of information unavailable to the *Times* was Pattie Weaver, a 31-year-old woman now living in northern California.

Weaver was brought up in a lesbian household in southern California in the 1960s. She told us, "When I hit my teens I went out looking for a positive male role model in a very self-destructive way. I know now I was looking for a man to take care of me. . . .

"I had great difficulty forming stable relationships because of the way I was brought up, which emphasized hypersexuality. Children benefit from the complementarity of male and female parents and I wish I could have had that in my youth. I look back now and I wonder that I managed to live through it all."

a critical thinking activity

Recognizing Deceptive Arguments

 People who feel strongly about an issue use many techniques to persuade others to agree with them. Some of these techniques appeal to the intellect, some to the emotions. Many of them distract the reader or listener from the real issues.

A few common examples of argumentation tactics are listed below. Most of them can be used either to advance an argument in an honest, reasonable way or to deceive or distract from the real issues. It is important for a critical reader to recognize these tactics in order to rationally evaluate an author's ideas.

a. *bandwagon*—the idea that "everybody" does this or believes this

b. *categorical statements*—stating something in a way that implies there can be no argument or disagreement on the issue

c. *scare tactic*—threatening that if you don't do or believe this, something terrible will happen

d. *slanter*—attempting to persuade through inflammatory and exaggerated language instead of through reason

e. *testimonial*—quoting or paraphrasing an authority or celebrity to support one's own viewpoint

f. *strawperson*—distorting or exaggerating an opponent's ideas to make one's own seem stronger

The following activity can help you sharpen your skills in recognizing deceptive reasoning. The statements below are derived from the viewpoints in this chapter. *Beside each one, mark the letter of the type of deceptive appeal being used. More than one type of tactic may be applicable. If you believe the statement is not any of the listed appeals, write N.*

198

1. The response of straight America has been overwhelming in support of gay marriage. I believe we are seeing a tremendous shift in the public's perception of lesbians and gays.

2. Hollywood sitcoms such as the "Golden Girls" have run strongly supported shows in the issues of same-sex marriage. And to a large extent, as the "Golden Girls" go, so does America!

3. Some have said gay marriage is merely a shortcut. For us, the real shortcut is to give in to homophobia and give up without a fight.

4. Lesbians and gays should not marry because marriage can only occur between a man and a woman.

5. Marriage is an oppressive, patriarchal institution that lesbians and gays should remain free of.

6. In attempting to gain marriage rights, lesbians and gays would be forced to emphasize their sameness to married heterosexuals. This ends up ripping away the very heart and soul of what I believe it is to be a lesbian in this world. We end up mimicking all that is bad about the institution of marriage in our effort to be the same as the straight couples.

7. Americans are uncomfortable with the notion of gays as parents.

8. Many gays and lesbians are immorally conceiving children through such abnormal ways as artificial insemination.

9. Some people argue against homosexual parents because they believe the children will just mimic their parents' sexual orientation. But they should know sexual development is more complex than that.

10. Americans reject governmental authorization of homosexual parenting because they know such family arrangements are perverse, and in an age of AIDS and pedophilia, more dangerous than ever before.

11. America's homosexual activists have as their eventual goal the complete legitimization of homosexuality in every sphere of life.

12. Depriving gay Americans the free choice of whether to marry is a monstrous injustice.

13. The country of Denmark and the city of San Francisco both let gay people register as domestic partners, making it an idea whose time has come.

Periodical Bibliography

The following articles have been selected to supplement the diverse views presented in this chapter.

Katrine Ames et al. "Domesticated Bliss," *Newsweek*, March 23, 1992.

Gene Antonio "The Homosexual Political Agenda," *New Dimensions*, January 1990.

Mona Charen "Domestic Partners Want More than Tolerance," *Conservative Chronicle*, July 19, 1989. Available from PO Box 11297, Des Moines, IA 50340-1297.

Kittredge Cherry and James Mitulski "Committed Couples in the Gay Community," *The Christian Century*, February 28, 1990.

Craig R. Dean "Gay Marriage: A Civil Right," *The New York Times*, September 28, 1991.

Brent Hartinger "A Case for Gay Marriage," *Commonweal*, November 22, 1991.

Nan D. Hunter "Sexual Dissent and the Family," *The Nation*, October 7, 1991.

Walter Isaacson "Should Gays Have Marriage Rights?" *Time*, November 20, 1989.

James D. Marks "A Victory for the New American Family," *The New York Times*, February 1, 1992.

Elisabeth Nonas "Family Outings," *The Advocate*, September 10, 1991. Available from Liberation Publications, Inc., 6922 Hollywood Blvd., Tenth Fl., Los Angeles, CA 90028.

Dennis O'Brien and Jean Bethke Elshtain "Against Gay Marriage," *Commonweal*, November 22, 1991.

Andrew Sullivan "Here Comes the Groom," *The New Republic*, August 28, 1989.

Ernest van den Haag "Confirmed but Not Bachelors?" *National Review*, September 15, 1989.

Organizations to Contact

The editors have compiled the following list of organizations that are concerned with the issues debated in this book. All have publications or information available for interested readers. For best results, allow as much time as possible for the organizations to respond. The descriptions below are derived from materials provided by the organizations. The list was compiled upon the date of publication. Names, addresses, and phone numbers of organizations are subject to change.

American Civil Liberties Union (ACLU)
132 W. 43rd St.
New York, NY 10036
(212) 944-9800

The ACLU is the nation's oldest and largest civil liberties organization. Its Lesbian and Gay Rights/AIDS Project, started in 1986, handles litigation, education, and public policy work on behalf of gays and lesbians. It publishes the handbook *The Rights of Lesbians and Gay Men* and the monthly newsletter *Civil Liberties Alert*.

Concerned Women for America (CWA)
370 L'Enfant Promenade SW, Suite 800
Washington, DC 20024
(202) 488-7000
Fax (202) 488-0806

CWA works to strengthen the traditional family according to Judeo-Christian moral standards. It opposes gay marriage and the granting of additional civil rights protections to gays and lesbians. It publishes several brochures and *Family Voice*, a monthly newsmagazine.

Courage
c/o St. Michael's Rectory
424 W. 34th St.
New York, NY 10001
(212) 421-0426

Courage is a network of spiritual support groups of gay and lesbian Catholics who wish to lead celibate lives in accordance with Roman Catholic teaching on homosexuality. It publishes listings of local groups, a newsletter, and an annotated bibliography of books on homosexuality.

Desert Stream Ministries
12488 Venice Blvd.
Los Angeles, CA 90066-3804
(213) 572-0140

Desert Stream sponsors support groups for homosexual Christians who believe homosexual activity is immoral. The organization distributes several research papers on homosexuality, including *A Biblical View of Homosexuality* and *Hot Thoughts—The Effect of Pornography on Male Homosexuals.*

Dignity/USA
1500 Massachusetts Ave. NW, Suite 11
Washington, DC 20005
(202) 861-0017
Fax (202) 429-9808

Dignity/USA is a Roman Catholic organization of gays, lesbians, and bisexuals and their families and friends. It believes that homosexuals and bisexuals can lead sexually active lives in a manner consonant with Christ's teachings. Through its national and local chapters, Dignity/USA provides educational materials, AIDS crisis assistance, and spiritual support groups for members. Its publications include the monthly *Dignity Journal* and a book, *Theological Pastoral Resources: A Collection of Articles on Homosexuality from a Catholic Perspective.*

Equal Rights Marriage Fund (ERMF)
2001 M St. NW
Washington, DC 20036
(202) 822-6546
Fax (202) 466-3540

ERMF is dedicated to the legalization of gay and lesbian marriage and serves as a national clearinghouse for gay and lesbian marriage rights information. The organization publishes several brochures and articles, including *Gay Marriage: A Civil Right.*

Exodus International
PO Box 2121
San Rafael, CA 94912
(415) 454-1017

Exodus International is a referral network offering support for homosexual Christians desiring to become heterosexual. It publishes lists of local ministries and programs and bibliographies of books and tapes on homosexuality.

Family Research Council (FRC)
700 13th St. NW, Suite 500
Washington, DC 20005
(202) 393-2100

The council is a research, resource, and educational organization that promotes the traditional family, which the council defines as a group of people bound by marriage, blood, or adoption. The council opposes gay marriage and adoption rights. It publishes numerous reports from a conservative perspective on issues affecting the family, including homosexuality. These publications include the monthly newsletter *Washington Watch* and the bimonthly journal *Family Policy.*

Focus on the Family
420 N. Cascade Ave.
Colorado Springs, CO 80903
(719) 531-3400

Focus on the Family is a Christian organization that seeks to strengthen the traditional family in America. It provides resources for homosexuals seeking to change their lifestyle and has done extensive research on homosexuality and school programs, civil rights laws, and other public policy questions. Among its publications are the brochures *Help for the Homosexuals* and *The Ten Myths of Homosexuality* and the monthly magazine *Focus on the Family*.

The Hetrick-Martin Institute (HMI)
401 West St.
New York, NY 10014
(212) 633-8920

HMI is a nonprofit organization that offers a broad range of social services to gay and lesbian teenagers and their families. It also sponsors advocacy and education programs for gay and lesbian adolescents. HMI publishes the quarterly newsletter *HMI Report Card* and distributes articles, comic books, and pamphlets on homosexuality.

Homosexuals Anonymous Fellowship Services (HAFS)
PO Box 7881
Reading, PA 19603-7881
(215) 376-1146

HAFS is a nondenominational Christian fellowship of people who desire to change their homosexual orientation. Members meet in small groups and follow a fourteen-step program modeled on that of Alcoholics Anonymous. The organization publishes several pamphlets including *Can Homosexuals Change?* and *Freedom from Homosexuality*.

Lambda Legal Defense and Education Fund, Inc.
666 Broadway
New York, NY 10012
(212) 995-8585

Through test-case litigation and public education, Lambda works to defend the rights of lesbians, gay men, and people with HIV. Lambda won the first U.S. AIDS discrimination case in 1983. It publishes *AIDS Update* periodically and the *Lambda Update* quarterly.

Lesbian Mothers National Defense Fund (LMNDF)
PO Box 21567
Seattle, WA 98111
(206) 325-2643

LMNDF is a volunteer resource network that provides information, referrals, and emotional support for lesbians on the issues of child custody and visitation, artificial insemination, and adoption. It publishes the quarterly newsletter *Mom's Apple Pie* and a bibliography of materials concerning lesbian mothers.

National Association for the Research and Therapy of Homosexuality (NARTH)
16542 Ventura Blvd., Suite 416
Encino, CA 91436
(818) 789-4440

NARTH is an information and referral network for people interested in changing unwanted homosexuality through psychological treatment. It publishes a monthly newsletter and the book *Reparative Therapy of Male Homosexuality*.

National Center for Lesbian Rights
1663 Mission St., 5th Floor
San Francisco, CA 94103
(415) 621-0674

The center is a public interest law office providing legal counseling and representation for victims of sexual orientation discrimination. Primary areas of advice are in custody and parenting, employment, housing, the military, and insurance. The center publishes the handbooks *Recognizing Lesbian and Gay Families: Strategies for Obtaining Domestic Partners Benefits* and *Lesbian and Gay Parenting: A Psychological and Legal Perspective* as well as other materials.

National Gay and Lesbian Task Force (NGLTF)
1734 14th St. NW
Washington, DC 20009-4309
(202) 332-6483

NGLTF is a civil rights advocacy organization that lobbies Congress and the White House on a range of civil rights and AIDS issues and works on the state level to abolish sodomy laws. The organization also works to eradicate prejudice, discrimination, and violence against homosexuals. It publishes numerous papers and pamphlets, including *Anti-Gay/Lesbian Violence Fact Sheet* and *Twenty Questions About Homosexuality*.

Oregon Citizens Alliance (OCA)
PO Box 407
Wilsonville, OR 97070
(503) 682-0653

OCA is a political organization that opposes minority status "special rights" for homosexuals because it believes homosexual behavior is wrong and injurious to public health. OCA distributes brochures and information packets.

Parents and Friends of Lesbians and Gays (P-FLAG)
PO Box 27605
Washington, DC 20038-7605
800-432-6459

P-FLAG is a national organization that provides support and educational services for gays, lesbians, bisexuals, and their families and friends. It works to end prejudice and discrimination against homosexuals. It publishes and distributes pamphlets and articles, including *Why Is My Child Gay?*, *About Our Children*, and *Coming Out to My Parents*.

Reconciling Congregation Program (RCP)
3801 N. Keeler Ave.
Chicago, IL 60641
(312) 736-5526
Fax (312) 736-5475

RCP is a network of United Methodist churches that welcome and support lesbians and gay men and that seek to end homophobia and prejudice in the church and society. Its national headquarters provides resources to help local ministries achieve these goals. Among its publications are the quarterly magazine *Open Hands*, the book *And God Loves Each One*, and pamphlets, studies, and videos.

Regeneration
PO Box 9830
Baltimore, MD 21284-9830
(410) 661-0284

Regeneration is a Christian ministry serving men and women seeking to overcome their homosexuality. Its Regeneration Books division sells a wide selection of books on homosexuality from a Christian perspective.

Sex Information and Education Council of the U.S. (SIECUS)
130 W. 42nd St., Suite 2500
New York, NY 10036
(212) 819-9770

SIECUS is one of the largest national clearinghouses for information on human sexuality. It publishes articles and bibliographic listings on homosexuality in the bimonthly newsletter *SIECUS Report*.

Spatula Ministries
Box 444
La Habra, CA 90631
(213) 691-7369

Spatula Ministries is a support group for Christian parents coping with their children's homosexuality. It publishes brochures and a newsletter listing similar groups across the United States and distributes books, including *Splashes of Joy in the Cesspools of Life*.

The Universal Fellowship of Metropolitan Community Churches (UFMCC)
5300 Santa Monica Blvd., Suite 304
Los Angeles, CA 90029
(213) 464-5100

UFMCC is a Christian church of the lesbian and gay community with three hundred churches in sixteen countries. It publishes a wide range of materials on topics concerning religion and homosexuality, including *Not a Sin, Not a Sickness* and *Homosexuality and the Conservative Christian*.

Youth Networks
2215 Market St., No. 479
San Francisco, CA 94114-1612

Youth Networks distributes nationwide educational materials for and about young lesbians, gays, and bisexuals. Among its publications are *We Are Here*, a listing of community resources and services for gay and lesbian teens, and numerous pamphlets. Interested youth can obtain information by sending a stamped, self-addressed envelope to the above address.

Bibliography of Books

Martha Barron Barrett *Invisible Lives: The Truth About Millions of Women-Loving Women*. New York: William Morrow and Company, Inc., 1989.

Irving Bieber et al. *Homosexuality: A Psychoanalytic Study*. Northvale NJ: Jason Aronson Inc., 1988.

Roger E. Biery *Understanding Homosexuality: The Pride and the Prejudice*. Austin, TX: Edward-William Publishing Company, 1990.

Warren J. Blumenfeld and Diane Raymond *Looking at Gay and Lesbian Life*. New York: Philosophical Library, 1988.

Warren J. Blumenfeld, ed. *Homophobia: How We All Pay the Price*. Boston: Beacon Press, 1992.

Darlene Bogle *Strangers in a Christian Land*. Old Tappan, NJ: Chosen Books, 1990.

Susan Cohen and Daniel Cohen *When Someone You Know Is Gay*. New York: M. Evans & Company, 1989.

Andrew Comiskey *Pursuing Sexual Wholeness*. Lake Mary, FL: Strang Communications Company, 1989.

William Consiglio *Homosexual No More*. Wheaton, IL: Victor Books, 1991.

Joe Dallas *Desires in Conflict*. Eugene, OR: Harvest House Publishers, 1991.

William Dannemeyer *Shadow in the Land*. San Francisco: Ignatius Press, 1989.

Martin Duberman *Cures: A Gay Man's Odyssey*. New York: Dutton, 1991.

Martin Duberman, Martha Vicinus, and George Chauncey Jr., eds. *Hidden from History: Reclaiming the Gay and Lesbian Past*. New York: New American Library, 1989.

Rob Eichberg *Coming Out: An Act of Love*. New York: Dutton, 1990.

Lillian Faderman *Odd Girls and Twilight Lovers: A History of Lesbian Life in Twentieth Century America*. New York: Columbia University Press, 1991.

Richard C. Friedman *Male Homosexuality: A Contemporary Psychoanalytic Perspective*. New Haven, CT: Yale University Press, 1988.

Chris Glaser *Come Home!* San Francisco: Harper & Row, 1990.

John C. Gonsiorek and James D. Weinrich, eds. *Homosexuality: Research Implications for Public Policy*. Newbury Park, CA: Sage Publications, 1991.

Richard Green	The "Sissy Boy Syndrome" and the Development of Homosexuality. New Haven, CT: Yale University Press, 1987.
David F. Greenberg	The Construction of Homosexuality. Chicago: The University of Chicago Press, 1988.
Benedict Groeschel	The Courage to Be Chaste. New York: Paulist Press, 1985.
James P. Hanigan	Homosexuality: The Test Case for Christian Sexual Ethics. New York: Paulist Press, 1988.
John F. Harvey	The Homosexual Person: New Thinking in Pastoral Care. San Francisco: Ignatius Press, 1987.
Gilbert Herdt, ed.	Gay Culture in America. Boston: Beacon Press, 1992.
Ivan Hill, ed.	The Bisexual Spouse. McLean, VA: Barlina Books, 1987.
Mike Hippler	So Little Time: Essays on Gay Life. Berkeley, CA: Celestial Arts, 1990.
Jeanette Howard	Out of Egypt: Leaving Lesbianism Behind. Tunbridge Wells, England: Monarch Publications, 1991.
John W. Howe	Sex: Should We Change the Rules? Lake Mary, FL: Creation House, 1991.
Morton Hunt	Gay: What Teenagers Should Know About Homosexuality and the AIDS Crisis. New York: Farrar, Straus & Giroux, 1987.
Nan D. Hunter, Sherryl E. Michaelson, and Thomas B. Stoddard	The Rights of Lesbians and Gay Men: The Basic ACLU Guide to a Gay Person's Rights. Carbondale: Southern Illinois University Press, 1992.
Richard A. Isay	Being Homosexual: Gay Men and Their Development. New York: Farrar, Straus & Giroux, 1989.
Rik Isensee	Growing Up Gay in a Dysfunctional Family. New York: Prentice Hall, 1991.
Marshall Kirk and Hunter Madsen	After the Ball: How America Will Conquer Its Fear and Hatred of Gays in the '90s. New York: Doubleday, 1989.
Jeff Konrad	You Don't Have to Be Gay. Hilo, HI: Pacific Publishing House, 1992.
Karen Linamen and Keith Wall	Deadly Secrets. Colorado Springs, CO: NavPress, 1990.
Helen B. McDonald and Audrey I. Steinhorn	Homosexuality: A Practical Guide to Counseling Lesbians, Gay Men, and Their Families. New York: Continuum, 1990.

John J. McNeill	*The Church and the Homosexual*. Boston: Beacon Press, 1988.
David P. McWhirter, Stephanie A. Sanders, and June Machover Reinisch	*Homosexuality/Heterosexuality: Concepts of Sexual Orientation*. New York: Oxford University Press, 1990.
Roger J. Magnuson	*Are Gay Rights Right?* Portland, OR: The Multnomah Press, 1990.
Eric Marcus	*Making History: The Struggle for Gay and Lesbian Rights, 1945-1990: An Oral History*. New York: HarperCollins, 1992.
Lawrence Mass	*Homosexuality and Sexuality: Dialogues of the Sexual Revolution*. New York: Harrington Park Press, 1990.
J. Gordon Melton	*The Churches Speak on Homosexuality*. Detroit: Gale Research Inc., 1991.
Deborah A. Miller and Alex Waigandt	*Coping with Your Sexual Orientation*. New York: The Rosen Publishing Company, 1990.
Neil Miller	*In Search of Gay America*. New York: The Atlantic Monthly Press, 1989.
Richard D. Mohr	*Gays/Justice: A Study of Ethics, Society, and Law*. New York: Columbia University Press, 1988.
Joseph Nicolosi	*Reparative Therapy of Male Homosexuality*. Northvale, NJ: Jason Aronson Inc., 1991.
Judith A. Reisman and Edward W. Eichel	*Kinsey, Sex, and Fraud: The Indoctrination of a People*. Lafayette, LA: Huntington House Publishers, 1990.
Robert B. Marks Ridinger	*The Homosexual and Society: An Annotated Bibliography*. New York: Greenwood Press, 1990.
Michael Ruse	*Homosexuality: A Philosophical Inquiry*. New York: Basil Blackwell, 1988.
Michael R. Saia	*Counseling the Homosexual*. Minneapolis: Bethany House, 1988.
Vincent J. Samar	*The Right to Privacy: Gays, Lesbians, and the Constitution*. Philadelphia, PA: Temple University Press, 1991.
Suzanne Sherman	*Lesbian and Gay Marriage*. Philadelphia, PA: Temple University Press, 1992.
Elaine V. Siegel	*Female Homosexuality: Choice Without Volition*. New York: The Analytic Press, 1988.
Charles Silverstein, ed.	*Gays, Lesbians, and Their Therapists*. New York: W.W. Norton & Company, 1991.
John Stott	*Homosexual Partnerships?: Why Same-Sex Relationships Are Not a Christian Option*. Downers Grove, IL: InterVarsity Press, 1985.

Meg Umans

Like Coming Home: Coming Out Letters. Austin, TX: Banned Books, 1988.

Gerard van den
Aardweg

On the Origins and Therapy of Homosexuality: A Psychoanalytic Reinterpretation. New York: Praeger Publishers, 1986.

James D. Weinrich

Sexual Landscapes. New York: Charles Scribner's Sons, 1987.

Kath Weston

Families We Choose. New York: Columbia University Press, 1992.

Index

Achtenburg, Roberta, 189, 190
ACT-UP, 77
adoption, 168
  homosexuals and, 71, 165, 185-186
Agrast, Mark, 68
Ahrens, Carol, 33
AIDS (Acquired Immunodeficiency
  Syndrome)
  brain studies and, 19, 20, 24
  Centers for Disease Control
    reported cases of, 65
  children with, 197
  church policies and, 152
  discrimination and, 65-66, 84-85
  domestic partnership laws and, 164,
    170
  education about, 110
  gay parenting and, 187-188, 193
  homosexual behavior and, 20, 170
  lesbians and, 20, 85
  media coverage of, 175
alcoholism, treatments for, 131
Alfred C. Kinsey Institute for Sex
  Research
  studies on sexuality
    causes for sexual orientation, 55,
      114
    curing homosexuality, 135
    sexual orientation scale, 47, 53-55,
      144-145
Allen, Laura, 20
Alter, Jonathan, 75-76
American Psychiatric Association
  on homosexuality, 190
androgen
  homosexuality and, 49
androgyny, 128
animals
  homosexuality and, 20, 21
artificial insemination, 185-187, 191

Bailey, Michael, 40
Ballard v. United States, 168
Barinaga, Marcia, 17
Berrill, Kevin, 64
Bieber, Irving
  study on causes of homosexuality,
    37, 51, 135
bisexuality
  causes for, 47-48
  prevalence of, 53-54
Blumenfeld, Warren J., 54

Bowers v. Hardwick, 168
brain
  hypothalamus
    effect on sexuality, 18, 19, 20, 26
  research on
    differences may determine
      sexuality, 17-22
    con, 23-27
    problems with, 20, 24-25
  suprachiasmatic nucleus, 20
Britt, Harry, 72, 164
Brougham, Tom, 163-164
Burger, Warren, 193
Bush, George
  Federal Hate Crimes Statistics Act
    and, 66
Busse, Michael, 151
Byne, William M., 25

Capote, Truman, 90
Cass, Vivienne C., 56
Catholic church
  homosexuality and, 130-131
celibacy
  through psychotherapy, 128
Centers for Disease Control
  reported AIDS cases, 65
Cheney, Dick, 100
children
  AIDS and, 197
  born to homosexual parents, 165
  gender nonconformity of, 39-42
  heterosexual parents are best for,
    168, 171, 196
  raised by homosexual couples
    are not harmed, 50, 55, 83,
      189-191, 194
    con, 168, 194-197
  reactions to homosexual parents,
    190-191, 195, 197
Christianity
  can change homosexuality, 140-147
  con, 148-155
  homophobia and, 150, 151
  opposes domestic partnerships, 166
Citrus House, 112
civil rights laws
  for homosexuals
    are necessary, 78-86
    con, 87-95
    discriminate against others, 72-74,
      91, 95

will not help homosexuals,
178-179
purpose of, 79, 86, 179
Clatts, Michael, 57
Cohen, Susan and Daniel, 138
Coles, Matthew A., 78
Cook, Colin, 140
co-parents, 191
Cutting, Ginny, 166

D'Souza, Dinesh, 167
Dannemeyer, William, 92
Davies, Bob, 146
Dean, Craig R., 172
DeCrescenzo, Teresa, 111
Denmark
homosexuals in the military, 97, 98,
99
District of Columbia
Human Rights Act
homosexual discrimination and,
173-174
Dixon, Sharon Pratt, 173
Dobbs, William, 76
domestic partnership laws
AIDS and, 164, 170
are changing, 71, 72, 163-164,
165-166, 169, 170
Christianity opposes, 166
National Gay and Lesbian Task
Force on, 72, 174
see also marriage

education
about homosexuality, 97-98, 100,
109, 115, 166
Erikson, Erik, 49
estrogen, 49
Ettelbrick, Paula L., 177
Exodus International, 151

family
dysfunctional
can cause homosexual behavior,
29-35
fathers
can affect homosexual behavior,
29-35, 127, 128, 130, 139,
con, 36-44, 55
Federal Hate Crimes Statistics Act, 66
Fein, Bruce, 167
Feinstein, Diane, 164
Frank, Barney, 90
Freud, Sigmund
theories of sexual behavior, 47, 49

Gay and Lesbian Alliance Against
Defamation, 66

Gay and Lesbian Community
Services Center, 112, 117
Gay and Lesbian Parents, 186, 188
Gay Rights Platform, 118
gays
definition of, 127, 179
legalizing marriage of
would harm homosexuals,
177-183
would help homosexuals,
172-176
movement goals, 178
relationship problems, 127-128
see also homosexuals
Gelman, David, 56
gender
identification problems, 127
nonconformity of children, 39-42
roles are oppressive, 179
socialization and, 46-47, 50
genetics
as a cause for homosexuality, 40
con, 127
Geshwind, Norman, 25
Gill, Patrick, 173
Glaser, Chris, 148
Goodman, Diane, 188, 191
Gorski, Roger, 19, 20
Griffin, Carolyn Welch, 36
Griffith, Bobby, 108, 109
Growing American Youth, 107

Hackworth, David, 99, 100
Haldeman, Douglas C., 136, 151
Hamill, Pete, 75
Handler, Alanna, 185, 186, 189, 191
Handler, Helene, 186, 189, 191
Harrelson, Don, 186
Harris, Jean, 74
Harris, Scott, 184, 193-194
Harrison, Barbara Grizzuti, 23
Harvey Milk High School, 111
hate crimes, 64, 66, 68
Hayton, Bradley P., 196
Helms, Jesse, 75
Herek, Gregory M., 67, 84
Hersch, Patricia, 52
heterosexuality
brain structure and, 18, 20
causes for, 46, 49, 54
Hetrick-Martin Institute, 108,
110-112
HIV, discrimination and, 65-66
Hoffman, Gloria, 20
Holland
homosexuals in the military, 97-98
Holtel, Rene, 97
homophobia

Christianity and, 141-147, 150, 151
homosexual marriage and, 166,
  173, 176
of gays, 127, 139, 178, 188
homosexuality
  as deviant behavior, 29, 92, 95,
    115-116
    con, 44, 153
  as natural, 139
  causes for
    brain structure may influence,
      17-22
      con, 23-27
    child abuse, 33
    conscious decision, 25
    genetic, 40, 127
    hormones, 49-50
    may be multiple, 45-51
    poor parent-child relationships,
      28-35, 127
      con, 36-44
    seduction
      con, 43, 50, 55
    uncertainty of, 45-51
    unimportance of, 52-57
    unknown, 43
  compared to addiction, 131, 146
  cure is possible, 141, 147
    con, 149-155
  dangers of, 115-116
  denial of, 29
  disease and, 115-116, 196
  immorality of, 94-95, 143
    arguments against, 80-81
  in various cultures, 18, 50
  medical treatments for, 26
  myths about, 37-44, 50, 82-83
  percentage of, 53, 114
  prisoners and, 53
  psychiatry and, 127
  psychotherapy can change, 126-132
  psychotherapy should help with
    acceptance of, 133-139
  sex hormones and, 18, 21, 25, 49-50
  six stages of, 56
  social restrictions against, 57
  society should accept, 63-68
    con, 69-77
  studies on, 18, 37, 47-48, 51, 53-55,
    114, 135
  support for, 29, 37
  twins and, 40
  voluntary therapy for, 56
homosexuals
  affirmative action and, 73, 74
  AIDS risk groups and, 20, 170
  anti-sodomy laws and, 76, 84, 168,
    193
  as religious clergy, 71
  civil rights legislation
    discriminates against others,
      72-74
    is necessary, 78-86
      con, 87-95
  discrimination against, 65-67, 83
    employment, 79-80
    housing, 79, 84
    legislation against, 68, 71
    military service, 79, 84, 103-104
    unproven, 89-92, 94
  have extensive rights, 90-91
  male friendships and, 127, 128,
    132, 147
  marriages of, 71
    heterosexual, 128, 130, 136-137
    illegality of, 82, 162, 164, 168
    should be legal, 162-166
      con, 167-171
  military service and
    in other countries
      homosexuals are successfully
        integrated, 97-101
    should accept homosexuals,
      96-101, 176
      con, 102-105
  parenting by
    adoption and, 71, 165, 185-186
    children born to, 165
    custody and, 71, 82, 190
    does not harm children, 55, 83,
      189-191, 194
    reasons for, 188
    should have greater rights,
      184-191
      con, 192-197
  percentage in population, 53, 114
  physical differences in, 21
  promiscuity and, 93, 115, 128
  radical behavior is harmful, 70,
    74-77
  teenagers
    suicide of, 68, 108, 114
    support programs for
      are harmful, 113-119
      are helpful, 106-112
    violence against, 64-65, 67, 151
      radical behavior will increase, 74,
        76-77
  see also gays
Hooker, Evelyn, 56
hormones
  imbalance causes homosexuality,
    49-50
    con, 127
  sexuality and, 18, 21, 25, 49-50
Horn, Patricia, 161

Horowitz Carl F., 69
Human Events, 192
Human Rights Campaign Fund, 71, 174
Hunt, Morton, 48
Hunter, Joyce, 108, 111, 112
hypothalamus
  sexuality and, 18, 19, 20, 26

Isay, Richard A., 133
Israel
  homosexuals in the military, 97, 99, 100

Johnson, Adelaide, 134
Jones, Stanton L., 131

Kennedy-Hawkins Civil Rights Act, 73
King, Martin Luther, 72
Kinsey, Alfred
  studies on sexuality, 37, 48
    causes for sexual orientation, 55, 114
    cures for homosexuality, 135
    sexual orientation scale, 47, 53-55, 142
Kirk, Marshall, 75
Kirkpatrick, Martha J., 189, 190, 194, 195
Knight, Robert, 194
Kolb, Lawrence, 134
Konigsberg, Eric, 96
Kowalski, Sharon, 162-163, 174
Kramer, Larry, 77

Lambda Legal Defense and Education Fund, 71, 166
Landis, Dennis, 18
Lazarus Project, 149
Le Vay, Simon
  findings on homosexuality, 18-20
    are inconclusive, 24-26
legislation
  homosexual civil rights
    discriminates against others, 72-74, 91, 95
    is necessary, 78-86
      con, 87-95
    prohibiting homosexual discrimination, 68, 71
Lesbian and Gay Health Conference, 110
Lesbian Rights Project, 190
lesbians
  AIDS and, 20, 85
  artificial insemination and, 185-187, 193

consciously choose lifestyle, 25
custody battles and, 191
early abuse causes behavior, 33
in the military, 97, 98
movement goals, 178
physical differences in, 21
violence against, 64-65, 67
see also homosexuals
Levi, Jeff, 72
Los Angeles
  programs for gay teens, 109-110, 112, 114-118

Madsen, Hunter, 75
Magnuson, Roger J., 87
Mapplethorpe, Robert, 75
March on Washington for Lesbian, Gay, and Bi Equal Rights and Liberation, 107
marriage
  definitions of, 162
  gay
    legalizing would harm homosexuals, 177-183
    legalizing would help homosexuals, 172-176
  heterosexual
    as best for children, 168, 171, 196
    homosexuals in, 128, 130, 136-137
  homosexual
    illegality of, 82, 162, 164, 168
    should be legal, 162-166
      con, 167-171
    legal rights of, 162, 163, 173-174, 178
    oppressive institution of, 178, 182
    Supreme Court on, 162-163
  see also domestic partnership laws
Masters, Roy, 28
media
  gay issues in, 174-175
military service
  in other countries
    homosexuals are successfully integrated, 97-101
    should accept homosexuals, 96-101, 176
      con, 102-105
Milk, Harvey, 111
Miller, Deborah A., 45
Mirken, Bruce, 106
Money, John, 26, 49
mothers
  can affect homosexual behavior, 29-35
    con, 36-44, 55

National Center for Lesbian Rights,

214

187, 189-190
National Education Association
  position on homosexuality, 118-119
National Gay and Lesbian Task Force
  discrimination ordinances and, 71
  domestic partnership laws and, 72,
  174
  on hate crimes, 64, 68
  radical behavior of, 77, 118
National Gay Rights Advocates, 195
National Lesbian and Gay Health
  Foundation, 108
National Organization for Women, 174
New York
  gay culture in, 74
  gay rights laws in, 166, 170
  programs for gay teens, 108, 110-
  111
Nicolosi, Joseph, 30, 126
Noriega, Celia, 186, 191
Norway
  homosexuals in the military, 99

Ovesey, Lionel, 134

parents
  can affect homosexual behavior,
  29-35, 47
    con, 36-44, 55, 189
Parents and Friends of Lesbians and
  Gays, 174
Paul, Nick, 190, 191
Pavlov, Ivan
  conditioned response study, 30
pedophilia, 193, 194, 197
Peters, Jeff, 63
Pillard, Richard, 40
Pomeroy, Wardell, 135
progesterone, 49
Project 10, 109-110
  is harmful to teenagers, 114-119
promiscuity
  in gay relationships, 93, 115, 128
psychotherapy
  can change sexual orientation,
  126-132
  is harmful, 134-139, 151
  should help homosexuals with
  acceptance, 133-139
Putka, Gary, 118

Queer Nation, 70
Quintanilla, Michael, 111

rape, 33, 196
Raymond, Diane, 54
Reinisch, June M., 50
Reisman, Judith, 195-196

relationships, alternative
  need recognition, 179-183
religion
  can support homosexuality, 148-155
  homosexuals as clergy, 71
  opposes homosexuality, 140-147,
  166
Remafedi, Gary, 108

Salk Institute
  studies on homosexuality, 18
San Francisco
  AIDS cases in, 85
  gay culture in, 74
  gay rights laws in, 164, 166,
  170-171
  homosexual parents in, 165, 186
Sanders, Stephanie A., 55
schools
  programs should support gay teens,
  106-112
    con, 113-119
Schroeder, Pat, 103, 105
sensitivity training
  homosexuality and, 97-98
sexual orientation
  cannot be changed, 134-139
  Christianity can change, 140-147
  Christianity should support,
  148-155
  discrimination based on, 173
  psychotherapy can change, 126-132
  is harmful, 134-139, 151
  psychotherapy should help with
  acceptance, 133-139
  studies on, 55, 114
  scale, 47, 53-55, 142
SHAPE: Stop Homosexual Advocacy
  in Public Education, 109
Sheldon, Lou, 109, 115, 118
Smith, Patricia, 113
Socarides, Charles, 94, 134
society
  needs to recognize alternative
  relationships, 179-183
  should accept homosexuality, 63-68
    con, 69-77
  should sanction gay partnerships,
  161-166
    con, 167-171
sodomy
  laws against, 76, 84, 168, 193
Spong, John S., 153
Stoddard, Thomas B., 161
Supreme Court
  on marriages, 162-163
Swaab, Dick, 20, 22
Sweden

homosexuals in the military, 97, 99
Switzerland
  homosexuals in the military, 99

Taylor v. Louisiana, 168
teachers
  as homosexuals, 43, 71, 80, 117,
    118
teenagers
  homosexuality and, 68
    harassment of, 109-111
    need support, 106-112
      con, 113-119
testosterone, 21, 49
Thompson, Karen, 162-163, 174
Traditional Values Coalition, 109, 119
Tucker, P., 49

Uribe, Virginia, 109, 114, 116-118

Vaid, Urvashi, 65, 77
Van Gelder, Lindsy, 25
violence

against homosexuals, 64-65, 67, 151
  radical behavior will increase, 74,
    76-77
in homosexual relationships, 196

Waigandt, Alex, 45
Warren, Barry, 163-164
Weinstein, Hallie, 97, 101
White, Byron, 168
White, Dan, 76
Wilson, Pete, 185
Wirth, Arthur G., 36
Wirth, Marian J., 36
Witelson, Sandra J., 21-22
Wolfson, Evan, 166
women
  abused
    can become lesbians, 33
  oppression of, 178-179, 181-182

Ziemba-Davis, Mary, 57
Zisterer, Bruce, 189, 190-191
Zisterer, Joel, 189, 190-191

216